ALOHA
NUI
LOA

A Pineapple Plantation Story

ALOHA NUI LOA

A Pineapple Plantation Story

Yvonne Lee McIntire

ARPress
ILLUMINATING IDEAS
EMPOWERING VOICES

ARPress
45 Dan Road Suite 5
Canton MA 02021

Hotline: 1(800) 220-7660
Fax: 1(855) 752-6001

Ordering Information:
Quantity sales. Special discounts are available on quantity purchases by corporations, associations, and others. For details, contact the publisher at the address above.

Printed in the United States of America.

ISBN-13:   Paperback   979-8-89356-615-4
                eBook   979-8-89356-617-8

Library of Congress Control Number: 2022902319

A word from our readers!

"*Aloha Nui Loa* is a story of REAL life in Hawai'i. A must read." Susan Atay, Maui, HI. Allstate Sales Manager

"A delightful love story set in days gone by that recreates Old Hawai'i with evocative imagery and language that transports the reader back in time. The author skillfully weaves culture and history into a tender story of love, social class and change, drawn from her own personal experience of growing up on a pineapple plantation in Hawai'i in the 1950's and 60's. This exotic adventure brings to life the essence of aloha, the beauty of the islands, and will have you rooting for love all the way!" Cathleen Nardi, Osprey, FL. Teacher, Quillo-ist, Artist

"Sure didn't think that a kid from a small town in Kentucky could relate to a love story on a pineapple plantation in Hawai'i. Yvonne McIntire in her novel, *Aloha Nui Loa*, proves that wrong! Five stars to the roller coaster of emotions I felt while reading this book. In the end my heart was smiling and more proof that 'God is the God of the second chance.'" James Michael Strait, La Grange, KY. Machinist-Instructor

"The pace of this wonderful love story will keep the reader turning pages. McIntire's setting of a Hawaiian pineapple plantation with its distinctive culture and characters is imaginative and successful. Very highly recommended." Ted Baer, Palo, Alto, CA. Retired Chemist

More from our readers, page 309.

Introduction

Many moons ago, I decided to do something really different. After years of living on my own and celebrating Mother's Day with my **'ohana**, I decided to spend that day with my dear parents. At that time, they were still living on the pineapple plantation on the island of O'ahu, Hawai'i, where I was raised. I was happy when my husband and son gave me their blessings, saying we could have a special dinner when I returned home. Yes, I've been back to the plantation many times, but on this occasion, as I said, it was different. It was truly a nostalgic journey to return to "The Old House" of all my childhood dreams. I was in for a big jolt. The house had aged even further. The plantation had seen more prosperous days. My parents were patiently waiting for the day dad would retire and hoping they would someday be able to purchase their own home. It pricked my heart.

Was it coincidence that while I was visiting, the place was to be inspected by the plantation manager and the head engineer? Living in their commodious homes, management had little inkling as to how the other half lived in their close quarters. The homes of the plantation workers needed maintenance, and the gentlemen were there that day to assess the need. It so happened that I was casually lounging in my old room, when my dad, the plantation manager, and the head engineer popped in totally unexpectedly. It was hilarious. The humorous situations of that day inspired me to exclaim to my mother, "Wouldn't today make a great chapter in a book?" Mom was nonplussed. "What would happen," I continued, "if there really was a plantation owner's son who fell in love with the daughter of the union man? What challenges would they face? Could their relationship work with the big differences in their socio-economic backgrounds?" Mom being Chinese, reserved judgment. For me, it was great fun to think up adventures for our main couple to experience together as their relationship deepened. Though based on a real place and on real characters and events, the story between the main characters is a work of fiction. However, the picture presented of plantation living is true. Pineapple growing played a big role in the agriculture of the 50th State. To help preserve its place in Hawaiian history, I felt it needed to be shared.

It is my hope that you enjoy meeting the Andres and Alexander families in this story, as much as I enjoyed presenting them to you. I'm an optimist at heart. I love a book with a happy ending. Underneath this lighthearted story of first love flows a deeper current, one of redemption. With the reading of Eden and Ben's love story, may you find your own happy ending, and of course, redemption.

Yvonne Lee McIntire
Maui, Hawai'i

Dedication

To my parents, Willie and Janet Abear, for all the sacrifices they made for us kids, and for teaching me in the ways of hospitality.

Acknowledgements

David M. McIntire for his tireless hours of editing and for the back cover photographs, Henry Parrilla of Local 142 for his wealth of plantation and union history, and Dr. Ryan Fusato for invaluable medical advice. Bob Jones, former news anchor of KGMB TV, Honolulu, for his insight, Peter Savio, of Savio Realty Ltd, Honolulu, and Donald Horner, CEO of First Hawaiian Bank, for saving my old home. Mahalo nui to Bill King and Kumu Kuʻualohanui Kauliʻa for expertise in the Hawaiian language. Special thanks to friend Mary Gates of Dallas, for her many hours of tech support. Gratitude to Rick Ortiz of **the macpro**, and Lori and Isidro Soriano for tech help! Much appreciation from the bottom of my heart to Jason Collins of Author Reputation Press for his confidence in me, and to Elle Murray, Hannah Lopez and the staff for their excellent service. Thanks to Ikaika Enos of Haiku House of Maui, for his aloha and generosity, and to Dana and Tatiana Monteiro for the cover photo shoot.

Author's greeting:

A-L-O-HA!

I know that most of you, my readers, are familiar with the word Aloha. It has several meanings: hello, goodbye, love. Having the 'aloha spirit' is the very essence of Hawai'i. This is the slice of Hawai'i that I love.

Of a truth, I wrote this book on a whim in 8 weeks one summer. It was to entertain and pay tribute to my parents. They say that if you want to write a book, write about what you know. So, I set the story in the very plantation where I grew up, with family members and friends as characters. I had no idea it would come into print, or that others would enjoy not only a love story, but the story of plantation living. I also wrote it when I was much younger. It sat in my old Mac in storage for a long time, as life has a tendency to take over. Then one day, I wanted to print out a copy of the story. Lo and behold the computer was gone from its storage place. Where did it go? Yes, an overzealous hubby in cleaning up the space, tossed it out. OMG!

I thought of many things I could do, but I refrained from hitting him on the head with a fat pillow. He was so penitent that I forgave him easily, but not until I showed him my faded hard copy which he had to type into the new computer. Ha!

While he read the whole manuscript, I could hear him laughing and sniffling intermittently. When he was done, he encouraged me to get it published. We weren't experts in book publishing, but we worked together diligently in editing and did manage to get a few copies printed. Then I had to deal with a moderately serious health issue, so the book was put on the back burner once again.

On January 4 of this year, I was contacted by Jason Collins of Author Reputation Press. I was very surprised. Thanks to him, I was encouraged to rebrand the book, as he said it was my heritage and I shouldn't leave it stored in a box! He really believed in me! After much inner wrestling and thought, I agreed. It gave me a chance to make all the corrections and additions that were needed and to polish up the story to give it that certain je ne sais quoi. It was an amazingly satisfying process. I shed a few tears. I laughed. I saw things I didn't know I wrote, for instance, the inner strength of the young heroine. Yes, you could say this book is partly autobiographical, but it is mostly made up in my big imagination. I followed the usual formula, for want of a better word, required for a modern romance: boy meets girl, they fall in love, conflict arises, they part ways, they reunite, and finally, they get married. Et voila, a happy ending!

While the book is based on a real place, the story is really about the main characters of Eden Andres and Ben Alexander. Yes, there really was an Irish plantation manager and a head engineer (Robert Redford look-alike) who came to the house to inspect for repairs. No, the main characters are not my husband and me, though one incident that happens between them is true to life.

In the process of making revisions, I pondered on what it was like growing up on the plantation. It was a halcyon childhood. We had no tv, computers, cell phones, or media devices. We were perfectly happy without them. Instead we played outside with homemade toys. We were a close-knit community of a mix of ethnicities, preparing a Christmas program where all attended and shared a huli-huli (rotisserie) chicken dinner afterwards. Bags of apples, oranges and nuts were given to all the families and gifts were given to all the children. We had camp picnics, kite flying contests, baseball and volleyball tournaments with other camps, and working in the pineapple fields during the summer when we were of age. It was a somewhat idyllic, simple, and carefree life. And I had great fun putting it on paper.

Why am I rebranding? Well, we were able to publish a few books of the original. The book was printed with a few mistakes and errors, minor but noticeable to me. Some of the narrative had to be converted to conversation. The cover was beautiful, but not my original choice. Actually, this whole process has changed or rather is changing my life. I agreed to rebrand Nuiloha (made up name) to Aloha Nui Loa which means a very big aloha or all my love. The story remains unchanged, just enhanced.

With the passage of time, my memory dimmed a bit. So, for ease of writing, the timing of the book had to be updated to accommodate certain modern touches, such as the use of cell phones, and present day mentions of Hawaiian music and singers, vehicles, etc. I had to contrast the lifestyles of the main characters. My parents and siblings, and others on the plantation were exaggerated characters of the real ones, to emphasize personalities, with name changes! In hindsight, I wrote not knowing I was pouring myself into the heroine and felt the emotions only years later when I am 74. I wanted to show a part of Hawai'i that is now history, a remembrance of good times, and I wanted to honor my parents. Though the plantation closed down in 2008 and operations were moved to Costa Rica, the camp remains. Thanks to Peter Savio and Donald Horner, it was saved, but that is another story! Retirees now own their own places, and the old house has a new family living in it. My parents were able to purchase their own home nearby.

Soon after my parents moved into their new home, my sister Joyce and I took a ride to the old plantation camp. We drove all around and stopped to view the homes we lived in. The first one had only 2 bedrooms, and 5 kids had to share one room. I asked my sister if she remembered the short cement walkway that our dad made in front of "the little house." She had no recollection. I got out of the car and much to my delight, there was that cement walkway of my memory. You see, when the cement was still wet, Dad told me to go to the kitchen and get a chopstick so he could write our names into the walkway. I was only 4 at the time. Here it was 41 years later. You could tell there were names written in each block, blurred by time and the elements, BUT my name was the only one still legible. I got chicken skin, or goosebumps! My sister looked at me in awe and said, "It's up to you, Yvonne, to tell our story!" We drove to the other house, "the old house" where my parents lived for 37 years. It was a poignant moment. Another family had moved in. We realized that it was no longer ours. We shed a few tears as we bid goodbye to the house we dearly loved and hurried to the new home where Mom had dinner waiting for us!

So, here is a plantation story, intermingled within a modern-day Cinderella tale. I hope it brings you joy, and that it gives you a glimpse of the Hawai'i that I love with all my heart. Come visit soon!

Aloha Nui Loa, (all my love)

Yvonne Lee McIntire

I would love to hear from you! You may write to me at: pineapplegirl9@yahoo.com

Note to reader

There are many words and phrases in this story that may be unfamiliar to someone not raised in Hawai'i. For this reason, they have been **bolded** in the text and can be found in a glossary which has been included at the end of the book.

The eight major islands of The Hawaiian Islands:

Kaua'i	**"The Garden Isle"**
O'ahu	**"The Gathering Place"**
Moloka'i	**"The Friendly Isle"**
Maui	**"The Valley Isle"**
Lana'i	**"The Pineapple Isle"**
Hawai'i	**"The Big Island"**
Ni'ihau	**"The Forbidden Island"**
Kaho'olawe	**"The Target Isle"**

To help the reader visualize all the beautiful places mentioned in the story, may I suggest that you look up the Hawaiian place names on a current map of the Hawaiian Islands and check out photos online. Enjoy!

Table Of Contents

CHAPTER 1
Daughter of the Union Man

The blazing sun in the western sky dipped closer to the horizon, coloring the sky with brilliant hues of orange and red, with a trace of lavender. Its rays slanted over the **Wai'anae Range** and spilled onto the rows of neatly arranged young pineapple shoots planted in the **red soil**. Eden Andres stood at the entrance gate of **Aloha Nui Loa** Plantation, taking in the glorious sight, grateful it also presented a warm welcome to the returning field workers. They were a jubilant bunch who disembarked from the last **labor truck**, she noted, as she watched them march in small groups toward the plantation office.

The slim young woman, marvelously tanned, waited for her father to appear among the similarly clad **palaka** shirted workers, unbeknownst that she, too, was the object of interest from another quarter. Standing at the viewing window of the executive office, Ben Alexander, having completed his weekly survey of the plantation, was also observing the workers returning from the fields. Eden caught his eye immediately, as she was dressed so differently from any other plantation girl he'd seen. She was en vogue in fitted bell bottom jeans and a **tapa** print cropped top that had thin straps. Her long dark hair was glorious in the late afternoon light.

"Who is she?" he asked himself out loud and wondered why she was lingering at the gate.

"Boss, you have a conference call in 15 minutes," his secretary Chloe Dinez, called out to him. At length, when he looked back at the gate, the girl was gone. He frowned, feeling let down, his previous dour mood returning.

"Wait a minute," he upbraided himself, "what am I doing?" After all, he was only at the plantation temporarily. His dad, Barnes Alexander, the chief stockholder of the Alexander Corporation, or "The Company," as dubbed by the plantation workers, had done the unthinkable and shocked everyone by eloping with his personal assistant, a woman half his age. In addition to that, the chief consulting engineer of the plantation, Matthew Campbell, was out recovering from surgery. Coerced by his dad to fill in for both him and Matt, Ben was pressured to agree, postponing a long-planned trip to New Zealand. A freelance engineer, he was on hiatus from his work, and recovering from certain health issues. He felt a little edgy at the thought and sighed heavily.

Eden, however, was smiling broadly. She was doing something she loved since childhood: paying homage to her father, Gil Andres, by greeting him after work and offering to carry his denim hold-all home. Her heart swelled with pride as she spotted him moving out ahead of the crowd. Short in stature but athletic in build, he walked in brisk, energetic strides, overtaking more clusters of workers. He had an air of authority about him, and it showed in every confident step he took. Gil Andres was the kind of man people noticed, because his vibrant personality was irresistible and drew admirers like a magnet. Folks teased Eden frequently about her likeness to her father, and she was warmed by that thought. She was so happy to see him, her childhood hero.

Workers greeted Gil amiably as they walked toward the plantation office. He also was smiling, his dark eyes dancing in merriment as he removed his favorite Yankees cap and fluffed up his thick but matted down hair. As he replaced the cap on his shock of unwieldy hair, Eden noticed that he had gone grayer at the temples since she was home last Christmas. Still yet, he had a boyish appeal, and one couldn't easily place his age. The handsome face, weathered by the many hours under the Hawaiian sun, looked younger than that of one who was approaching his fiftieth birthday. Gil spotted his daughter at the gate and waved, very pleased to see her waiting for him.

"Give me fifteen minutes," he shouted to her.

Eden nodded, then elected to sit under the shade of the nearest coconut palm tree and leaned against its trunk. Knowing full well her dad's penchant for **talking story**, she expected that she had at least a half hour wait ahead.

Out of his daughter's view, the usual joy on Gil's face was replaced with a furrowed brow. He had a lot on his mind. First, he wasn't certain how he could mediate the **small kine** feud between his beloved wife Janie and their second daughter, Eden. Then, there was the upcoming plantation house inspection to deal with. Last, there was the union contract renewal with the company to sort out. As one of the union representatives, it was this latter problem that was uppermost in his mind. Nearing the plantation office, he mulled over the union's demands concerning the new contract. The deadline for drawing up the document with the company was close at hand, and he was a little uneasy about a few of the union's demands, which he felt were unrealistic in these economic times. Glancing ahead, he spotted his old friend Lefty Shimizu, and his face lit up.

"Hey, Lefty, wait up. I need to talk with you."

The other man stopped in his tracks. What a contrast they made, for the younger man towered over his shorter counterpart. With the ease of a lifetime of camaraderie, they walked shoulder to shoulder and joined the throng of workers who had filed into the plantation office to clock out for the day.

The atmosphere inside the office was one of elation. It was Friday. Satisfaction of having put in a full week of work was apparent on every face. Their noisy chatter filled the office hallway as they busily exchanged the events of the week. In the crowded hall, the two friends waited their turn and were at the tail end of the long queue of workers.

Gil took the opportunity to scan the line ahead of him. The workforce came from many ethnic backgrounds, good folk, hardworking, some youthful and enthusiastic, others not so young anymore. Yakking away, they reminded him of a flock of eager **myna** birds. The din gave him a perfect cover for what he had to say to his giant of a friend. He faced Lefty and looked him squarely in the eyes.

"**Eh,** no worry, bro, tomorrow is another day! Sleep on your decision," he said rather pointedly. "Let's also bring up more suggestions with the members at the next union meeting. I'll call you sometime in the week when we can talk about what happened today, okay?"

Lefty wanted to protest but hesitated. Uneducated and lacking in social graces, he was painfully aware of his clumsy speech. To make matters worse, he was unpopular with the plantation folk. Fortunately for him, Lefty Shimizu, the **hānai** son of immigrant laborers from Asia, was normally mindless of people's opinions of himself. The sort to be proud of his ignorance, he barely qualified for his job at the plantation. His pay was rather meager by present day standards, but it was enough for him to provide for his aging father and young sister, Michiko.

On the other hand, Lefty's charismatic friend Gil Andres, like his daughter Eden, enjoyed immense popularity. Gil was generous, self-sacrificing and hardworking. To the plantation folks, he epitomized the folk hero, a modern-day Robin Hood, and he wore his crown with flourish and style.

No one really understood the deep friendship between Lefty and Gil. Rumor had it that Lefty had saved Gil's life in a hunting accident that had occurred up in the mountains, and that in a tough situation, Gil had become indebted to the young hothead.

Most of the plantation folk, however, believed Lefty was the only one who gained from this unusual alliance. He took advantage of his mentor's social position in the community and continually broke the rules of convention. He was always getting into trouble. Once, he was nabbed cheating at a **Paiute** card game. If Gil hadn't intervened, the angry gamblers would have manhandled the blatant cheat and thrown him down the big gulch behind the chicken coops. Another time, he was caught poaching on private land, and Gil's skill at **hoʻomalimali** had charmed the landowners so much that they let Lefty go scot free. "Not right, unfair," tongues had wagged when the story got around the plantation. Whatever his foibles, however, Lefty remained faithful to Gil and to the union. In these two areas, he could not be faulted, not even by the great man himself.

Lefty hitched up his old army fatigues, retrieving a cheap cigar from a side pocket. He chewed on it for a moment, lit up, and took a few puffs. His habitual sneer softened.

"Yeah, yeah, yeah, I know I have to think about it." he conceded. "You're right." Gil was always right. He didn't know of a time when his old friend wasn't. Lefty was too aware of his own bad temper and his tendency to mouth off for nothing. Most of all, he knew he needed to chill out and take time to think about what had happened at work today. Rubbing his stubbly chin with his free hand, he decided that it was wiser to listen to Gil than to start a revolt. "Okay," Lefty finally agreed, "we have plenty of time to talk about this thing later." He looked his companion straight in the eye and had to admit to his admiration for the man. Not only was Gil always right, but he could keep his cool in any crisis. It was no wonder that the union members had unanimously and repeatedly voted him in as one of their representatives. They needed someone who could display complete self-control and diplomacy in difficult situations.

Gil was visibly relieved when the giant acquiesced so easily. He had expected a grumble at the very least and was genuinely glad that Lefty hadn't made a scene. Feeling the knot in his stomach loosen, he gave the big man a friendly slap on the shoulder as they clocked out and proceeded towards the foyer.

Lefty halted at the door to wait for his friend and watched as Gil paused to charm the office staff. His mentor was not only a trusted friend, but he was also an honest man. At times, he was too honest, Lefty brooded. Hearing the laughter and giggles of the office ladies, the big unshaven man chuckled, revealing a missing front tooth.

"Yeah," Lefty said to no one in particular, nodding his head, "we made the right choice! Gil was born to be a union rep."

Meanwhile, sitting in the sun, Eden got restless and went in search of her dad. She made her way to the lobby of the office and plopped down on a comfy chair in the waiting room reserved for visitors. It was unusually warm there, but she forgot all about the humidity when she noticed the row of books on **Hawaiiana** on the **koa** wood shelf opposite the reception window. Out of curiosity, she picked up one of the brochures on Aloha Nui Loa. When she came to a photo of the compound, she read out loud, "The main office, also known as Headquarters, is the heart of the Alexander Corporation, which employs thousands of workers on pineapple plantations on three different islands: Molokaʻi, Kauaʻi, and Oʻahu. Aloha Nui Loa Plantation, located on the island of Oʻahu, is the largest one, and the oldest. The majority of the workforce is comprised of men, descendants of contract laborers from Asia and the South Pacific, a small percentage of women, and high school and college students who are hired seasonally. The company provides on-the-job training programs with better pay as incentive for more committed workers." Eden smiled at that statement, sighed deeply and added silently to herself, "Thanks, Dad!" The union, with their members' best interests at heart, had long ago lobbied hard to insure fair wages and benefits for the plantation workers.

She supposed she was lucky. Her dad had made certain that each of his six children had learned the meaning of "Hard Work." When they were of age, they were urged to work in the fields during the summer months. "Do you want to slave away at manual labor all your lives," he often reminded them at the dinner table, "or do you want an education so you can get good jobs you really want?" Gil reiterated this all their growing up years, and she and her siblings had paid heed to their father's advice. Eden was no exception.

She turned several pages and began reading again. "Located at the edge of the compound, the office building in its heyday was originally the elegant homestead of a prosperous landowner. The company saved it from ruin and the former estate was preserved. The gracious old stucco house has been meticulously remodeled and divided into several offices. Here, CEO Barnes Alexander, the plantation manager, Ray Mulroney, and Gracie Sato, his plantation secretary, reign supreme. Their staff, which consists of junior clerks, the accountant, the engineer and the health nurses, are all comfortably accommodated."

Eden tried to stifle a yawn. Rubbing her eyes, she stood up and walked over to the picture window. It was way too warm in the room. Feeling the heat, she fanned herself for a few minutes with a magazine she picked up from the coffee table. She could see the flagpole that stood in front of the portico. The Hawaiian and American flags hung limply. She gazed up above the red tiled roof at the coconut palms that lined the winding driveway and marveled at their great height. To the right of the palms, the pagoda-like bulletin board with its minuscule tile roof was a focal point for the returning workers. Every Friday, she knew, one of the junior clerks posted the various company news bulletins and the work schedule for the coming week.

The adjacent large, grassy parking lot was being emptied of vehicles and was now serving as a gathering place for the local youth. It normally was a breezy idyllic spot, a perfect place to park under the palm trees on a sunny day and wax the family car. Several mahogany skinned lads were lounging around a shiny restored 1966 Mustang parked in one corner of the lot. A couple of them were strumming ukuleles in the **kanikapila** way. Eden loved the **falsetto** rendition of "Praising Him Island Style."

Her gaze turned to the interior of the compound. There were huge steel hangars with metal roofs that housed the trucks and field machinery, a machine shop, and a company store where the mail was also sorted in the olden days. Lastly, there was the paymaster's station where the paymaster and his faithful assistant doled out the paychecks every payday. Eden looked at the tall chain link fence that enclosed the entire operation. It was interrupted by two gates, one leading to the bumpy road out to the fields, and the other to the **camp**, the area of the plantation where the homes of the workers were situated.

Nothing seemed to have changed much in the two years that she had been on Maui. She recalled telling her college roommate Francesca Henley all about life at Aloha Nui Loa. Hailing from the remote seaside town of Hana, Maui, Franny was all ears. She and Eden became instant friends from the moment they met.

"Every workday between 7:00 AM and 3:30 PM," Eden shared, "the plantation hums with activity." Franny, who liked to sleep in, wrinkled her nose. The pineapple girl chuckled. "You get used to getting up early! That crisp mountain air is very invigorating. In the morning the field workers can be seen walking up the planks to the labor trucks to be driven to the outlying fields. The whistle is sounded promptly at seven, proclaiming the start of the workday. It is very loud, so you can hear it from all over the camp. **Luna**, who are the work gang supervisors, like my dad, get their instructions from the field bosses and guide the stronger workers in the arduous tasks of planting or harvesting. The jobs that don't require as much physical strength are assigned to the older men and the women. Depending on the season, they can be seen in their gangs at **hoe-hana**, commonly known as weeding, or **cutting suckers or pulling slips**, which are the different shoots from the mother plant. Once stacked and dried over a period, these shoots are used for planting new fields. Of course, most of the kids on the plantation worked summer jobs in the fields."

Franny, well versed in cattle ranching but knowing almost nothing about pineapple, listened with such rapt attention that Eden had continued in that serious vein. "Eleven is lunch time, and gang members can always be seen gathered at some secluded corner of a dirt road with their **kau-kau tins** spread out like in a boarding house. This really is the highlight of the day, looked forward to by all. You can imagine what great fun it is sharing lunches with everyone! At 3:30 PM, the whistle is blown again to mark the end of the workday, and the process of loading and unloading the labor trucks begins all over again."

The **pau hana** whistle had long sounded and Gracie Sato cleared her desk and turned off her ancient Mac computer. Old fashioned to the core, she left the newfangled PCs to her junior secretaries. A firm believer that she had to be the exemplary model of perfection, she carried punctiliousness to the extreme. Her grooming, from her glossy black hair that was pulled back from her round face into a severe chignon, to her sturdy, serviceable black pumps, was impeccable. The ever-present sharpened pencil over her right ear helped to project that starchy, old-fashioned school marm look. As always, fresh flowers, this time **proteas** in a clear vase, adorned her tidy desk.

Gracie stood up and straightened her polyester gabardine skirt and prim Laura Mae blouse. She took notice of the two men who were just about to leave the office. Her homely face brightened when she saw Gil Andres and Lefty Shimizu. Dropping her usual stiff, secretary voice, she called out warmly, **"Aloha,** Mr. Shimizu and . . ."

Lefty grunted in disgust, cutting her off in mid-sentence. As far as Mr. Shimizu was concerned, Gracie was a traitor. She had chosen to serve management who gave her a sizable salary instead of accepting the minimum wage secretarial job the union offered her. Never mind that Gracie was the sole provider for her widowed mother. Lefty wasn't a reasonable man. Gracie Sato tried his patience. Deliberately showing his disapproval, he refused to acknowledge her greeting and turned his head in the other direction.

Oh, but Gracie was not one bit deterred. Ray Mulroney, plantation manager, was rightfully proud of her single-mindedness. She also wasn't one to take a hint, and Lefty's rebuff rolled off her like water off a duck's back. Instead of feeling snubbed, she gave him a superficial smile that made her already slanted eyes disappear behind two slits above her flat, Asian nose. Everyone thought it was part of her charm, but this gave her a comical look and bugged Lefty no end. It really looked like she was making fun of him and did not ingratiate her in his eyes. Some men are gluttons for punishment, but not him. He snorted and walked away abruptly. This longstanding feud between Lefty and Gracie was well known. Gil laughed outright.

Of all the luna, Gil Andres was Gracie's favorite, and whenever she got the chance, she made time to chat with him. She often heard him jesting with the office girls and watched as they in turn lavished him with attention. True to form, Gil approached her desk with his warm and carefree manner. "Give it up gracefully, Gracie. Why don't you just marry the guy?" Ignoring his teasing, she turned to gather her lightweight raincoat from its hook and changed the subject.

"Nurse Emily told me your girl Eden was in to see her today. She left vitamins for her, Gil. Do take it with you." Gracie placed the bottle on her desk in front of him and offered him a cup of tea.

"No thanks, Gracie. You know I'd love to have tea and talk story, but I must be off. Eden is waiting at the gate for me, and I promised Janie to be home promptly as she's preparing a welcome home and twentieth birthday dinner for our number two girl. Oh, about the house inspection, it should take place sometime next week, eh?"

"No, it probably won't be that soon, Gil. I should have the schedule ready by the end of next week. I'll let you know when I have your appointment time. Please do wish Eden a happy birthday for me and remind Janie to bring over her famous cheesecakes for the 4-H Bake Sale. I have room in my chest freezer to store them for her."

"Yes, I will. No need worry, I won't forget about the cheesecakes. Please thank Nurse Emily for Eden's vitamins. She never forgets!" Gracie smiled and bobbed her head.

"I bet you're glad to have Eden home again."

"Yep, the house has been way too quiet without the kids. At least we'll have one kid home, and my father Milton will be coming to stay for the whole summer. He's bringing one of his dogs with him and that should keep us busy. Although, you know how busy Janie is. These days, she's in the **tūtū** mode and longs for one of the kids to get married and give her **moʻopuna**. That is, if she can find spouses for them all. Typical Chinese, you know how she likes to matchmake!" A good friend of Janie's, Gracie chuckled.

"And please give Milton a hug for me. He must be enjoying retirement!" Gil nodded. Everyone in the camp knew how Milton loved socializing with his friends.

Checking his watch, Gil added, "I'd better hit the road! Eden will be wondering where I am." He picked up the bottle of vitamins, thanked the office manager politely as he flashed her a **shaka** sign, and then tipped his baseball hat gallantly. He headed toward the lobby and his awaiting daughter. Gracie watched him take leave, remembering fondly how all the girls of the plantation had crushes on the handsome Gil, but he only had eyes for Janie.

"T. G. I. F.," she sighed aloud. With one final look around the office, she was ready to go home and relax. In her practiced, sedate manner, she closed the door and departed for the day.

An overheated Eden could hear her dad talking with Gracie Sato in the next room. The warmth of the lobby was getting to her. She decided to get a drink of water and peek into the new conference room and staff lounge. Just as she stepped into the hall, the door of the supply room was opened abruptly. A new office girl pushed out a tall trolley piled high with office paraphernalia, and Eden was forced to stand against the door to the office of . . . she couldn't quite make out the name.

"Eh, watch out," Eden uttered.

"Oh, sorry eh," whoever was behind the trolley said, "I didn't know you were there."

Eden flattened herself against the door behind her, and as she did, it opened suddenly, and she came into contact with someone who was facing into the room. Whoever it was, turned completely around at the same instant she did, and she found herself face to face with an immaculate but colorful turquoise print **Reyn Spooner aloha shirt**. She looked up into the greenest eyes she had ever seen. Faint from the heat, she swayed. Those green eyes widened in surprise.

"I beg your pardon," a deep male voice blurted out.

Apologetic, the trolley clerk seeing who it was quickly disappeared down the hall and Eden was forced into the arms of the green-eyed stranger. As Ben Alexander caught her, he exclaimed, "Well, isn't this just dandy." He picked her up and carried her to the infirmary.

"Why, it's Eden Andres! She's coming to, Boss!" Malia, the nurse's aide, rushed to his side. Ben Alexander was grateful she was still in and breathed a sigh of relief.

"I'm alright, Malia," Eden said softly, her eyes rolling open slowly. "If this hunk in shining armor will put me down, I can go home with Dad. I heard him talking with Gracie."

At a loss for the proper thing to do, Ben Alexander obeyed her and let her down gently onto the examining table. He had thought her attractive from a distance, but now, seeing her up close, she was so lovely, he suddenly felt disoriented.

"Uh, I'll go look for your dad," he stammered, and went out into the hall. To his irritation, he was met by Chloe who reminded him that Ray Mulroney, who was off island, was due to call him in a few minutes. Entering his office, he instructed over his shoulder, "Tell Gil Andres his daughter is in the infirmary, will you?"

Chloe's message had Gil rushing to the infirmary to find his daughter with a dreamy look on her face, lying on the examining table, attended to by Malia.

"Eden...Malia, what happened?"

"I'm alright, Dad," she reassured him, as she sat up and smiled wanly.

After a polite inquiry as to his daughter's condition, Gil was satisfied. With his hands firmly on her shoulders, he ushered her out of the infirmary, thanking Malia kindly and bidding the nurse's aide a good day.

Standing at the viewing window of his office, Ben Alexander, still on hold with his call, watched as Gil and Eden walked arm in arm across the compound and out the gate toward the camp. They made quite a striking pair, this union man and his daughter. Carbon copies, they had the same big disarming smile and playful sparkle in their dark brown eyes. Ben bemoaned his lousy timing, but then recalled Eden's innocent comment. "Hunk in shining armor," he repeated, and laughed out loud.

CHAPTER 2
Aloha Nui Loa

"Are you sure you're okay?" Gil inquired as he looked his number two daughter over and affectionately ruffled her hair. "This bag is heavy." Eden took the denim hold-all from him and hefted it over her shoulder.

"I didn't faint, Dad. Look, see, I've been working out." She flexed the muscles of her free arm.

"Skinny as always," he thought but smiled approvingly. He knew his daughter was an aerobic nut, the most energetic of his four girls.

"It was that guy who thought I did," Eden added. "Who was he anyway?"

"What guy," her father replied, enjoying their repartee and his daughter's discomfiture.

"Must be some new office staffer, offering assistance," she explained to herself.

"I won't mention this to your mother if you promise me to eat enough protein at each meal," her father admonished gently. "Do you want old Emily on your case again? She left another bottle of vitamins for you, you know." Eden rolled her eyes. Nurse Emily was always hovering over her brood, as she liked to call the offspring of the plantation workers.

"Dear Emily, she was overjoyed to see me today. Dad, you fuss over me just as much as she does. For heaven's sake, I'm a chef-in-training. I eat very well, thank you! It's just that the heat in the visitor's lounge was unbearable. What are they trying to do, scare the tourists away? What happened to the air conditioning? Shouldn't they get it repaired? Summer's hot weather is just around the bend."

"No need to worry, the AC has been acting up lately. It's been on the blink for the last couple of days. I'm sure they'll have someone in soon to repair it."

"Geesh, Dad," Eden let out, as she heaved the denim bag to her other shoulder. She couldn't resist teasing him. "What do you have in here, gold?" It made Gil laugh.

"I told you that bag was heavy. Phil's dad gave me some purple sweet potatoes from the Kunia experimental farm. "The Company" hopes to diversify next year. From what Mike says, they're even sweeter and a deeper purple than the **Okinawan sweet potato!**"

"Really, they're a darker purple? Wow, this I gotta see. I can hardly wait to try them. You know how I love sweet potatoes!"

"Yep, darker even than the Moloka'i sweet potato! Maybe you and mom can put your heads together and concoct something with them in the kitchen," suggested her dad, always the negotiator, smoothly guiding his daughter to work together with her mother.

"Well, they do sell **manju** and **mochi** using the Okinawan variety on Maui. They're so **ono-licious**. I brought home some Maui goodies from Sam Sato's and Homemade Bakery. Wait until you try the ones made with peanut butter and lima beans. Mom was ecstatic after her first taste." Her father smiled, feeling successful at this slick maneuver of his to encourage his daughter and wife to begin to mend fences.

Eden was quiet for a moment as she took in the fragrant air. At the far end of the large park, **keiki** were still out playing. Father and daughter could see their tiny figures in the section of the park known as "the playground." Her favorite shower trees that line the road were just beginning to bloom with dewy pink blossoms.

"Oh Dad, look at the **shower trees**! My favorite. How I've missed them!" She began to hum bars from the song, "Shower Tree" by Nathalie Ai Kamauu. Gil sang along, enjoying the camaraderie. He had a good voice and when the kids were young always had song fests with them.

It was the tail end of the rainy season and the land looked newly washed. The rain had been heavy earlier that week and had left its mark everywhere. Water had indeed widened the potholes, making **Hau'oli** Way look much like an obstacle for Boot Camp. The sight of the potholes brought back the words of an article in *Plantation Living* that Gil had been looking at. He pulled the magazine out of his back pocket and read out loud to his daughter now.

"Hau'oli Way, the main street of the Aloha Nui Loa Plantation, is just wide enough for two cars to pass each other safely. It is made of asphalt and the frequent rains have carved out a multitude of potholes in its surface. Dodging all the holes in any kind of vehicle has proven to be a challenge and has become an object of friendly competition between the residents of this small community. It seems that everyone vies wholeheartedly to be the 'champion pothole dodger.'" The author had grown thoughtful and had continued with words that had pricked Gil's heart, though he didn't share this with his daughter. He continued reading with a lighter tone than he felt. "No complaints about the potholes are forthcoming though, no matter how long it takes to repair the road, for in rainy weather, it is far easier to negotiate than the dirt road it replaced. Over the years this road has come to symbolize the permanency so lacking in the lives of immigrant field workers. Permanency means homes that the 'The Company' provides for the workers at a nominal rent. Since most of the workers are descendants of immigrants to Hawai'i, the plantation is an ideal place to put down roots. They all look upon this opportunity as a great resource in life and accept it gratefully with humble hearts. To them, a home on Aloha Nui Loa plantation is the doorway to the American Dream."

Gil glanced at his daughter to gauge her reaction to this last statement, but Eden looked straight ahead and kept her thoughts on this subject to herself. Here, he came to a stop, sticking the magazine back into his pocket. Article forgotten for the moment, he and Eden turned to watch the sun slide behind the mountains. The temperature dropped slightly, and he breathed in the air deeply and felt at peace with himself.

"After a full day at work," he said finally, "I'm happy to be going home." Eden beamed then and put her free arm through his once again.

"Me, too, Dad, me too! Thank God, it's cooled down." She sighed contentedly. They walked in companionable silence. It was so very comforting to Eden. Her dad was her first childhood hero, the first man she loved. He always made her feel cherished and protected.

The first row of homes that lead up to the Plantation Store, which sat prominently at the top of the road, came into view. So dear and familiar, the sight reminded Eden of a documentary she had seen recently of General Washington leading his beleaguered revolutionary troops to their well-worn winter camp. These houses had a similar vibe. They were simply too old, and in great need of renovation. Thriving in the tropics, the hungry termites had done their destructive work. Funny, Eden thought, how everyone in the camp took the situation lightly and joked that the houses were still standing because all the termites were holding hands. Her parents informed her a few weeks before coming home that management had decided that it was not feasible at this time to tear down the houses and build new ones. So, regrettably, they decided to continue with the repairs. Eden had mixed feelings about the news and her parents were disappointed, but they knew there were economic realities that could not be ignored. "The Company" always did their best by them and would continue to do so. They were grateful for that.

Eden looked at the camp objectively. Despite the need for internal repairs, she was pleased the exteriors of the houses were well maintained and presentable. Fashioned out of rough-sawn lumber, with the simplest of floor plans, they varied in size. Each was painted white and sported a hunter green metal roof which made them all look exactly alike. The Andres' lot was the only exception. It was pie shaped and situated in the bend of Hau'oli Way. Her father, being an avid gardener with the proverbial green thumb, had miraculously transformed the ordinary plot of ground into a veritable paradise. It made up, generously she thought, for the worn-out condition of "the old house," and surely took the sting out of having to wait so long to purchase a new home for their large family.

They finally reached their domain and walked across the velvet lawn. It always made Eden feel a little luxurious, coming home to the soft grass. The lush green foliage surrounding "the old house" beckoned them to the comfort awaiting them inside. Along the front of the house, flanking the steps up to the front door, Gil had planted birds of paradise, and along its length, **anthuriums** and **maidenhair ferns** grew in abundance. Standing over them were the gigantic tree ferns he and Lefty had hauled down from the mountains. Orchids of all varieties hung in pots, and **mondo grass** grew profusely in the backyard.

In her vegetable garden, their neighbor Henrietta called out to Eden, who graciously handed the denim hold-all back to her dad and walked over to the fence. Gil waved hello and went around to the back of the aged building and on through the **banyo**, which housed an old G.E. washer, a large sink, piles of shoes and slippers, his wife Janie's broom and mop, work clothes on hooks, and garden supplies. Slipping past laundry that was neatly arranged on plastic lines stretched the length of the small room, he went up the tiny wooden step.

"It must have rained all day," he surmised, "otherwise, Janie would have had the laundry all piled neatly in the baskets, folded and ready to be put away." At this time of day, he knew she would be busy preparing dinner in their crowded kitchen. He opened the door gingerly and was immediately assailed with the pleasant aroma coming from the adjoining room. As he entered the hub of their home, Janie looked up from the kitchen table and gave him a tender look. His wife of thirty years was in her element, and dinner was well in progress.

"How was it today, Dad, and where's Eden," she asked him affectionately, as she took his denim hold-all from him and automatically emptied the contents into the sink.

"She's out gossiping with old Henny." Gil removed his hat and tossed it gently onto the formica table of their ancient dinette set. "The purple sweet potatoes are from Mike Castro." Janie looked at the purple sweet potatoes.

"They're perfect, dear!" Gil was always bringing something home in his hold-all. When the kids were little, she remembered, they thought it was a "magic bag," full of treasures.

"I told Eden you two ought to try doing something with them, you know, and she liked that idea." He paused at the sink to wash his hands, drying them on the towel hanging over the can opener that was attached to the pantry shelf. Lowering himself onto a chair, he bent over and untied the laces of his work boots. He waited as Janie performed her daily ritual of greeting. First, she handed her husband a tall ice-filled plastic tumbler of water, then knelt and removed his boots and socks, placing them next to the kitchen door. It was something she never got tired of doing for him.

Gil's appreciation for his wife showed on his face as he watched her wash vegetables under the tap and return to her dinner preparation at the table, all the while keeping her attention upon him. Smiling warmly, she admired his usually bushy hair now matted down, and listened as he began his daily after-work monologue.

"We had a rough patch today," he started slowly. "You know what Lefty can be like. He took an instant dislike to acting head engineer, young Alexander. Ben is his name. Must be named after the old man, his grandfather, I guess. He's pleasant enough but needs to learn how to be personable with the men." Between great gulps of water, he continued, "The boy has plenty of schooling, so he's sharp in that way. The brilliant type Eden would love," he chuckled. "Oh, by the way, they met today." So absorbed in his talk, Gil didn't notice his wife's raised eyebrows at the mention of Eden meeting Ben

Alexander. "Though," her husband continued, "I can't say I care too much for his formal style."

"**And then**?" she egged him on, still working away at her chopping board, this time keeping her eyes on her work. Another indulgent smile played on his wife's ruby lips. She knew only too well how her husband could ramble on with just a wee amount of encouragement.

Catching her drift, he reached over and pinched her cheek. Though spots of white now showed in her dark hair, and fine wrinkles lined below her almond eyes, to him she was still the provocative beauty he had fallen in love with so many years ago. When she put her mind to it, she could still raise a spark in him.

"Well," he continued, "he looks the part, plantation owner's son and all. A handsome guy if you ask me. Makes me wonder why he's still single." Janie's ears perked up to this intriguing tidbit, but her interest escaped her husband once again. "He talks like he thinks too much. In my opinion, he doesn't seem to be enthusiastic about his current assignment, his father being away and all." Gil shook his head. "Yep, he's a deep one, a different kettle of fish from Ray Mulroney, who is easygoing and diplomatic. It will take some time getting used to young Alexander's ways. Whew. He's not **high maka maka**, but that smooth voice droning on and on was just too much for Lefty," he recounted the story with amusement in his eyes. "That guy couldn't make heads or tails out of that highfalutin speech. You know how Lefty feels already about the bosses," Gil added on a sobering note, "he thinks they lord it over the laborers as it is. He threatened to quit again today after meeting Alexander, but I got that hot head to simmer down. I promised him we'd talk at length after this inspection business is over."

Janie Wang Andres looked up and the smile froze on her lovely face. "Oh no, you know how stubborn Lefty is," she lamented, "I hope he doesn't get out of hand. I never understood how anyone as sweet as his sister Michiko could be related to an old mule like him!" Up went her cleaver into the air.

"Hear, hear, Mom," Gil warned loudly, putting his empty tumbler down with a thump, "I hope you don't get out of hand yourself. With that cleaver, you look like an avenging angel, and I'd hate to have you on the other side of the bargaining table. Easy does it, that thing is sharp, you know!"

His wife quickly heeded his reprimand. She could be inscrutable, which was only natural, as she was mostly Chinese. She could also be brutally frank and to the point as well, traits Gil viewed as necessary tools for a union man, and he greatly admired them in his wife.

Pulling out Eden's vitamins from his jacket pocket, he conveniently placed them next to his wife's chopping board. He was looking forward to dinner. Janie, an accomplished cook, had prepared Eden's favorite meal, Swiss Steak, which was simmering on the stove. The aromas filling the kitchen had his mouth watering.

"By the way," Gil said with an impish gleam on his face, "before I forget, Gracie wants your cheesecakes before D-Day next Saturday." He playfully snitched a piece of carrot, deftly avoided his wife's attempt to slap his hand, and crunched on it pleasantly.

"The Annual Bake Sale is Gracie's big thing," Janie added. "You know that event always causes a flutter with the ladies of the plantation. I look forward to it every year myself, and I'm relieved that Eden is back to lend a hand with the baking. That girl is a natural baker. She has a way with pie crusts. I taught her the basics, you know, when she was only eight. Look at her now. She can help with the cheesecakes too."

Gil took in the peaceful look on his wife's face and knew she was immersed in her task at hand. He stood up slowly, rubbing the back of his neck before heading to the parlor to read the newspaper.

"It is comforting to have Eden home again, Mom. And no need to worry, Lefty was just mouthing off and I can handle him."

"You're right, dear," she called out to him on an optimistic note. "Ah, dinner will be ready in a few minutes. I see that nurse Emily remembered Eden's vitamins. I hear the old girl's taking a leave of absence to visit her daughter on the mainland. How nice of Mike Castro to feed the chickens today for you, dear. Oh, by the way, Phil Castro's home from **U.H.** He picked up Eden at the airport. I've already prepared her old room for her, so we'll have lots of time after dinner to figure out how to get ready for the house inspection."

Gil answered her with a satisfied grunt as he lowered his tired body into his favorite recliner. Though somewhat pressed for space, Janie ran a well-organized home. It was going to be good to have at least one of the kids home, he reminded himself again. He was glad that Eden was safe at Aloha Nui Loa and not on her own on a neighboring island. In the time she'd been on Maui, he'd really missed her perky enthusiasm. In fact, he had to admit, he missed all the kids, especially the companionship of his boys. The events of the day faded away as he opened the sports section of the Honolulu Daily News.

CHAPTER 3
The Old House, an Introspection

Eden was ensconced tightly but cozily in her old bedroom. The room was smallish and over the past two years had served as a guest room, storage for her Uncle Mick's golf clubs, old schoolbooks, her father's mini trampoline, extra bedding, and not to forget, the old clothes all the kids had outgrown. She was sitting on the sagging bed with its colorful, pieced Hawaiian quilt. In a quirky mood, she was ingenuously attired in odd-fitting clothes. Having risen early that morning, she had engaged in an energetic round of circuit training and aerobics. Now, feeling languid from the heat, she plopped down onto her bed with elbows up, legs bent at the knees. She was showing off smooth tanned legs and tiny, Cinderella feet. Reeboks had long since been discarded, and socks and leg warmers, along with her mother's extensive collection of cookbooks, were strewn on the bed. She was daydreaming.

Reflecting on the last few days, she gave herself a mental shake. If only Francesca hadn't fretted at her earlier than planned departure from Hāna, she thought ruefully, there would have been plenty of time to get to the Maui Airport. She had wanted to savor the drive on the Hāna road one last time. Too soft-hearted for her own good, she had sought to comfort Franny, who wanted to persuade Eden to stay an extra week. As a result, she had to be driven to Kahului in a big rush. She could have easily taken the small plane from Hāna to Kahului, but it meant accepting a loan from her college roommate to purchase her ticket. Dear, sweet Randy, Franny's beau, had been more than willing to drive her over to the **'other side.'** Though he was a skillful driver, a mudslide at Keʻānae and the inconvenience of the remodeling at the Maui Airport had caused her to miss her scheduled flight. At the end of May, the place was packed with tourists, and Eden didn't enjoy being jostled about. Feeling partly nauseous from the speedy winding drive and a little emotionally drained, all she wanted was to get home to Aloha Nui Loa.

To make matters worse, Phil Castro, her childhood friend who was always fretting about her, was anxiously waiting for her arrival at the Honolulu Interisland Terminal. Luckily, she was able to get on another flight, but by the time she arrived in Honolulu, looking much like a bedraggled world traveler, her joy at seeing him was short lived. Instead of being happy she got home safely, he gave her a sermon on the importance of being on time.

"Eden, how could you miss your flight?" he said with exasperation, "weren't you paying attention?" She could have cheerfully throttled him, especially when she found that her luggage had been waylaid. Instead, she gave him a big bear hug in answer, which totally threw him off.

So, here she found herself at home, without her own clothing or belongings. Fortunately, she was able to rummage through her sisters' old clothes and could keep herself decently clad until her precious suitcases and box of books were found. According to her mother, she resembled a Barnum and Bailey clown. She wouldn't be in this fix now, Janie had reemphasized over the last few days, if she had been better organized. It wasn't exactly the homecoming she had envisioned, even though they had a cozy birthday dinner together. Janie had been placated when Eden had turned out the scrumptious cheesecakes. She loved to bake, and inheriting her mother's innovative ways, made several cheesecakes using the purple sweet potatoes. It was such a clever idea that Janie was delighted with the results and had to compliment her daughter's ingenuity.

"What a great idea to use the purple sweet potatoes," Janie said. "So yummy. They should sell well at the bake sale, don't you think?"

"I think so, Momsy," Eden had responded. "They came out so much better than I anticipated. My pastry instructor at the college is a whiz at making desserts using local fruit. I still want to try making a cheesecake using **breadfruit**. I must admit, this is just as good as the ones made with **liliko'i!**"

Breakfast that morning, however, was another story. Eden grimaced at the memory. Her mother had thrown a royal fit when she had appeared at the table wearing the atrocious turquoise exercise suit. The outfit had fitted her sister Abby of the ample bosom like a glove but was unsuitable for Eden's trim frame. She looked like a kid playing dress up. It was the pig tails that did it.

That eventful day, Eden was feeling self-conscious about her exposed legs, so she had added the ridiculous hot-pink shorts, a.k.a. Abby's first sewing project, and those chartreuse leg warmers that had belonged to the twins. Her clown 'costume,' as Janie labeled it, and the kiddie hairstyle, made her look like a rebellious teenager instead of a responsible twenty going on twenty-one. Secretly, it made her want to chuckle inside when Janie was irked to the max. It seemed to Mrs. Andres that she was always remonstrating her daughters for their impulsive ways. In her opinion, Eden took top honors. She was famous for acting before thinking and repenting at leisure. That morning was par for the course.

"Eden, do you do it on purpose?" Janie had accused. "That outfit is ridiculous! Until your suitcases are found, you may borrow some of my clothing!" Eden had turned a deaf ear to her and continued to eat her yogurt while leafing through a magazine. Failing to get an appropriate response, Janie had tried glowering at her daughter. That, of course, hadn't worked.

"Relax, Momsy," Eden chimed in. "You're getting worked up for nothing. You have no idea how intense it was during Finals, and I just want to hang out and be comfy. Anyway, who's going to see me looking like this, Gramps? He's out for the day!" She had no idea she would eat those famous last words that very afternoon.

The much-used Big Ben windup clock ticked noisily from its perch atop the black metal shelf that stood directly behind the sagging bed. Eden had cleared a space for the ancient typing stand with its rusty metal legs and had pushed it next to her old bed. Its white Formica top with the gold speckles in it was covered with a pile of books and papers. Sitting precariously on top of the heap was a glass of diluted **guava** juice. The two large windows that covered the wall fronting Hauʻoli Way were opened wide, but the air was still and the heat in the small room was slightly oppressive.

She loved "the old house" and her crowded bedroom. These were familiar to her and made her feel welcomed. Not that she hadn't been welcomed by Franny's family in Hāna, but family was family. She really believed that one didn't have to achieve fame or wealth with family. One was loved for being family. Holding down a part-time job while in college had been more grueling than she expected, and dorm living was great fun but not altogether restful. The week in Hāna on a cattle ranch had been enlightening. That delectable sea breeze while walking along the beach of Hamoa, the one that Mark Twain called "the most beautiful beach in the world," soothed her soul. She had enjoyed her stay with Franny's family, but she was relieved to be back in Aloha Nui Loa where she could just be her own free self. Except for the early morning tussle with her mother about her frivolous clothing, she was truly comforted to be back in the sanctity of home. Somehow, life on the plantation seemed more real to her, or perhaps it was just life as she was accustomed to living.

The Andres home, Eden decided, had character. In comparison to Franny's affluent lifestyle and beautifully appointed home, "the old house" was full of 'junks,' as her mother liked to call her motley collection of furnishings. In every available space, there was a pile of something or other, as plantation homes were not originally designed with storage space in mind. The rattan furniture, still intact after many years of service, with their cushions covered in a tropical flower print 1950's style **bark cloth**, had been redone several times. On the walls of the single wall frame house were found calendars from various businesses in the neighboring town of **Wahiawā**, an odd assortment of prints and posters, and lastly, the high school graduation pictures of the older children. Live plants in pots and dried flower arrangements added a jungle-like flavor. Eden knew it was a constant battle to keep the place orderly with the burgeoning family and their accumulation of earthly possessions. The everything-has-a-place-almost-minimalist-look of *House Beautiful* that Janie Andres favored eluded her and seemed even more remote with the passage of time. After years of trying to keep up, she had given in gracefully and had chosen to live in homey clutter.

It was not that the place was unkempt. Goodness knows, her mom was the "Cleanliness is next to Godliness" type. There just wasn't enough space to store everything. It gave the house its lived-in look and made it a haven for their many friends and relatives. They came from all over the islands to bask in the warmth of her father's hospitality, and to sample her mother's diverse styles of ethnic cooking.

They were lucky, Eden reminded herself, for the Andres' house was one of the roomier models which were built expressly for the larger families. Her father was fortunate to have secured it when the children were youngsters. To make room for their steadily growing accumulation of furnishings, Gil had built shelves in every place possible. When these, too, were filled, he built a storage shed out back to store his tools and an extra freezer. In return for his many deeds of generosity, the freezer was usually filled with carefully wrapped packages of wild caught fish, game and farm raised meat that were gifts from his many friends. To the shed, he had added a small greenhouse, where he and Janie kept their potted plants. Most of them were started from cuttings obtained from friends. Ferns and orchids hung gaily from wood slats that made up its ceiling. Next to the greenhouse, Janie had planted ginger, garlic and lemongrass around the base of a mature **kalamungay** tree that had been carefully pruned by her husband.

On the other side of the shed, a small chicken coop was being built. Behind that lay the carefully tended vegetable garden with its border of healthy-looking **taro** and **cassava** plants. Beyond the garden was the dirt road that separated the fields, now full of pineapples, from their yard.

Eden could hear her dad pounding away at something out back and returned to her reading. Gil was busy working at the picnic table. His project was a doghouse of reclaimed lumber for Jack, his father's dog. He checked his watch intermittently as it was the day of the house inspection. At lunch hour, the hottest time of day, the day workers ceased from their labors, and a sleepy quiet had come over the plantation. The tiny **black pineapple bugs** seemed to multiply by the minute. Gil's morning had been jarring enough. He had launched headlong into this woodworking project with the outcome of the last union meeting still occupying his mind. The combination of the midday heat and his unsettled feelings were causing him some degree of stress. A carpenter he was not.

Slam! The kitchen door was opened roughly and banged shut with a vengeance. The loud, abrupt sound startled Eden and she sat up, ears alert. She gathered that her father had come in when the silence of the day was broken by his yowling. Expletives of all sorts, some not so mild, were pouring forth, first to the frig, then to the kitchen sink, and finally to the air. Mrs. Andres dropped her crocheting and quickly ran to his aid.

"Gil dear, what happened?" Seeing he had merely hammered his left thumb, and there was no cause for real alarm, she invited him to sit down while she ministered first aid to her aggrieved husband. One look at her adored face, and the furious brow was immediately erased and replaced by another of his brilliant smiles.

Eden got up and quietly closed her bedroom door. Whatever the problem was, she was certain that her mother would soon have it under control. Sure enough, the crisis passed in no time at all. She could hear her mother's soothing voice, cooing comfort to her traumatized husband, and soon the gruffness left his own staccato sentences. The peace and tranquility of mid-day was restored, and Eden returned to the perusal of her mom's treasured cookbooks.

Mr. Andres tried not to look exasperated as he dressed for work. Part of his annoyance, besides having a sore thumb, was that the house inspection time had been mistakenly set for late in the afternoon. He was scheduled this week to work the night shift, and to insure being on time for work, he had to leave the house at 2:30 PM. He couldn't possibly meet with the bosses at the same time. He had gravely corrected this gross error with Gracie. Taking it in her stride, Gracie had rescheduled the inspection for 12:30 PM. Now here it was, going on one o'clock. The Inquisitors –Janie jokingly called the inspectors– were already half an hour late.

The Andreses now sitting together in the parlor looked deceptively serene. So serene that only their children, Eden especially, would guess at the insecurity that had plagued them all their wedded life. It was bothering them now, but they both hid it well. The improvement of the old house meant more to them than they let on.

Having to still rent a place to live and the uncertainty of not knowing how long they would be able to live there, however, didn't stop them from being happily married. They were well-matched and complemented each other perfectly. Their friends commented on it frequently. After thirty years of a blessed and happy marriage, they still looked the attractive couple they had made the day they wed. Their children loved them dearly, and Eden, the sensitive, idealistic one of the bunch was the most demonstrative about it. Their happy union had produced six handsome children. Abigail, the oldest, had come first. Another few years passed before Janie was with child again. It was with great expectation that the Andreses awaited the birth of their second baby. Instead of the boy they hoped for, they had another girl, who was born premature. It was a tense time for all. The tiny babe was not allowed home until she weighed five pounds, having to stay three months in an incubator in the hospital. With the tender loving care of plantation nurse Emily Hodges, the concern for her weight gain had quickly passed.

Gil and Janie, having prepared only a list of names for boys, gratefully gave the honor of naming the baby to Miss Emily. A Bible thumping Presbyterian and an avid gardener, she had christened the infant, Eden. Gil had lovingly tacked on Sabina, in memory of his dear mother, for the baby had the look of her grandmother.

Eden was very active and darling, but Janie had bemoaned the fact of not giving her athletic husband the son he hoped for. Her husband was generous with his love.

"We have lots of time to have more kids, my dear," he comforted as he picked up the tiny babe. "Let's thank the good Lord for giving us such a lively one. Look at her squiggly arms and legs," he had urged his wife. "She doesn't weigh more than a T-bone steak. See, she can fit in the palm of my hand." The baby grew under the tender care of her nurse, who was forever plying her with vitamins. Her father's words proved to be prophetic, and the growing child remained as boney as ever. For this reason, she was affectionately called every nickname under the sun associated with thinness, "Bones" being the most popular of them all.

The Lord was good indeed. He heard Miss Emily's **"Prayer of Hannah"** for the Andres family, and four other children were born in succession. Two hefty sons, named Robert and Albert, were born a year apart, and to their utter joy, three years later the precocious identical twins, Gwen and Vera, were added to the fold. The twins shared the single name of Guinevere, for by that time Mrs. Andres, with so many little ones running under her busy feet, had not had the time to think of another name, let alone two. Abigail, having just discovered the joys of medieval stories, had suggested Guinevere, Gwen and Vera for short! Gil and Janie reminded everyone of two sparrows in the Spring, proudly boasting of their brood as their 'cheaper by the half dozen bunch!' Gil didn't mind the daily sacrifices he made to insure his children's future. The rising cost of living in the Fiftieth State constantly ate up what precious little savings he was able to set aside for his family's dream home. What a source of frustration it presented to the children, as they grew into adulthood and watched their parents' dream of owning their own home fade away.

Abigail, the beautiful, frustrated at teaching for what she called a mere pittance, found work in a modeling agency and, because of her unusual beauty, had branched into free-lance modeling in Honolulu. Eden had saved up her after school earnings working at Cornet Store in Wahiawā and had opted to attend the newly accredited cooking program at the UH-Maui College. The boys, Robert and Albert, both joined the Air Force right after high school, and set their hearts on attending college using the G.I. Bill. Robert was stationed in Minnesota, of all places, enjoying the change of seasons, while Albert was in Georgia, loving the southern comfort. Fortunately for the Andreses, Gwen and Vera, the brainy twins, were blessed with well-off godparents who generously offered to augment their scholarships at a Catholic girl's school in Honolulu. They were currently in California on a student exchange program for the entire year. For financial reasons and others not so easily defined, the Andres family still lived at 199 Hauʻoli Way, on Aloha Nui Loa Plantation, just outside of Wahiawā.

CHAPTER 4
The Inspection

It was a scorcher of a day. "The old house" was due to be personally inspected by Raymond Mulroney, Aloha Nui Loa's manager, and Ben Alexander, the acting head engineer. For the past few days, Gil Andres had been rambling on and on about the differences between the two men, but since her father normally shared his opinions aloud, Eden had paid scant attention to his revelations. She wasn't **niele**, like Abby, and took the meeting of her father and his bosses as just an everyday plantation event.

To be ready on time, however, had taken all their attention, and Eden and her parents had worked at a feverish pace the last couple of days. The clutter of the old house was under control, and there was the distinct scent of Pine-O in the air.

Gil paced the parlor floor. He was a stickler for punctuality, and those guys were going on half an hour late. He sank into his favorite chair but got up immediately and walked to the screened front door. There was nothing to be seen but the heat waves on the horizon, and nothing to be heard but the sound of the Army bombing practice above **Schofield Barracks**. He shaded his eyes and squinted in search of the missing duo. They were nowhere in sight. His faded green Army field jacket that was hanging on the nail next to the front door was stuffed into his denim hold-all at his feet. There, he was ready for work. Now, if only Ray and Ben would show up, he would be on time for work.

Earlier that week there had been another scene with Lefty, and Gil was feeling unnecessarily pressured and a little strained. He sat down once more to unload his burden onto his obliging wife, seated on the sofa crocheting away.

"Had some trouble at the last union meeting," he began with a deep sigh. "I thought I had squared away all of Lefty's doubts when we talked last week, but I was too optimistic. Somehow, he's developed a dislike for young Alexander, and of all the crazy things, Lefty's name was pulled to introduce Alexander to the union men. It could have been a well-timed icebreaker, but that rascal got puffed up with self-importance and tripped up on his words. The more he tried, the more he stammered. The more he stammered, the more ridiculous it sounded. I tell you, he brought down the house. How could the staid Alexander help himself? Everyone else was cracking up. All he did was break a little smile, but Lefty took it all wrong. If I didn't have to be so fair, I would laugh it off, but after the bosses left, that darn hothead threatened to call a strike. It exasperated me so much, I wanted to wash my hands of him."

"Gil, dear," Janie commiserated, "this has happened before. Lefty always wants to call a strike for some wild reason or other. It makes him feel important. The very idea is disgusting, considering how intolerant he is of anyone, especially the bosses. You'd think he didn't have anything else to do but put on airs."

"I know, but this is different. Why young Alexander? He's been away from home since graduating from college. Yale it was, I think, in engineering, then further studies at UC Davis in tropical agriculture. His father has been heading this whole operation for years. Why pick on the son? He's still carving out his engineering career and is only going to be here until his old man returns."

"Perhaps," Janie responded, shaking her head, "he's envious of Ben's Ivy League education. Who knows, Lefty certainly isn't reasonable. We all know that."

"Well, Ben is the heir apparent. As much as I can see how he's just filling in for his father right now, he will be a big part of the company's future. He stands for all that is despised in Lefty's eyes."

"So," his wife retorted, "why should that make a difference? You said yourself that Ben Alexander was an educated man. It seems to me that at least he took his schooling seriously. Lefty doesn't even come close in comparison. Why, he scraped through grade school, and never got through the ninth grade! He should have stayed in school like the rest of us and shouldn't have sneaked off all the time to go hunting. Besides, don't you think it's high time he took his responsibilities seriously? At least Ben Alexander isn't shirking his." Janie belonged to the camp that believed Lefty took advantage of everyone, especially her husband. She glanced up from her crocheting and continued without sympathy. "Lefty is always the one for biting the hand that feeds him."

"Now, dear," Gil reproved his wife mildly, "the part about Lefty was minor. The big thing was the talk about the company wanting to pull out entirely from Aloha Nui Loa. Surely, they must be losing some profit with the labor costs in Hawai'i," he sighed. "The pineapple grown here is top class, possibly the best in the world, but how can they continue to compete in the global market with labor so cheap in other countries? If they pull out, this land will revert its lease to the Alexander Land Trust, and the houses will all come down. You know what that would mean. I would be jobless at my age, and we'd have to find another place to live."

"What about all the others?" Gil continued rubbing his forehead with concern in his eyes. "Can you see some of the old timers trying to make a go at new jobs? No way! Plantation life is the only life they know. Who would hire them? They're too old to train for anything else. No, my dear, if it was only my own family's problem I had to cope with, maybe I would bail, but there are hundreds of others to think of. I can't allow this one incident to jeopardize the lives of so many. Not now, anyway, with all the rumors of a shut-down. I can't allow Lefty to have his childish tantrum. He thinks that a strike would solve all the problems and forgets the hardships that go hand in hand with it." Gil shook his head. "Personally, I don't understand his vendetta against young Alexander. Lefty doesn't even know the man."

Janie could see that this impassioned speech wasn't getting her husband anywhere. To comfort him, she got up and patted his shoulder.

"There, there dear, it's too distressing to contemplate life without the plantation. This is where we met, Gil, remember, the girl next door!" Gil's countenance turned tender at this statement by his wife. "I'm sure," she continued, "that between them, the union leaders and the bosses will work things out to keep the whole operation going." Fishing through her handbag, she pulled out a letter from the twins, knowing it would cheer him up. "Here, let me read Gwen and Vera's letter. They seem to be enjoying themselves, and I'm so relieved. Aren't you? They're going to Disneyland next week."

In her room adjacent to the living room, Eden could hear her parents talking. She felt a little guilty about eavesdropping, but she had heard the same story almost all her life. The uncertainty, the possibility of losing their home, had gotten to all of them. So much so, that none of the Andres children talked openly about it anymore. The subject was too painful and made them feel quite helpless.

Plantation life couldn't go on forever. She knew this fact well. In the old days, the plantation provided everything a family needed: a job, a home, a company store, medical, community activities, upkeep of the houses and camp proper. Hawai'i became the 50th state. Modern industrialization, higher education, big businesses, all in the name of progress, changed everything. Nothing would ever be quite the same as it was in her grandfather's or her father's day. Along with that realization came the gnawing truth that the kids of her generation were slowly trickling out of the aging plantation. Driven away by the high cost of island living and lured by the promise of big paying jobs on the U.S. mainland, many of her friends had moved away after college. They loved Hawai'i, even longed for and missed it tremendously, but they were not inclined to continue the tradition started by their grandparents, who had traversed the globe in order to work the Hawaiian plantations. It was somewhat sad, but in the name of progress, the once thriving plantation communities of her grandfather's day were in decline.

It was already one-thirty in the afternoon. Eden looked at the clock and yawned. She felt indescribably lazy. How amazing, it seemed to her, that, in just two weeks' time, her rigid school schedule had been quickly dispensed with and replaced by the bad habit of procrastination. She groaned with distaste when she thought about whipping up enough energy to change out of her outlandish outfit. Since coming home, she'd slipped back almost too easily into her role of second daughter. Gone was the efficient college student, and back was the slightly carefree plantation girl. Perhaps that's why her mother picked on her so much. She wanted Eden to be just like Abby, much to her distress. Not that it would hurt to look chocolate box beautiful like her big sister, but her mother's meddling was a bit much. Janie sometimes couldn't leave well enough alone.

Temporarily forgetting the meeting with the big bosses, Eden's eyes fell onto a color photo of an elegantly appointed dinner table. Scribbling furiously for the moment, she was immediately transported into the culinary world of Emeril Lagasse and Morimoto San, her mother's favorites, and to Ming Tsai and Roy Yamaguchi, her favorites. So intrigued was she with the exquisite recipes, the tantalizing sauces, the delicious scents wafting from her dream kitchen with its gleaming copper batterie and her stainless-steel restaurant stove, that she didn't hear the four-wheel-drive vehicle come to a grinding stop on the gravel driveway. Neither did her brain register the sound of her father's congenial welcome to the two men outside, nor did she hear his invitation to begin their inspection of "the old house." In fact, so engrossed was she that she was taken completely by surprise when the door to her room was rudely opened, and in-filed her smiling dad and two handsome men. Three pairs of eyes stuck like glue to her person, taking in every detail. The first expressed total surprise, the second brimmed with amusement and the third held admiration.

Momentarily dumbfounded, Eden sat up transfixed, mouth gaping. When her father had mentioned the names of the plantation manager and the acting head engineer, she had pictured them as his contemporaries. Somewhere along the way, she had totally missed the boat. She never expected two very robust men in the prime of their lives to be standing in her old bedroom, inspecting the termite destruction of the floor. Both were tall, tanned, and exuded vigor, dwarfing her short, albeit athletic, father. Horrified to be caught in such an uncomely fashion, heat spread over Eden's cheeks. Lowering her eyes, she stood up suddenly, inadvertently hitting her head against the bookshelf Robert had so proudly fashioned in woodshop in high school. To her further dismay, papers scattered in all directions. She bent quickly to retrieve the mess as the older of the two khaki clad gentlemen did likewise. Their heads had the misfortune to meet somewhere in mid-air and Eden, the smaller of the two, fell backwards into an ungainly heap on the floor.

That did it! The scene was just too much for the fun-loving girl and the hilarity of the moment hit her funny bone. She rolled back her head and broke into hearty laughter. At this unconventional behavior, her father, normally the loquacious member of the family, was rendered speechless. The plantation manager joined in her laughter. Rubbing his head in mock pain, he offered her a helping hand

"I dare say, young lady," he began affably, "I must beg your pardon." Eden was ceremoniously helped up, but her carefree mood came to a sober halt when she noted the beginnings of a frown on her father's face. She quickly composed herself like the gentle, well-mannered young lady that she was, and her father, ever the diplomat, expediently covered the awkward moment by making introductions.

"Raymond Mulroney, Ben Alexander, this is my number two girl, Eden Sabina," he announced proudly. Eden Sabina winced at the mention of her full given name. To her chagrin, her dad still saw her as his little girl.

Ben Alexander held back a smile as he covertly observed Gil's number two girl. He had been surprised but secretly pleased to discover the identity of the swooning gate girl. He watched her shake hands daintily with Ray Mulroney, who had so gallantly helped her up. Ray, who was slightly portly with just a streak of gray in his auburn hair, was liked on sight, and Eden beamed widely for him, showing off her dimple. For some inexplicable reason, Ben felt something akin to the 'green eyed monster,' and he quickly covered his interest.

It was then that she focused in on him and there her smile froze. The hunk in shining armor was none other than Ben Alexander, the heir to the Alexander Corporation! Shades of a major faux pas, she thought, eyes blinking wildly. She found herself blushing to the roots of her hair and didn't know when she was ever more embarrassed in her life.

There was an odd silence as Eden took in Ben's appearance. It was like she was seeing him anew. He was the handsomest man she had ever had the good fortune to behold. At least ten years younger than Mulroney, he was taller than the plantation manager and incredibly well-built. His rather long, sun-bleached blond hair was superbly cut, and his pointed nose melded into the contours of his sun-browned face. The jaw was well chiseled, and the mouth held just a ghost of a smile, but it was the regal emerald eyes that held her spellbound. For a few seconds, she couldn't take her eyes off him. Though neither acknowledged it, the chemistry between them instantly kindled a spark.

Feeling flustered and thrown off kilter, she finally remembered her good manners and proffered her hand to the golden Adonis. When he hesitated to take it right away, she felt quite frivolous. With a curt nod of his golden head, he shifted his gaze away from her and caused his ratings in her eyes to drop rapidly from a ten to a zero. So much for looking like a nobleman, she thought, if there was one thing she couldn't stand, it was a conceited hunk. The shining armor was quickly dismissed!

Puzzled, she peered up at him again, but somehow the spell had been broken, and a subtle change had come over him. In place of that little smile was a mask of censure. Baffled and feeling quite snubbed, Eden felt the need to get away from those disturbing eyes and gathered her papers into a pile and excused herself politely. Her father winked as she made a quick getaway for the kitchen.

Holding her head high, she sashayed down the hall. Once in the sanctuary of the kitchen, she yanked open the door to the frig and grabbed a Red Delicious out of the bin. Leaning back on the fridge door, she chomped viciously on her apple. After a few minutes she felt her calm return and peered around the fridge and into the hall. The men were making their way to the front door. She waited until they were out of the house and breathed a sigh of relief. Deeming it safe to make a reappearance in the living area, she sauntered casually into the parlor, sat down in her dad's recliner, and acted as if nothing out of the ordinary had happened. She wasn't one to hold grudges, because her merry heart always did her good.

Her mother was sitting on the old rattan sofa, crocheting another baby sweater like it was going out of style. Despite their morning hassle, Eden observed her with affection. Janie's obsession with having grandchildren before she reached a ripe old age had become a joke with the kids. In friendly rivalry, they had made a bet to see who would be the last to give in to their mother's endless matchmaking schemes. Eden was confident she would be the winner. She was the only one not dating.

Looking so dear with her John Lennon spectacles low on her nose and her eyes darting from side to side, Janie queried in a hushed voice, "Seen the bosses, have you, Eden? Attractive, aren't they?" Eden choked on her apple. Her mom had a knack for always saying the right thing at the right moment. Oblivious to her daughter's jangled feelings, she eyed her outfit with distaste, but forbore bringing up that heated subject again. "Darling, you should have your hair done," she continued in a whisper. "Those pigtails are so childish! Besides, you have beautiful hair. You should wear it loose instead of your usual ponytail all the time. Don't . . ."

Her voice trailed off as Eden picked up a magazine from the coffee table and chose to zone out her mother's suggestions. Questions bombarded her brain. Why is mom whispering? Why is she crocheting so wildly like she has a deadline to meet? Why is she going on about my hair when she already knows how I feel about beauty salons?

Unable to bear her daughter's Raggedy Ann appearance any longer, Janie got up and hurriedly pulled the rubber bands from Eden's hair.

"There," she exclaimed, pleased with her fast work, "you look ten times better. I wish you would consult with Abigail and have her advise you on a more fashionable hairdo. You really could do something with your appearance if you would only . . ." Her mom sat down once more and resumed crocheting at that furious pace.

Eden shook her head and her hair fell like a curtain around her slim form. Her mother was acting very strange. She was beginning to wonder if something was seriously wrong when a voice from behind her spoke out.

"Are there any leaks in the ceiling?" It was low, cultured and well-modulated. Ordinarily, she would have drooled over anyone who sounded so dreamy, but this one rather turned her off. It was that Alexander man.

"Drat, it's him again." she mouthed to herself as she waited for her mother's response. When none was forthcoming, Eden pulled her magazine an inch below her eyes to peer at her parent. Her mom was a little hard of hearing, but who could fail to hear the condescension dripping from that voice?

"Does the ceiling leak?" Ben Alexander asked once more, attempting another approach. Giving the two women a cursory glance, he merely presumed that they had not heard him.

Eden stifled a giggle. How quickly the tables had been turned! "What fun," she thought. "Why, Mr. High and Mighty actually sounded a bit human this second time around." She would have loved to see the surprise on his snobbish face. While the drama in her wanted desperately to curtsey to His Dibs and blurt out, "Why kind sir, this is how the other half lives, you know," but the quelling look her mom gave her quickly dispelled the ridiculous notion from her head. Instead, she clamped her mouth shut. Seconds which seemed like eternity ticked by. Eden began to feel uncomfortable in the silence that ensued. Why was her gracious mama giving this total stranger the freeze? She placed her magazine on the coffee table and tried to get her mother's attention by making faces at her. Plainly, she saw that her mom was upset, but whatever for?

Ben debated what course of action to take next. It was finally apparent to him that the two women were ignoring him. The soul of discretion, his good manners prevented him from reciprocating in kind. He probably deserved it, he figured, judging from the reaction he'd received from Andres' number two girl. Why had he given her the royal snub, anyway? Perhaps it was because she seemed overly friendly. He wasn't much of a socializer himself, and he felt extremely out of place in her home. For the life of him, he couldn't even begin to understand how Ray could fit in so easily. Nothing ever bothered Ray, it seemed.

Ben shrugged. The sooner the inspection was done, the sooner he could get out of this confined atmosphere. The place was a little run down, and it depressed him. Everywhere he looked, there was something needing repair, peeling paint here and there and a couple rooms with termite-eaten floors repulsed him. He felt grieved that the company hadn't been able to do more for them. He was beginning to feel claustrophobic in the cluttered house, or was it the heat that was making him feel uncomfortable? He couldn't be sure. Anxious to get out, he walked to the front door.

The very slight breeze welcomed and cooled him immediately. He took out his handkerchief and wiped his brow. The moment in time seemed vaguely familiar, yet he knew it couldn't be a déjà vu. After his bout with malaria in Thailand, parts of his memory had remained a mystery. The doctors had reassured him that all would come back to him in time, yet he still felt a twinge of sorrow about his memory loss.

So absorbed with his thoughts was the man, that he didn't notice that Eden was admiring his hunk proportions. The back of his fine head of hair curled in the heat and gave him a rakish appearance. Spun gold, it was Eden's favorite color. The indecision and vulnerable look on Ben's face pulled on her heart strings, and suddenly, she felt remorseful for laughing at him. She was forced to admit that it was unfair to treat the man so unkindly, especially since he'd come to her rescue, even if it had been by coincidence. Intuitively, Eden knew that something was not all right with him, and she wondered what was going through his mind. The silence was getting to her, and she began to squirm in her chair.

Ben put his hand to the door, pushed it open, and then closed it again. He looked a little unsure of himself and very young, but Eden guessed him to be in his thirties. She didn't know why, but she suddenly felt drawn to this somber man. She had to keep herself in check because the only thing that was preventing her from rushing up to him and hugging the hurt away was her mother's daunting presence! Just for a moment, Ben's beautiful mouth quivered. Not able to resist a minute longer, Eden dove right in to rescue him.

"Mr. Alexander, sir, I don't live here full-time anymore, you know. I don't think the roof leaks, but it did five years ago when we had a big **Kona storm**. Quite a bad one it was, too. The corner of the roof at the back end of the house lifted completely. It was scary because Dad and the boys had to nail it back down in the pouring rain. The carpenters had a tough time getting it fixed up right!"

Surprised and unprepared for her answer, Ben turned slowly to face her, reorganizing the strained look on his face. Once more, at the sound of her musical voice, he was puzzled and surprised. Where had he heard it before? The quiver threatened to return, making him look more boyish.

"Yes, I noticed the roof had been repaired," he said guardedly, and proceeded on a friendlier note, "it seems to have held up well, I see."

Eden offered him a chair and a cold drink. When he politely accepted, she gave him her best smile. The smile did something to Ben's equilibrium. He felt the beginnings of a cold sweat. Was she flirting with him? He blinked and studied her again. He thought she looked like a rather fetching elfin, a Pierrot, in that wild getup. She was all eyes, and he couldn't help but notice that her ears stuck out from beneath her glorious hair, that she had unbound. He nursed the fruit punch, which was too sweet for his liking, and followed her with disguised interest as she walked to the potted plant next to the TV. Such tiny feet she had, and as his admiring eyes traveled up her tanned legs, he decreed they were a definite plus. She clipped off several brown leaves and suddenly looked up. Once more, he averted his brilliant eyes.

Their conversation took on an even friendlier tone and he began to feel more at ease. Meanwhile, Janie Andres listened to their exchange and gave her daughter looks branding her a traitor. Eden ignored her completely. She admitted to herself that Ben Alexander's presence both unnerved and excited her and she was sure he reciprocated, though somewhat cautiously. While he scrutinized the family pictures in the frames on the shelf next to the TV, she took advantage and feasted her eyes on him. He was the kind of man her dorm mates would tag, one of "God's Gorgeous Creations." She wondered how many women had fallen for him because of his good looks. For a while there, he had looked so alone and unhappy. If only she knew what was really bothering him. In that moment, she vowed she would do everything in her power to ensure his happiness and to bring a big smile to this man's solemn face.

His eyes, once again intent on her, blazed green in the afternoon light. Lord, she had never seen such mesmerizing eyes before! She was grateful when her dad and Ray Mulroney reappeared in the parlor to tell Ben his opinion was needed for repairs to the back bedroom.

CHAPTER 5
Invitations

With their laughter carrying through the long hallway of "the old house," the three men made their way once again to the parlor where a more than curious mother and daughter were waiting on tenterhooks. Eden was relieved that the inspection ordeal was coming to an end. As she mulled over the whole set of events, she concluded that, contrary to her previous perception, plantation life was not simple at all, but full of complicated surprises. Her mom's inexplicable behavior was unprecedented, but what happened next was even more incredible to her. She heard her dad's friendly voice extend a luncheon invitation of Chinese food to the plantation manager and the acting head engineer the Saturday after the repairs were done. She felt, more than expressed, her concern at this development. What was Dad thinking? Social interaction between management and the employees was virtually unheard of. Why, the only exception she could think of was on Christmas Eve when the entire plantation got together for the annual Christmas program and the **huli-huli** chicken dinner. The dinner was a gift from "the company," of course, but it was the plantation folk who prepared the feast. She thought to herself, "Doesn't Dad realize he's placing my mother in a rather awkward position?" Besides, she didn't think she could take another minute of Ben Alexander's piercing green eyes, let alone have lunch with the man. Neither could her mom, by the look of her, as panic flashed through Janie's eyes. What had happened to her family in the time she had been gone?

What the two men must be thinking of them by now, she didn't have a clue.

Ray Mulroney carefully avoided the quizzical look Ben Alexander shot him. With an appreciative sparkle in his blue eyes, he poured his attention unto the women. The rich auburn hair with copper glints only emphasized his charm.

"I can hardly wait to try your cooking, Mrs. Andres. I've heard only fabulous reports about it!"

"Well," Janie Andres responded and stood up tall, secretly thrilled at the compliment . . . "I hope it will be to your satisfaction, Mr. Mulroney. Gil and I enjoy having guests. Our daughter Eden is training to be a chef, you know." Eden watched in astonishment as her mother quickly transformed back into her gracious self.

"Please, do call me Ray," Mulroney replied, his blue eyes burning brilliantly, "I have known Gil for some time now, and I hope I can presume to call you Jane." Janie nodded. His simple honesty melted her reserve.

Ray Mulroney rose a few notches on Eden's list of people to esteem. She could very well understand why her father spoke so highly of him. As Ray turned to face Eden, disapproval showed in the green depths of his partner's eyes.

"My dear," he spoke gently, "it's been a double pleasure meeting you!"

"Mr. Mulroney, I . . . ." At this, Mulroney put up his hands.

"Oh no, that would never do. Let's not stand on ceremony, please. Call me Ray, Eden. I do hope we get to see more of you this summer. Your father has already related to me that you are home on break from cooking school on Maui. I hear that the tourists are swarming to the Valley Isle these days." Before she could answer properly, he glanced at the clock above the TV and smoothed down his mustache. "Well, excuse me, but we do have another appointment to keep. Sorry again for the delay, Gil. We'll send the carpenters over next week to start in the back room!"

Looking mighty pleased, Gil shook hands vigorously first with Ray and then with Ben. "I appreciate it, Ray, Ben. I must be off to work. Don't want to be late, you know." They laughed at the private joke. Gil placed his arm around his stunned wife and headed for the kitchen. "Gentlemen, our daughter will gladly see you out!"

Before she could protest, Ray took Eden's arm and led her out to the dark green Range Rover in the driveway.

"Your father tells me that you are quite an accomplished cook. Mealtimes at your house must be lively, my dear."

"Mr. Mulroney . . ."

"Ray," he interrupted.

"Ray," she paused, unused to being so informal with the boss, "Yes, I am home for the summer. I do love to cook, but I feel warranted to inform you that my mother is the cook of our family. When it comes to Chinese food, no one can hold a candle to her. You are in for a treat!"

As they approached the Range Rover gleaming in the sunlight, Eden couldn't help but admire it and gasped with delight. It was the latest in sports vehicles.

"The Queen of England drives one, you know!" she quipped.

Both men appeared amused by her youthful enthusiasm. Ray, especially, was enjoying this little dalliance. The child was as refreshing as the welcomed breeze that blew a strand of his perfectly combed hair out of place.

"Actually," Ray replied, turning to face the Range Rover's owner, "this belongs to Ben. He's allowing me the pleasure of driving it today, to see if I like it." Looking up at his partner, he suggested cleverly, "If you ask prettily, perhaps he might be persuaded to take you for a drive." Taken aback at Ray's suggestion, Ben's eyes clouded but Ray continued unperturbed, "Unless you would prefer to go out with an old fogey like me!"

"Oh please, Mr. Mulroney," Eden responded, "I mean Ray. I didn't mean to inveigle an invitation. Besides, you're not that old! I mean, you must be Dad's age." Realizing her spontaneous opinion had placed Mulroney in her father's age bracket, she burst out, "Oh, brother, how did I get myself into this one?"

"How refreshing, young Eden, that girls your age can still blush! But I'm only teasing, you know." Tickled, he held up Eden's right hand and pressed it gently to his lips. Eden's face grew even hotter under the increasing disapproval in Ben Alexander's eyes and quickly pulled her hand back.

"However," she retorted saucily, "since you are so much like Dad, I refuse to call you Sir unless you behave." To this rejoinder, Mulroney threw back his head and roared with laughter. The girl had spunk, and the compliment pleased him enormously.

Feeling excluded from the conversation, intolerance finally got the better of Ben Alexander. What was wrong with him? One moment he felt like laughing, and now he felt irritated to his bones. His mentor acting like a lovesick calf was annoying him tremendously. He got into his SUV on the passenger side, had the windows rolled down to let out the heat, and pretended not to notice while Ray took his sweet ole time to show Eden the vehicle. After what seemed like an eternity, Ray got into the driver's seat.

"Don't forget now, we're looking forward to seeing you at the luncheon," he threw out and waved carelessly as he headed up Hau'oli Way.

"Wow, what an extraordinary day this has been," Eden said out loud as she glanced down at her hand. "Mr. Mulroney actually kissed my hand!" She wondered what her parents would think of that as she blew her bangs from her forehead. With mixed feelings, she was relieved to see the two men depart. She stood at the edge of the yard watching the Range Rover as Ray drove away.

Her eyes turned dreamy as the quirky side of her personality took over. She fancied herself at a Ball, fluttering her fan coquettishly at her beau. It was then it dawned on her that instead of being dressed in a gorgeous silk gown, she was still attired in her crazy clothes. "Ohhh," she wailed, "me and my big ideas!" She laughed at herself. "Oh well," she uttered with a shrug, "the Saturday luncheon will be the last time we'll ever see those two in close proximity again."

Looking up to heaven, she daintily lifted her skirt and curtsied. Her beau bowed low to the floor. Taking her hand in his, Miss Andres was waltzed around the dance floor, and later she made a graceful exit into the dimly lit garden terrace, which was the safety of her rambling home, "the old house."

Drumming his fingers on the outside of his door, Ben caught a glimpse of Eden in his side view mirror. He blinked and looked hard. What was she up to? Of all the wacky things, she was dancing in broad daylight! Up went the thick, honey-colored eyebrows. That little smile threatened to return. In fact, at the sight of her perfect imitation of a frivolous Victorian maiden, he began to laugh silently. What was happening to him? He couldn't even remember the last time he felt like laughing. He sobered immediately.

He watched as Eden disappeared into the old house. Somewhere in the back of his mind, a familiar thought was nagging at him. Yes, he admitted reluctantly, something about that girl had struck a chord in him. He didn't know or understand exactly what it was, but he aimed to find out. Her pure and childlike quality was certainly appealing, but by present day standards, was she really the innocent she portrayed to Ray, or was she a flirt? He couldn't know for certain, and the thought puzzled him. The reminder of Eden's exotic looks and how they could be enhanced with stylish clothing tantalized him. "Why was she wearing such odd clothing, anyway," he wondered with the beginnings of a smile. "It was so unlike the other day at the gate. It's probably the flippancy of youth," he reasoned.

He caught himself short. To think, he was all set to dismiss the Andres family as just simple folk, but the moment he saw the genuine concern for him on Eden's open face, he knew somehow that she could figure in altering his well-arranged life. Without him really realizing it, the icy barrier that he had carefully built around his hardened heart began to thaw.

What Eden didn't know didn't hurt, but the conversation in the Range Rover turned out to be very gratifying to one man at least. Once they were clear of the potholes, Ray glanced briefly at Ben. Not present during the interchange in the parlor between his companion and Eden, he began in earnest.

"Ben, my boy, what's eating you? You were so stiff back there. Unbend a little, why don't you. I think you've been away from the islands too long. You've forgotten about the **aloha spirit**. Andres is an important man to us, and we need his support. If we can persuade him to join forces with us, the battle is half won." He watched as his friend struggled for control.

"What do you mean by 'join forces' with us?" Ben demanded, not one to beat around the bush.

"As a matter of fact, I offered him a supervising job!" Ray replied.

"Well," Ben answered after some thought, "that's reasonable. The company would be enhanced considerably by a man of his caliber, and I'm certain he would enjoy the benefits of a better paying job. What did Andres have to say?"

"Oh, he wants time to think it over. He'll give me his answer in a week or so."

"Listen, Ray," Ben got out, feeling weary of all the political talk, "perhaps I didn't make myself clear the first time. I want you to understand that I'm here only to fill in for my old man and Matt Campbell. If I had my druthers, I would be headed for New Zealand by now. How could I have known that you were going to need my help because Dad was going to do a foolish thing like elope with his personal assistant? Look at it from my point of view. They'll be back from their honeymoon shortly, and you'll be rid of me. If you don't mind my saying so, you'll probably be glad to see the back of my head."

Ray glanced sharply at his friend. The boy was being difficult. "You know full well that Matt is out on sick leave, and we need your expertise," he retorted rather harshly. "Your dad is preoccupied with his personal happiness at the moment. He deserves this vacation. You, of all people, must know that the plantation runs more smoothly with one of you being here. Remember, Matt is in recovery and will be out all summer."

"Grant you, Andres is a leader," Ben interrupted, deaf to his friend's argument, "but it's the way he's had to live that bothers me. I saw enough poverty in Asia to last me a lifetime. I mean," he spat out, "it was quite a shock to see it so blatantly in force here in Aloha Nui Loa. So much for this being a tropical paradise! You'd think we could do something better for the workers, but as it is, the plantation has slowly but steadily lost profit trying to keep up the show!"

There was a strained silence in the vehicle for both men were aware of the truth of the words just spoken. Ray understood that even more so than Ben.

"I know there is more at stake than fixing up a bunch of old houses." He had the decency to look terribly vexed at the reminder, until Ben couldn't hold it in anymore.

"And furthermore," the younger man countered with a hint of disdain, "did you have to do the Beau Brummel act with that . . . the Andres girl! Good grief! It was a bit melodramatic at your age, don't you think?"

"So, that's it," Mulroney snorted as his eyes widened in surprise, and Ben was rankled even more when his father's right-hand man had the audacity to burst out laughing. He continued in a tormenting vein, "I must be getting old and losing my touch. I wondered why you were so uptight back there. I should have known; it was the girl who unsettled you."

Ben opened his mouth to protest but thought otherwise.

"Got under your skin?" Ray added, as if to further provoke his younger colleague. Recalling Eden's innocuous teasing, he pondered aloud, "What was that she called me? Sir Ray... hmmm. A delightful girl. I admire your good taste." As he quickly viewed the scowl on Ben's face, his suspicions were confirmed. "Aha! I am right! You are jealous!" he exclaimed in amazement. This brand of realization was just too much of an enlightenment for the older man, and the knowledge tickled him to the utmost. "My friend, you've just made my day! I must not be losing my touch after all," he gloated gleefully. "The girls were right, Chloe especially! The hunk in shining armor has finally met his match."

"Chloe has a big mouth, and so does Malia," Ben defended himself hotly, growing more indignant by the minute. He'd have to have a word with his staff about the joys of being loyal to one's boss. "Don't be absurd," he continued, "I've seen a lot of beautiful women in my time. The girl is just a kid!" he pointed out as if Ray didn't know that for himself. "Keep your eyes on the road. And by the way, you can cut out the cute act! You may fool others, but you're not fooling me one bit!" With his green pools narrowing, he eyed his friend suspiciously and accused, "Come off it, Ray, I know you're up to something. The whole scenario smacks of one of your calculated schemes. I can even hear the wheels turning over in that crafty head of yours. I've seen you in action too many times to be taken in. You might as well come clean. All this social business has something to do with winning Andres over, hasn't it." When his friend returned his scrutiny with a guileless smile, a satisfied smirk formed on Ben's handsome face. He cautioned, "Ray, this is too wild a scheme, my friend. You're treading on perilous ground. Take my advice and don't involve the family, especially the daughter. You know how locals are about their kids! You might wind up in a situation too hot to handle."

Ray didn't pay any heed to his boss' son and began to hum a nameless tune. Ben shut up, knowing it was useless to pressure Ray. Once the great Mulroney made up his mind about something, that was it. His unconventional methods in the past had earned him promotion after promotion. Ben knew that no matter how sly Ray's methods seemed, the plantation Board of Directors would back him up. He just hoped that Ray was right this time.

Momentarily, he closed his eyes. Why was his head throbbing so much? Perhaps he hadn't gotten acclimatized to the heat yet. Opening the glove compartment, he took out his dark glasses and slipped them on. As he leaned his head back against the headrest, the passing of the incredible events of the last couple of months flashed through his mind. His dad eloping with a gal half his age was too much for him to contemplate. Being handed the tedious job of helping at the plantation during the contract renewal with the union when he had other plans, had upset him. He thought about Sylvia --Lord, how could he even momentarily have forgotten Sylvia! --and her moneyed elegance, and the postponed trip to New Zealand to meet her family. Was it only a few weeks ago that he was in Napa Valley dining with her at Thomas Keller's, The French Laundry? It all seemed like a dream that took place a long time ago. In this present plantation environment, he was set apart from Sylvia and her ritzy lifestyle. He felt torn between two vastly different but real worlds.

His head began to throb more. Pressing his forehead with his large hands, he closed his eyes tighter. The vision of Eden's long tresses and sloe eyes came unbidden. Those eyes, so soft and entreating, where had he seen them before? They could easily move any king to offer her all his worldly goods, even to the half of his kingdom.

It bothered him more than he wanted to admit, but Ray had been right about one thing. Meeting Eden had stirred up long buried emotions. He admitted truthfully, he wanted to see her again, and soon. Noting where his thoughts were leading him, he chided himself, lest he find himself guilty of what he had so self-righteously accused his father's trusted friend of. Good Lord!. What was happening to him?

Ray glanced briefly at his younger companion. Yes, if he could just pull off this next scheme of coaxing Gil Andres to join management, he would tremendously enjoy the promotion that would come with it. Perhaps he could even contemplate early retirement. The thought was extremely pleasing to him. As he turned from their present course and drove onto a dusty road, a clever stratagem was being formed in that master brain of his. Plan A was in effect!

CHAPTER 6
The Great Tree

With the dawn came the promise of an uncomplicated, do-as-you-please morning. Eden forced herself out from under the covers, pushed aside the pink and white checked curtains her mother had sewn eons ago, and peered out into the dim morning light. It was way too early to be up and about, but up she got. Dawn was just about to break, and that sight always buoyed her spirit. True, she was a sunset person at heart, but this was different. She had been away, and she had missed the sights of home. Today was the first chance she had to visit her secret pal.

She hugged herself and shivered as her dainty feet touched the wood floor. Brrr. It was cool, as it always was in the early morning near the foothills of the **Ko'olau Range**. The house was silent. In her parents' room, adjacent to hers, it was quiet except for their gentle snoring. Rather than wake them up precipitously with her scurrying to and fro, she got dressed, flicked a comb through her untidy hair, and headed for the bath on tiptoe. It felt good to be wearing her own clothes again. Her old **puka-puka** jeans had evoked enough comment from her mother to last a lifetime and she gladly relegated them to the back of her closet for the rest of the summer. Instead, she donned a pair of lightweight Dockers, a bright orange tank top and a U.H. sweatshirt.

She made her way from the bath to the kitchen and noticed her grandfather's slippers were gone from the shoe rack next to the kitchen door that opened to the banyo. She pictured him on his way to feed the chickens at the coops that were located at the edge of the plantation. To make sure, she peeked into his room and found it empty with the single bed made up neatly. Telling herself that she would have oodles of time later in the day to catch up with him, she moved stealthily back to the kitchen. She poured herself a glass of **liliko'i** juice, and its tartness gave her a jolt. Suddenly, she felt wide awake. After downing the contents of her glass, she rinsed it and left it on the drain board. After all, she didn't want to disregard the years of careful training she had received from her mother. With a family of eight, the assigned glasses had to be used over and over during the day. Growing up, none of the kids relished the job of washing glasses all day long.

She turned on the light in the banyo and rummaged around until she found what she was looking for. It was a pair of well-worn black rubber **zori**, and she slipped them on. Slowly pushing open the squeaky exterior banyo door, she secured its rope leash to the nail on the exterior wall and stepped into the cool air. The air was crisp and delicious and being outdoors so early rejuvenated her even more.

The sun was about to make its debut and brighten up the surrounding countryside. Eden could barely make out the leaves of the pineapple plants and the multitude of spider webs outlined with dew. Palm fronds rustling gently in the light breeze welcomed her. Despite all the upheavals of the last few days, she had to admit, she was glad to be back in Aloha Nui Loa.

Life is full of odd, funny moments, she thought, as she made her way to the path that led to her favorite childhood haunt. How misguided she had been as a youngster. Her humble background had been a source of great embarrassment to her, and she had vowed to get as far away from it as she could. Yet, here she was, after only two years of being away, painfully but tenderly aware that the aging place was her heritage. Yes, the house was old, but it held wonderful memories and it had played its part in the history of plantation life in Hawaiʻi. How could she have been so blinded, so ashamed of something that was so much a part of her? At least now she could begin to accept it all with awakened eyes and felt remorseful that she had been so ashamed of her roots. This sobering thought offered much comfort.

Reaching the path, she was taken aback to see that it was partly overgrown with weeds and **California grass**. As she tramped over the tall grass, she remembered the first time that her brother Robert had discovered the trail, and how excited they had been to explore it. Their plans had been found out by their dad, who warned them sternly of the dangers they could encounter if they ever ventured down to the stream without being accompanied by an adult. There was only one time they didn't pay heed to their dad's admonishment.

Robert had dared her and Albert to follow him. A great one for plans, he had insisted that they would make a fortune by selling the **swordtails** that they could catch in the stream. With enthusiasm, they took up his dare and had snuck out at nap time, carrying empty jars to the secluded spot. It had rained unexpectedly, and the stream had risen suddenly. Albert had fallen into the water, dropping his jar of swordtails. Thankfully, he had gotten hooked up on a fallen branch and with Robert's aid, had been able to scramble safely onto the bank. Badly shaken, they had not returned to the stream until they were much older. Not a word was breathed to anyone about their misadventure. Mrs. Andres had noticed their subdued behavior at dinner, but she never questioned them about the wet clothes she found hidden at the bottom of the clothes hamper. Thinking about her zany brothers, she missed them. The thought of her being so gullible, especially about their get rich schemes, made her chuckle. Theirs were the halcyon days of childhood, precious memories now.

The sun popped up and her way was made clearer. She sighed deeply as she plodded onward until she arrived at her very favorite spot on the plantation. There on an elevation near the stream stood her guarded secret, a gigantic **Mindanao Gum** tree. This was her special hiding place as a child where she let her hair down. As a teen, she had come here frequently to pour out her soul to her stalwart companion of the forest. The tree seemed to listen when no one paid much attention to her ramblings.

The pungent scent of the surrounding eucalyptus trees invaded her senses. Touching the smooth bark of the Rainbow tree as it's also called, she greeted her friend and gave it a hug. Then, she leaned her back against its trunk and slid down to its base. She looked up at the sky. She could see tiny **mejiros** flitting about. A red cardinal was high in the tree, singing to his heart's content. What a relief it was to be home where everything was familiar. "If only life could always be this peaceful," she murmured sleepily.

A song played on her lips, and she gave it voice. Hers was a soft, sweet voice that carried into the woods. She sang for a long time –several short, lively Hawaiian tunes, a couple old ballads, and then soulful songs of plantation life. Tears streamed down her cheeks as the financial struggles her parents had weathered together came to mind. She loved them so, even though Janie plagued her most of the time. At least she knew her mother deserved to have her own home someday, she thought with a huge sigh. The sun rose higher in the sky.

Spent from pouring her heart out, Eden fell into a fitful sleep at the foot of her beloved friend.

It was in that very spot that he found her. Benjamin Alan Alexander had been out for an early morning jog when he thought he had heard voices coming from the eucalyptus grove at the head of the stream. Wondering if the sound was just the wind in the trees or possibly **menehunes**, he hiked down the trail. Hearing nothing, he decided it must have been the wind. On his return, he spotted the magnificent Mindanao gum tree and wondered how he had missed it before. With a minor in tropical agriculture, and a love for trees especially, he made a beeline for it to take in its tremendous height and beauty. Stopping to catch his breath, he pulled out a handkerchief from the pocket of his knit shirt to dab the sweat off his forehead. The gum tree was a gorgeous specimen and the biggest of its kind he'd ever seen in central Oahu. He leaned forward to touch its smooth and colorful trunk. When he noticed the recumbent form laying against the other side of the base of the tree, he stepped back, startled. The handkerchief dropped from his hand unnoticed.

Gazing down, he saw that it was the Andres girl, fast asleep. He took another step backwards. Immediately, his polite upbringing told him to leave her in peace, and he reluctantly turned to walk away. It was here that the inner struggle between his mind and his heart surfaced. Common sense told him that there was no future in furthering their acquaintance, and yet, his heart yearned to find out who the girl reminded him of.

He stopped in his tracks and glanced over at the sleeping girl again. She resembled a wood faerie with that glorious hair wrapped around her tiny form, and he noticed the beaded garnet and jade bracelets around each childlike wrist. "Good lord," he muttered to himself, "she looks about fourteen and too unprotected to be out on her own." He wondered what she was doing out so early and all by herself. This was the second time he'd caught her in some odd, vulnerable moment. Concern showed on his handsome face. Seeing her like this, so unguarded, brought out the odd protective streak in him, and he knew he had felt something akin to this, sometime, somewhere . . . but where? For the life of him, he couldn't remember, and it frustrated him.

Ben observed the girl with a longing he couldn't deny, and then his mind prevailed over his heart. Without looking back, he walked quickly up to where his Range Rover was parked and sat behind the wheel. He periodically took sips from his bottled water, waiting until Eden got up. Hidden by the hanging branches, she never saw him.

Twenty minutes slipped by, and Eden awoke with the nuzzle of a cold nose in her face. Her eyes flew open, and she sat up quickly. There, whimpering beside her, was old Jack, her grandfather's **poi dog** who was named after Jack Benny. She grabbed his fluffy body and let him lick her face.

"Oh Jacky, where did you come from? You've been out with Gramps this morning, haven't you? At Jack's short bark, she gurgled, "You funny, funny dog. I swear that you can understand any language."

Ben's green eyes softened as he watched Eden play with the brown and white mutt, and then bend from the waist to retrieve something. Letting Jack down, Eden noticed the handkerchief on the ground. She picked it up and saw the curious initials B.A.A. embroidered in one corner and wondered where it had come from. It had the faint hint of the aftershave Polo. Still in mint condition and too fine to throw away, she tucked it into her front pocket with the intention of taking it home and giving it a good wash. As she brushed the leaves and grass from her rumpled clothes, Jack looked up expectantly. He looked so silly and adorable.

"Come on dawg, let's go and find Gramps!" She raced up the trail toward the chicken coops with the fluffy dog yelping in hot pursuit.

When she was out of sight, Ben started up the Range Rover and headed slowly to his family's old mansion on the hill. The scene he had just witnessed brought a tender look to his face.

Eden broke into a hard run when she identified her grandfather's hunched form heading for home. He was sporting a cane and muttering to himself. She sneaked up from behind him and covered his eyes, "Guess who, Gramps?" As if he didn't know, he played the familiar guessing game with his pet grandchild.

"Now, let's see, it couldn't be Abigail, no, not with that skinny chest!"

"Gramps," Eden squealed, as she jumped in front of him and gave him a huge hug, "you are the limit sometimes!" The old man chuckled as he allowed his granddaughter to kiss him on both cheeks, then he did the same, sniffing as he kissed her appreciatively like he always did.

"Good morning, Milton! You're looking as fit as ever," Eden remarked as she looked him over. His hair was all silver now, but he still had that lively look in his yellowed eyes.

"Good morning, Sabina!" Ever since Eden was old enough to understand that she resembled her late grandmother, her grandfather had called her by his late wife's name. It somehow made her feel more accepted, especially when she was younger and had to bear endless teasing about her unusual name.

"I found Jack at the stream, Gramps," she said as she got in step with him and called out to Jack. The dog wouldn't heed and instead, he cowered when he saw his owner. "Why is he acting so wimpy? He usually never leaves your side"

"That monkey," Milton Andres muttered under his breath along with some mild oaths, "he's afraid of the big white rooster your dad bought from a breeder in Waipahu! As hard as I tried, I couldn't get him to help me catch that dang bird. He took off as soon as it started to make a fuss." He slid a look of pure disgust at the old dog, though his tone was kind. "I'm glad Jacky didn't get lost. He's forgotten his way around here, I expect!"

"Gramps," Eden let out, as she linked her right arm into his left arm, and inspected the scratch on her grandfather's forearm, "that looks bad. Better take care of that as soon as we get home. You don't want it to get infected. Remember what happened to your big toe? How did you get that nasty scratch anyway?"

"No big thing, Sabina," he grunted. "That white rooster who belongs to your dad," he emphasized, "is an ornery character. Just needs to be trained. I tried to get him away from Red, you know, the one I brought back from Stockton, California? Well, I'm proud of that bird. Four-time winner already, but in the last cockfight, he got badly cut. That big white, kept harassing him until I finally decided to put the rascal on a **higot**. Had a whale of a time catching that awful bird. So, when I finally had him cornered, and made a grab for him, he went wild and clawed me. I have a mind to make **tinola** with that one!"

Eden stifled a laugh. Gramps wanting to make soup out of the white rooster was a hilarious idea! Instead, she studied his face intently. Her grandfather never hid his feelings. For as long as she could remember, Milton Andres and his eldest son Gil, had both poured their hearts and souls into the raising of fighting cocks and they were bent on disagreeing heartily about the best way to raise them. Skirting around a touchy situation, she humored him along for a few minutes, then changed the subject.

"How long are you staying with us this time, Gramps? I haven't seen you since Christmas, and I've missed you."

"I could say the same thing of you, young lady," he said as he scratched his hoary head. "Your papa didn't want you to stay on Maui to work for the summer. I can guess at his reasons. How did you do on your finals anyway?" He smiled as Eden raised her arms up in triumph.

"Well, you are now looking at Aloha Nui Loa's newest chef," Eden informed him proudly. "I have my one-year certificate in Culinary Science and in one more semester, I should qualify for an A.A. Degree in Science. After that I have the option to go on for two more years to obtain a Bachelors. I can transfer to the Mānoa Campus in Honolulu and major in Home Ec., but perhaps, I think what I want most of all is to get married."

"Get married!" Her grandfather squeezed her hand. "Now Sabina, be serious. You're too young for all that." She looked up at him, pleased as pink.

"Got you, Gramps!" she crowed. He laughed and pinched her ear affectionately.

"I don't know why mom and dad were so adamant that I come home to work. There are tons of summer jobs on Maui.

I guess they didn't want me using up a chunk of my hard-earned wages on rent and all. Maybe they weren't too keen on my going to Maui because they still see me as a kid, and they worry unnecessarily about my health. Hey, I'm only five years younger than Abby!"

"They'll get over it. Maybe if you put some meat on your bag of bones, they might view you differently. Remember, Abigail was born old! Believe me, Sabina, by the time you're my age, you're going to wish you were younger. I'm mighty glad you're home while I'm here. I suppose I'll stay for a few weeks and then go back to Waialua and Aunty Michelle at Thanksgiving." Eden digested his news with surprise.

"Thanksgiving? That's a long way off, Gramps. By the way, how is our dear Aunty?"

"Well," he answered contritely, "since she's on a low-salt, low-fat, low-cholesterol diet, it's making mealtime tense for the whole family. There is a limit, you know, to what an old man can take. I'm looking forward to a whole summer of your mother's superb cooking!"

"Gramps, really, Aunty is an excellent cook and Mom is very nutrition conscious too, you know."

"I know, I know, Sabina, but the difference is that everything your mom cooks is very tasty, whereas your aunt's current style of cooking is healthy, but a bit bland to tell the truth. I mean, I like beans and oats, but beans and oats every single day is more than I could take."

"You mean, you actually came here to escape Auntie's healthy cooking! Gramps, that's so naughty of you and hilarious!" They walked home in easy companionship, very happy to be with each other, with old Jack tagging a safe distance behind them.

The table was set for breakfast when they got to the old house. Janie was just placing the last pieces of **Portuguese sausage** on a platter with pancakes when they walked in. "Oh, there you are Eden," Mrs. Andres sang out cheerily, "I suspected you had gone for an early morning walk!"

"Mom, I'll help you as soon as I see to this nasty scratch on Gramps's arm." Having taken care of it, she sat him at the table while she served him his usual bowl of rice, pouring fruit juice into his Knotts Berry Farm mug. They had an ample supply of orange juice because of the **kaʻu oranges** from Aunt Nan's bountiful tree in ʻEwa Beach.

"Give your dad a holler, Eden," her mother asked, flipping over more pancakes, "I don't want his food to get cold. I think he's working in the vegetable garden. He mentioned something about digging up some cassava for me for dessert tonight."

Eden made haste to the backyard. She found her dad, standing in the middle of the garden, leaning on a hoe. When he saw her, he lifted the U.H. baseball cap that Phil had given him off his head and wiped his brow with his forearm.

"Dad," she called out, "Mom has breakfast ready for you."

Her father smiled benevolently on his number two girl. With that small face and tiny chin, she was the spitting image of his own mother. The long ears were the tell-tale feature that distinguished her as a descendent of Sabina Roman Andres, and sometimes he worried that his dad openly showed his preference for this child. Gil himself had spent more time with the boys while Janie still doted on Abigail. Perhaps, it was human nature to be drawn to certain people, even your own kids. She was looking healthy at least. Much as he hated to admit it, her time on Maui had done her good.

The conversation at the table understandably turned to the house inspection by the bosses and Gramps listened with interest as they all told their sides of the story. He laughed with gusto when Janie recapped her nervous crocheting.

"Well, Gil told me not to say a word, so I didn't."

"Mom," Eden piped up, "Dad didn't mean for you to not answer any questions! You should have seen Mr. Alexander's face. I bet he never gets treated like that ever!"

"Women!" Gil said, shaking his head. "I'll never forget my shock when I opened your door, Eden, totally spacing out that you were home and wearing that crazy outfit. I was also in the dark about all that had gone on between you, Mom and Ben. The poor guy. And then I had the nerve to invite them to lunch!" More laughter followed, but they all had been pleased about the outcome of the inspection.

True to his word, Ray submitted the work order, and the carpenters were sent out the following week. Janie fussed over Roy Okada, the maintenance supervisor, and his crew, plying them with cold drinks and snacks. The floors of Eden's old room and the room that was shared by her brothers were patched. Painters followed next. Eden chose a pale yellow for her and blue for the boys, and the rooms were transformed in just a few days.

So pleased with the effect, Janie wondered if the entire house could be painted. When Ben was consulted by Roy, management's generosity proved to be unprecedented. He told Roy to do whatever the Andres' home needed, and not to spare any expense. The maintenance supervisor scratched his head in surprise. Gil wondered about Ben's decision too and suspected that Eden's presence had something to do with it but kept the knowledge to himself. Janic was to have her choice of paint colors for the whole house, and he had never seen his wife in such a flutter. He watched in awe as she excitedly selected a pale peach for the twins' old room, and soft green for the master bedroom. The parlor, kitchen, and bath were swathed in creamy white.

Gil and his family wholeheartedly undertook the job of painter's helpers. Within a week the interior of the house had been painted and the place looked renewed. An elated Janie had bought fabric on sale to sew new curtains for the parlor and kitchen. She made a sizable dent in her savings, but, along with the others, she couldn't help but be thankful to the two men who had given her old home a new updated look. It was with grateful hearts that the Andres family looked forward to returning the favor to their benefactors.

"I hear," Milton began, "that the Alexander boy has a fancy education. Manuel was telling me today that he was involved in an accident on the job and was ill with Malaria that caused some memory loss. Know anything about that, Gil?" Milton, retired from the company, still took a big interest in plantation news. His son chewed his food thoughtfully and then swallowed.

"Well, I heard he was part of a bridge building engineering team in Thailand. He caught a tropical bug, some form of malaria, they say. Not sure of the details. Also, he suffered a head injury from an accident on the job, and maybe those two things account for the memory loss. Had to bring him home because he was too weakened to take care of himself. The grandmother nursed him back to health. I heard that he's recovered, but patches of his memory are sketchy. He looks the picture of health, though. Always see him jogging or hiking around the plantation most days. Maybe that's why he seems so self-contained. Can't get him to relax, but he's easier to get along with since he inspected the house."

At the mention of Ben's name, Eden perked up. She tried hard not to appear so interested, but she wanted to know more about the plantation heir. Her grandfather, being wise and shrewd, and never missing a trick, took note of her high color.

"I've heard the stepmother is only a few years older than the boy, and he wasn't too pleased about being saddled with the plantation while the old man is honeymooning somewhere in the South Pacific."

"Well," Gil continued, "I guess it came as a shock. Can you imagine how I would have felt if you had done the same, Dad?" Milton Andres chuckled at the ridiculous notion.

"Yeah, I can see your point. Any word about the new contract?"

"You know how it is, Dad, I really can't say anything yet. The current contract will be up soon, and the union will just have to come to terms with the new one!" Gil always leveled with his dad, but, tempted as he was to share, he wisely dismissed the idea of saying anything about the ongoing Union-Company negotiations. He didn't want to worry his womenfolk unnecessarily.

"Yep, I understand," his father nodded in agreement.

"Thank you, Janie, that breakfast hit the spot!" Gil continued. His wife flushed with pleasure as the other two dittoed his sentiment. Her husband was attentive and always full of compliments. Gil pushed his mug toward Janie, and she poured him his favorite **pouchong tea**. After a few sips, he deliberately steered the conversation into safer waters. Not noticing that he had deliberately turned the conversation away from union talk, she started to clear the table. Milton knew he would have to talk to his son at a time when the women were not present. They all got up from the table, occupied with their own thoughts. Janie, intent on getting letters out to her children on the mainland, excused herself for the next hour. Eden began her morning chores, determined to obtain more information about Ben Alexander. Milton gladly went down for his mid-morning nap. Feeling content, Gil sat down in his favorite recliner to rest before he got ready for the night shift.

CHAPTER 7
Friends

The horn of the beat-up green 1952 Chevy was honked several times before Eden remembered --Phil Castro had kept his promise to drive her into Wahiawā town. Aside from Francesca Henley, Phil was her best friend. He and Eden had become fast pals the day when, as the newcomer on the plantation, Phil had loaned her his shiny red bicycle. Eden had practically dragged the shy lad into her circle of friends, and he'd never forgotten her act of kindness.

Janie Andres was constantly nourishing hopes that the two kids would eventually consider tying the knot. To please her mother, Eden tried to see Phil in that light, but when he gave her a peck on the cheek at his High School graduation party, she knew it was to no avail. Being kissed by Phil had felt like being kissed by one of her kin. Phil was and would always remain just a good friend and nothing more. Their friendship stayed intact all through their school years, and they made a pact to correspond with each other while Eden was away at college. Along with her parents, he wasn't enthused about her decision to not attend school on Oahu. He could understand why she chose Maui because of the acclaimed state-of-the-art culinary school, but he still vowed to keep an eye on her from a distance. Her dad gave in to her wishes only on the condition that she agree to come home at Christmas and summer breaks. Her mom wasn't as diplomatic. She vehemently voiced her disapproval. Eden left for Maui in mid-August, happy as a caged bird set free. As the two friends went their separate ways, Mrs. Andres fretted over her misfortune of losing a potential son-in-law.

Eden jumped up from the sofa and asked hurriedly, "Mom, do you need anything in town? I'm going for a ride with Phil." Her mother knew better than to dream, but her hopes rose perceptibly.

"No, dear, but it would be a big help if you would take the cheesecakes we made to Gracie's. She has room in her freezer to store them until the bake sale." Her mother got up from her chair and peeped through the lace curtain hanging over the front parlor window. There was Phil grinning from ear to ear, waiting patiently in his family's old car. "That jalopy doesn't look quite safe," added Mrs. Andres disparagingly. Daughter gave mother a warning glance before she disappeared into her bedroom. Janie chose to ignore her, kept up her chit chat and continued, "Oh well, do as you wish. I'm sure that you and Phil have a lot to talk about. You do need downtime before you start at the cafe next week."

Feeling slightly snubbed that the kids hadn't cooperated with her plans for them, Janie mumbled to herself, "Phil's a rather nice boy, but maybe he's too **hang loose** for Eden." Her second daughter surely needed someone with a firm hand to manage her. It didn't stop Janie, however, when her previous matchmaking plans were foiled. "Something else will have to be worked out," she harrumphed to herself. She sank back into her chair and pulled out the blue baby sweater she was working on. The idea hit her like a bolt of lightning, and immediately her sagging spirits were uplifted. Why, how could she forget about Ray and Ben, both single, who were coming to lunch in a few days' time? With her countenance aglow once more, she made her plans accordingly. Her crocheting took on a renewed vigor.

Eden, dressed in short shorts and bright red tank top, secured her long hair with a rubber band, and reappeared in the parlor. The sight of that dreadful ponytail didn't dismay Janie, who was now tickled pink with herself. At the last minute, she called out to Eden, "Don't forget to take your vitamins, dear!"

It felt like old times once again when Eden finally jumped into the old Chevy. She glanced at Phil Castro, taking in the glossy black hair, large eyes, and smooth brown skin. Phil's grandfather, Ignacio Castro, immigrated to Hawai'i from Ilocos Norte, in the northern Philippines. Milton Andres, on the other hand, left the Visayas, Cebu to be exact, a year earlier. In contrast to the fair skinned Visayans, Ilocanos were notably darker complexioned, and, when Phil and Eden were children, they teased each other constantly about the difference in their tans. He was very attractive, but she couldn't say the same thing about the dilapidated car.

"Gosh Phil, it's so good to spend time with you! I like your new haircut. By the way, whatever happened to the Sentra you drove to meet me at the airport the other day? This heap is BAD! Don't you ever wash it?"

Phil's grin widened. "Dad has the Sentra today. He's gone to pick 'ōpihi. Don't knock Nellie, you'll hurt her feelings. At least she runs smoothly," he said as he patted her dashboard. He began regaling Eden with school stories and had her in stitches in no time at all.

"I can just see you now," she wisecracked, "Wahiawā's newest dentist, driving around town in this thing. Why don't you get a Honda or Kia, they fit the image better you know?"

"Hey, give the boy a chance, I'm just a starving college student." An impish look stole across his face. The whites of his eyes contrasted sharply with his brown skin. "You ought to consider getting braces, Bones, you could be a knock-out if you did." At that jibe, Eden gave him a withering look which, of course, didn't faze him at all. The two friends glanced briefly at each other and grinned.

Passing the site of the **Kūkaniloko Birthstones State Monument**, the birthplace of Hawaiian **aliʻi**, and continuing in light banter, they crossed the Karsten Thot Bridge, the northern entrance to Wahiawā town. Surrounded by groves of eucalyptus trees, Wahiawā, the unofficial pineapple capital of the world, was located about three miles or so from the plantation. It hadn't changed much since Eden was a tiny tot and it certainly hadn't changed in her time on Maui. Small town as it was in comparison to Honolulu, it served the residents well with its various amenities.

There was the General Hospital, the post office, the new library, the remodeled police station and adjoining courthouse, a humongous bus depot, the DMV, several elementary schools, the Intermediate school, and Leilehua High school. Various churches dotted the landscape. Wahiawā District Park, which included tennis and basketball courts, two baseball fields, a swimming pool, a gym, and a recreational center, divided the town in two. There were various shops and small businesses, banks, gas stations, restaurants, bakeries, Drugs and Sundries, a movie theater and a shopping center. The main attraction was the famous Wahiawā Botanical Garden.

Phil grew pensive as he saw Eden close her eyes and lean back against the seat. Her self-appointed guardian angel felt privileged that she had consented to spend the whole day with him. For the first time since she got back from Maui, she seemed more at ease with herself. The morning sun brought out the red glints in her hair, and she looked serene. In fact, never had he seen her look so fresh and appealing. Being on Maui had matured her, he could tell. It was too bad he couldn't have visited her on the Valley Isle. His parents had finally decided to build a home on the lot they bought in Wahiawā, and the expense of the house precluded any leisure trips for him.

"Saturday morning shoppers are out," he spoke aloud, as he approached the business section. Phil was naturally modest and negotiated the narrow old streets of Wahiawā rather well, Eden thought as she opened her eyes to look around. She liked the familiarity of the town and the crisp mountain air. "Where's Gracie's house anyway," Phil asked. I'm not too familiar with this part of town."

"It's above the high school, somewhere. My folks took me there when I was little. Just go up **California Avenue** and I'll tell you where to go. She lives with her mother in a 1950's style house complete with stone fireplace and accents of glass block windows. Believe it or not, the walls are made of bleached redwood planks. It's a darling of a place." At the time, Eden hadn't understood why Gracie had never married. She voiced this now, as Phil turned up the street that led to that lady's home.

"Who knows," he answered thoughtfully, "maybe she doesn't want to be married. Or maybe, she could be suffering from unrequited love. You never know about these things. She seems to be pretty much into her work, but she doesn't strike me as the feminist type."

"Yeah," Eden nodded in agreement, "she's dedicated to the company, Dad says. She and Mom are old friends, you know. That's it, the white one in the cul-de-sac, see it?"

Phil spotted the house. He shifted gears as the old Chevy crawled up the quiet street and exclaimed, "Wow, look at that spread on the right, Eden. Wish my folks' yard could look like that!"

Eden followed Phil's pointing finger. Her eyes fell onto a beautifully kept estate bordering the gulch. The old Tudor style house and its coach house were in prime condition. Though the grounds were not extensive, it had a park-like appearance. It resembled a country house in the Cotswolds. Her eyes softened immediately.

"Why, it's charming. Look at all that weathered wood and those fantastic trees. Someone must love it to have spent so much time caring for it. I wonder whose it is. Do you see a name on the mailbox?" They drove past it and Eden craned her neck to get a longer look. "Wouldn't you love to live there?" she crooned dreamily.

"Now, Eden," Phil responded, "we must be content with what we have. The Lord knows what we have need of before we ask." Eden was accustomed to Phil's way of spouting off scriptures. He was raised in an evangelical church and aspired to go into the ministry someday. She couldn't help herself, but she was drawn to the old estate and felt the owners were extremely blessed.

Phil pulled into Gracie's driveway, careful to avoid parking too close to the rusty old Dodge truck. Eden recognized it right off.

"Looks like Gracie has company," she reasoned aloud. "Hmmm. That's odd. If I'm not mistaken, that's Lefty Shimizu's truck. I'd know it anywhere. I wonder what he's doing here. He and Gracie don't exactly hit it off, you know!"

With Phil carrying the goodies, Eden led the way up the cement steps to the front door and rang the doorbell. Gracie, a little breathless, wearing a frilly white apron over her short **mu'umu'u**, appeared at the door.

"Oh, there you are, Eden. Your mother just phoned to say you were on your way. Come on in. You too, Phil. I'm baking banana bread."

The aroma wafting from the kitchen reminded Eden of the old Kilani bakery, famous for its delicious butter rolls which she was going to purchase to add to their family dinner that night. Glancing around Gracie's home, she was impressed with its cleanliness. It was pristine white and as neat as the woman herself. There were brightly colored silk **zabutons** arranged beautifully upon the white cushions of the black lacquered wood furniture, and **tatami** mats covered most of the oak flooring. All around the living room, kimono-clad Japanese dolls stood in glass cases. Everywhere Eden looked, the bleached redwood walls were covered with scrolls of Asian art and calligraphy. On the sofa table sat a **bonsai** pine. Separating the dining room from the living room was a black and white **shoji** screen.

The pair followed Gracie through the spotless living room and into the kitchen. It was so classic 1950's style with the gleaming white stove, old fashioned refrigerator and shiny vinyl floor. Lefty Shimizu sat at the small dinette set and was sipping tea. Phil and Eden traded looks. This was certainly a twist, Eden thought, as her father's friend stood up, appearing slightly mortified to be caught trifling with the enemy.

"Why, hello there, Mr. Shimizu. Didn't expect to see you here!" Lefty raised his eyebrows in acknowledgement. Of all of Gil's kids, he liked Eden the best, and he was fond of Phil. Michiko, his younger sister, had a big crush on the boy.

Gracie stored the cheesecakes in her chest freezer. "These look great, Eden. Would you like some green tea and **almond cookies**? Mr. Shimizu just brought over some of Michiko's baked goods." Lefty's eyes narrowed and shifted from left to right. Eden was never sure what to make of him, even though he was one of her dad's closest friends. Ever since he had talked her mother into taking their pet rabbits off their hands and had roasted them over a fire for a barbecue, Eden hadn't trusted him.

"Ah, could we have a raincheck on the tea, Gracie?" Phil answered, looking at his watch. He knew if they stayed to chat, Gracie would talk story forever. "On second thought, we wouldn't pass up any of Michiko's cookies." He grabbed a couple and popped them into his mouth.

"Hey, speak for yourself," Eden chided and punched him gently in the arm. Phil feigned injury. Ignoring him and turning to Lefty, she asked, "How is Michiko, anyway?"

Michiko's brother evaded her eyes and replied in a low mutter, "Good, she's doing good, as usual."

Gracie handed Phil a bag of cookies, "Here you two, take these!" He thanked her, and nudged Eden toward the door. "We really must get going. See you all later!" he called out, leaving an even more flustered looking Miss Sato holding on to her white apron.

With Gracie thus distracted, Lefty attempted another getaway and this time succeeded. It was okay to talk to Gracie after work hours, but he would never talk to her at work. He followed the young couple out to the garage and watched them drive away in the old car.

It was the small local shopping center in the heart of Wahiawa that was their actual aim for the day, and Phil pulled into the parking lot near Foodland. The Chevy, parked next to the shiny, gold Mercedes SL convertible, looked ready for the junk pile in contrast to the low-slung automobile. The other vehicle was so sleek, they gasped at its sheer luxuriousness. "Wow, it's last year's model," Phil informed Eden. He was somewhat of an authority on new cars.

They got out of the green wonder and inspected the interior of the Mercedes. It was cream in color and the supple leather upholstery still smelled new. Phil was giddy just looking at it.

"Eden," he exclaimed, "a car like these costs as much as my folks' new cottage!"

Eden noted the California license plate and was pondering who it belonged to when the owner of it walked out of the deli with an unfamiliar female hanging onto his arm. The two friends, preoccupied with the splendid piece of European engineering, didn't notice Ben Alexander and the statuesque redhead clinging to him, as they made their way around the parked cars. The creature walking beside Ben was a goddess. With her brilliantly colored hair cropped short, her deep gray eyes heavily made up and her complexion flawless, she reminded one of a porcelain doll. A strapless hot pink and white flower print Betsey Johnson creation hugged her body, showing off legs that went on forever. On her head flopped a wide brimmed pink designer straw hat. Long, perfectly manicured nails were painted hot pink. Around her swan-like neck hung several strands of tiny white seed pearls, and simple white Jimmy Choo pumps completed her ensemble. It was unfortunate that the petulant pink mouth spoiled the effect.

Sylvia Reardon was in a high mettle. At the last minute she had altered her plans, and on a calculated risk, decided to stop over on Oʻahu enroute to New Zealand. It puzzled her that Ben had been attentive enough when he met her at Honolulu International but seemed distracted with something the last couple of days. Assuming that overseeing the plantation was wearing thin on him, she later dismissed that theory for a more excellent one. It must be, she presumed loftily, that his having to postpone his trip to New Zealand was a great disappointment to him. Knowing Ben, he was being tight lipped about it. She prided herself in understanding the male temperament.

Sylvia, overconfident, had not felt thwarted with his change of plans. There would be tons of time for him to meet her parents, who had recently purchased a spread near Lake Taupo on the North Island. She was not deeply in love with Ben, she admitted to a friend, but she was approaching thirty and it was time she settled down. Her family, nouveau riche, had been slighted by high society. Ben's family was old money, and with his connections, she knew being his wife would be the entree into the society columns. She could see the diamond sparkler on her left hand. How she would flaunt it! Ben was by far more handsome than any of her admirers. Her long string of wealthy suitors had left her excessively bored, but her vanity kept her from dropping them altogether, and so they dangled hopelessly at the end of the line. Only since meeting the heir to the Alexander Corporation did she feel sufficiently challenged, or rather, he intrigued her because he was always one step away from being within her grasp. Pampered, she was not used to being denied anything she wanted, and she really wanted to be Mrs. Benjamin Alexander. If she played her cards right, she told herself, he would come to heel and appreciate an alliance such as their marriage would be. It never occurred to her that Ben was more noble in his intentions than she supposed and would be otherwise inclined.

Her surprise visit had complicated matters but hadn't deterred Ben from his ambition to clear up this puzzle about his memory loss. He was fond of Sylvia, but he didn't want to think about the future until he had cleared up his past. In the last few weeks, he had at times felt almost desperate to get on with the rest of his life. This morning his spirits were high because O-ma, his grandmother, had called him from Switzerland. Her return to Hawai'i would coincide with the annual Summer Fête. "What a godsend!" he thought gratefully. He knew he could trust her implicitly with his confidences, and he needed her just now.

He must have told himself a thousand times over the last few days that his interest in Eden Andres was purely connected to his memory loss. Convincing himself she could be a significant key to opening his memory, he meant to pursue the premise as unobtrusively as possible. Ray had warned him that he was fostering the relationship for the wrong reasons, but Ben had brushed off his admonition. Mulroney wisely kept his own counsel. Reverse psychology seemed to be the best approach with Ben these days. After being introduced to Sylvia, the plantation manager, dismayed by the carefully hidden meanness of spirit beneath that glittering exterior, purposed to step up his plans and save his friend from what could be impending doom.

Ben's pleasure transformed his face when he saw Eden standing next to the Mercedes. She had constantly invaded his thoughts, until he wracked his brain for a way he could talk to her without attracting undue attention to themselves. He hadn't seen her since that interlude at the tree and that memory of her had found a niche in his heart. Now, here she was, conveniently positioned within a context that wouldn't give anyone anything to talk about. It was a God-given opportunity he couldn't miss. Glancing up, Eden saw the casual but elegantly dressed couple heading their way and put two and two together. With a sense of panic at being caught so conspicuously admiring Ben's car, she grabbed the surprised Phil by the arm and tried to pull him away. Ben, who had already anticipated her bolt, quickened his pace.

"Eden Andres!" he called out a bit too loudly, stopping the young couple before they had gotten very far. This at once alerted the antennae of both women. Face to face, the two females eyed each other squarely. Eden stopped in her tracks and couldn't help but smile generously, and Ben, oblivious to Sylvia's agitation, was charmed.

As the true reason for Ben's distraction was unveiled before her, the older woman felt an instant dislike for the younger girl. Feeling immediately threatened, Sylvia hung possessively unto Ben's arm and thought wickedly, "Men are such fools when it comes to sweet young things."

Both women turned to look at Ben, who made introductions. Covering up her feelings of gaucheness, Eden turned on the Andres charm.

"It's nice to meet you, Miss Reardon. I trust that you are enjoying our Hawaiian sunshine. This is Phillip Castro, my good friend and neighbor. He's on summer break from U.H. Manoa." At the sound of that melodious voice, Sylvia could only smile with affection.

Ben Alexander shook hands vigorously with Phil and the two talked about education and sports in general. "I follow the **Rainbow Warriors**," he said much to Phil's delight. Thrilled, Phil went off on a tangent about the intricacies of U.H. sports.

Temporarily left to themselves, Sylvia gave her rival a thorough scrutiny. The younger girl's clothes were homespun and had seen better days, and she was vainly amused at the comparison the two of them made. Her companion thought otherwise, as his eyes strayed from time to time to watch the glow in Eden's open face, and the beginnings of a smile lit up his previously solemn countenance. Alarmed, Sylvia thought to herself, "This is even worse than I thought." Ben had never smiled at her quite like that. Smugness momentarily escaped the Reardon heiress.

Eden, on the other hand, was quite happy to see Ben's face transformed and took the opportunity to study him. Today, there was something notably different, something indefinable about him. What was it? His friendly behavior seemed odd, because since the inspection, she had not seen hide nor hair of him. In the light of the information given at breakfast the other day, she looked for signs of his recent illness. He looked reasonably fit and healthy. In fact, he looked like he had stepped out of the pages of GQ. The thin-striped oxford shirt rolled up at the sleeves and the cashmere sweater tied carelessly around his neck just about did her in. True, the man looked more relaxed. The little smile which she was secretly beginning to love, surfaced and lurked beneath his bright gaze. She tried not to stare, lest she reveal her true feelings, but couldn't look away from those brilliant emerald eyes. Her face shone with undisguised admiration.

"Mr. Alexander, I do thank you for your help," Eden's lilting voice continued when the talk of sports came to an end. "Mom is in raptures about the repairs. You're in for a royal feast this Saturday. Chinese food is her specialty." Remembering her mother's treatment of him, she added, "I hope she didn't put you off by her behavior the other day. I can assure you that she really is the friendly sort. She was a little nervous, that's all."

"As a matter of fact, her actions puzzled me at the time, but I should be the one to reassure you. Gil has since explained the situation to me. Really, it's all forgotten. And please, I'd much prefer for you to call me Ben. This Mr. Alexander stuff is too formal." He couldn't help himself, and pushing his advantage, he wanted to encourage her, but to what end? He hadn't thought that far in advance.

They laughed together at the sheer absurdity of that eventful day, and then, slightly embarrassed and self-conscious to be seen talking so intimately in such a public place, they both colored. An awkward silence followed as their companions realized what was undeniable before their very eyes. The attraction between the young local girl and the tall blond gentleman was plain as day. With nothing more to talk about, the two couples bid each other a pleasant good day and parted company.

Phil placed a protective arm around Eden who seemed to him to be acting particularly goony. He was not devious in his effort to ascertain her feelings for the owner of the Mercedes, and he probed blatantly, "What's with you two, anyhow?" Eden, in a brown study, was not paying attention.

"What??" she answered absentmindedly.

"If I were you, I wouldn't get involved, Bones. He's way out of your league!"

"Involved? Castro, what are you talking about?"

Seeing her perplexed face, Phil decided to drop the matter. He knew her too well. It had not yet registered to her inexperienced heart that the man in question was even remotely interested in her. He decided to change the subject altogether. With a hint of relief in his voice he suggested, "Wanna go to see a movie tonight?"

Riding away in the luxury SL, Sylvia was more practiced in the art of subtlety. She took the gamble. "My, what an unusual young couple. I take it they're from the plantation." Ben grunted. He felt a headache coming on. She pressed on, "I thought it quite touching to see how well-matched they are. The boy seemed très proprietorial. Hmmm. I suspect there will be wedding bells soon." Ben, busy with his thoughts again, didn't catch the barb in her syrupy voice. Knowing his distaste for his temporary assignment, she continued more boldly, "A pity one can't do more for these people. Although, if the boy finishes his education, this couple might have a fighting chance." Her well-aimed comments hit their target. Ben winced. He didn't like to be reminded of the class distinction between Eden and himself, and he particularly didn't like the idea of her being linked up with the Castro boy. His head throbbed more.

Turning blank eyes to the calculating woman beside him, he responded dully, "Sylvia, my head is aching a little. Would you mind if I take you back to the guest house?" At this sudden turn to her advantage, Sylvia fussed over him until they reached the big mansion on the hill. Pleased with her clever move to put a wedge between Ben and this cheeky upstart, she cautioned herself to tread more carefully. No, she must not be too obvious with her machinations. Getting out of the car, she haughtily dismissed the whole incident as inconsequential and purred like a satisfied cat.

CHAPTER 8
The Luncheon Royale

Saturday arrived on a crystal-clear summer day. It was the kind of day where the sky remains a deep azure blue all day and small puffy white clouds, blown gently by **trade winds**, pass unhurriedly by. Gil Andres was feeling on top of the world. He was especially tickled at the honor the company was bestowing on him. Imagine, he was to be the first in Aloha Nui Loa's history to truly entertain members of the management in his humble abode. The privilege thrilled him, but even more so, he couldn't wait to extend his hospitality. It was something he was expert at, and he knew his guests were in for a treat. His wife Janie was famous for her innovative cooking, and he was very proud of that fact. He popped his head into the kitchen door and handed Abby some flowers from the garden. The old house was scrubbed so clean that Gil was impressed. "Janie," he declared, "I can drop scrambled eggs on the floor, scoop it up and eat it." Mrs. Andres shooed him away for the umpteenth time.

Janie was not only a terrific cook, but she was also ecstatic over Abigail's surprise visit. The girl was her pet, and she and Gil never saw enough of daughter number one. Working on a shoot at nearby Kemo'o Farms Pub and Grill, her firstborn had dropped in unexpectedly the evening before and had been persuaded to stay the weekend. The thought of entertaining two highly eligible bachelors when her two very available daughters were there to help her, was a dream come true. She was in a heightened state of anticipation. Recalling Abby's continuing contention, "I'll never get married!" didn't deter her. But even more than matchmake, Janie loved to entertain.

Wonderful scents of her Chinese specialties filled the whole house. To her, Chinese food was essentially easy to prepare, but necessitated exact timing. All the ingredients had to be carefully prepped beforehand as everything cooked quickly and had to be served immediately. This proved to be no problem whatsoever. Janie had timed the preparation for every dish down to the minute, and her girls were well-trained, experienced helpers in the kitchen. She wanted to make a good impression, one that would erase the memory of her odd and quirky behavior the day of the house inspection.

The menu included those bundles of joy called crispy **wun tun**, an old family recipe, a platter of **chow mein** topped with home grown vegetables in **oyster sauce**, a whole chicken braised in soy sauce with leeks and **star anise**, a large beautifully steamed red **kūmū** with **black beans**, Gil's favorite, egg drop soup, steaming hot rice and **almond float** with fresh early lychee and kiwi fruit for dessert. Eden, who loved cooking Chinese food the best, had prepared the dessert the night before, and had spent the last half hour frying the wun tun dumplings in her mom's old fryer. Abby was fast at work at the chopping block. What serious business cooking was in his house. Gil had known better and had opted to work out in the garden all morning.

Her kitchen detail done, Abby got started on the dining table. She was the artistic one in the family and was always eager to display her talent in **ikebana**. She found her grandmother's lace tablecloth and decided on a centerpiece.

"Mother, where have you stored that flat Blue Willow vase? I want to do a floral arrangement with these flowers Dad just picked."

"Ah, check in Gramps' room, Abigail," came the reply, "I think it's somewhere in there." Abby adored her grandfather, but she didn't relish stepping into his room, which smelled of home-grown tobacco. How could he stand the stuff, she felt, for once the scent got on you, it was difficult to get rid of.

"Where is our Gramps anyway," she demanded. "Shouldn't he be home for lunch?"

"Oh, you know him, he made plans to go out with Manuel again," Janie answered vaguely.

"Hmmm, I'll bet he's out gambling," she fretted. "Cockfighting is illegal, you know. Aren't you worried he'll get caught?" When no response came from the kitchen, she continued, "Didn't Doctor Santos tell him to quit smoking?"

Abby had the habit of talking to herself. Seeing as it was next to impossible to hold a conversation with their mother while she cooked, Eden took pity on her sister, and went to retrieve the vase from the bottom of the old wood shelf. It was stuffed to capacity with dishes seldom used and with small appliances wrapped in plastic bags to keep them dust free. She sneezed as she wiped the dust off the treasured vase before handing it to Abby. She glanced at her older sister for a moment. Abigail, the perfectionist, was already critically appraising her floral design. Eden returned to the kitchen. It was heaven to have her capable big sister home.

The Andres' half dozen was an attractive bunch, but Abigail was the celebrated beauty. Standing at the dining table, in her mint green **Bete Mu'u**, she was the stuff dreams were made of. Her short dark hair was curled in a tight cap around her heart-shaped face, and there was a hint of Joy perfume about her. Slender hands worked swiftly while she hummed a soft melody. Her husky voice had driven many a young man dizzy. Curiosity had gotten the better of her, and she had given up an important date to spend the weekend at home. The occasion was a special one, she agreed, but did it rate such a big to-do? Maybe. Goodness, you'd think they were entertaining royalty with the elaborate preparation for a noonday luncheon.

She placed her arrangement in the middle of the dining table and admired her handiwork. Satisfied, she joined her mother and sister in the kitchen. Sipping her Evian, she took out some postcards from her purse and read them aloud.

"Gwen and Vera seem to be getting along just fine," she said. "I sure miss their silliness. It's hard to believe they'll be gone all year. How can you stand it, mother?"

"Now, Abigail, I have enough on my hands without worrying about those two today. It wasn't easy to let them go but knowing they're in good hands has taken some of the load off my mind. Your father and I realize they deserved the trip."

Abby turned her attention to study Eden's figure. "How do you do it, sis? Some of my model friends would give their eye teeth to be as trim as you are." Eden looked up but didn't respond. She felt at home in her raggedy cutoff jeans and her favorite Celtics T-shirt. Her sister babbled on, "You should go and get dressed, our guests will be here within the hour. And do let me fix your hair. You'd look fantastic in a French braid." Abby, being the eldest, not only loved to arrange flowers, but she loved to arrange everyone else's life.

"Do get dressed, Eden," Janie agreed, "I can finish those," pointing to the Wun Tun dumplings in the fryer. Let Abigail do your hair!"

"Oh, alright. If you don't mind, I'll have a quick shower first. I feel sticky all over." She was out of the kitchen in a flash.

Although the girls shared a surname, that's where the resemblance ended. While Abby was steady, self-possessed and a bit commanding, Eden, in contrast, was a bundle of energy, sensitive and tended toward long-suffering. The sisters got on famously and had a healthy respect for each other's differences.

Mrs. Andres smiled sweetly. Abigail could always get her sister to cooperate in an area in which she, Janie, failed miserably. What Janie didn't know was that her firstborn managed her mother just as well. Janie sighed. She was glad for the love that existed between her two eldest daughters, and speaking of love, her thoughts once more returned to the preparations for her guests.

Eden splashed cold water onto her face and examined herself closely in the mirror. "No acne, thank God," she muttered to herself. The shower did wonders for her sinking self-confidence. She was accustomed to hiding her light under a bushel whenever Abby was around, and for once she was glad of it. For some reason, she was not looking forward to this meal. No, that wasn't completely true. She loved her mother's cooking. She felt a little nervous. Perhaps a certain gentleman had something to do with her feelings, which she had refused to examine since the encounter in the parking lot. However, on the other hand, she had a mind of her own too. She wasn't so swayed by good looks, was she?

She lavished herself with moisturizer and surveyed her wardrobe, considering outfits one by one. She could never decide what to wear, and this recurring nightmare of never having something suitable for the occasion constantly beset her. Each outfit was discarded, and the pile of no-no's mounted on her bed. Abby came in while she was trying to decide between the red jumpsuit and the pale pink sundress.

"Oh, the red, sweetie, it will go well with your dangling white shell earrings. We Asians are Winters. Bold, vivid colors, or icy pastels suit us. If you sit, I'll start on your hair." Eden gave herself up to her sister's ministrations. It was so easy to revert into their childhood roles, Abby as leader and Eden as follower.

"I'm relieved you are home, sis. I've been longing to have a talk with you."

Abby nodded. She was full of affection for her younger sister. They shared everything in their youth and could share confidences easily. Although, most of the time, it was the older sibling doing the sharing and the younger sibling doing the listening. Abby could see that something was eating away at her sister. Eden herself had been feeling a little mixed up lately and needed a good soul-to-soul talk with her older sister, who always seemed to know what to do.

With another nervous look in the long mirror behind her bedroom door, Eden practiced her smile. What was the matter with her? It was as if the hard-won independence she had gained living away from home had worn off. She'd never felt this high-strung before, but she reminded herself soberly that she'd never felt comfortable dressing up and rationalized that it accounted for the jitters in her tummy. Better than to examine the true reason. She had dallied over her toilette and the men had arrived before she was fully prepared to present herself. Abby, with her model's expertise, had been ready and welcomed their guests.

Doused with her sister's "Red" perfume and pumping herself up with a confidence she didn't feel, Eden headed for the dining room. Both men stood up as she entered. She greeted Ray warmly and said a quick hello to Ben. Ray was more than pleased to see her, and Ben, well, he was simply dumbfounded. He couldn't keep the stunned look off his face, nor could he believe his eyes. He had originally thought she was attractive, but he hadn't been prepared for the impact of seeing her so stylishly made up and well dressed. Was this the same scruffy young girl he had talked to just the other day? He couldn't get over it! The vision in red dazzled him. The hot color was the perfect foil for her burnished hair and showed off her suntanned shoulders to an advantage. He had heard in the last week that the Andreses had exceptionally good-looking daughters, but it didn't really sink in until today. If he had not met Eden first, he would have sworn that Abigail was the most beautiful girl he had ever seen. "Good Lord," he muttered to himself as he looked from Eden to Abby. The red and the green together reminded him of the dolls in his sister's collection. Yes, that's what they were, Christmas dolls. He wondered how Ray could display such equanimity at this startling discovery. If these two daughters looked like this, he could hardly wait to see how the younger two had turned out.

Ray was enjoying himself to the hilt. He shot Abby a conspiratorial wink and gestured from Eden to Ben. She was quick to catch on and immediately decided to play along. Ben, too occupied with the desire to look at Eden, and she, wanting to avoid eye contact with him, didn't notice. To be home to witness all this, Abby thought, was well worth the sacrifice of giving up her weekend date. Maybe, just maybe, she would be the one to win the bet after all!

Seated at the head of the table, Mr. Andres blessed the food. A Presbyterian, Ben was curious to watch everyone, Ray included, all follow suit and make the sign of the cross. He knew that most of the plantation folks were Catholic, but it didn't dawn on him that Ray was one, too. He didn't know why Ray being Catholic should surprise him. Ray was Irish to the core.

At each place setting, Abby had set chopsticks, a soup spoon, bowls of blue and white porcelain in varying sizes, scented homemade cloth napkins and simple clear glasses filled with iced water. The large round table filled with colorful oriental delicacies was a feast for the eyes. Ben was amazed that anything so fine could come from such simple folk. He had learned to love Asian food, and his mouth started to water. Thank God he was adept with chopsticks and cast a glance at the struggling Ray. Each mouthful was better than the last. He hadn't tasted anything as flavorful nor seen anything as beautifully appointed since he left Thailand. He looked up in awe at Gil, then at Janie. Some of his friends would pay big to have a chef like Mrs. Andres. She was a treasure.

"Why, this is out of this world, Janie," he blurted out. "Gil, you must be a satisfied man. It's a wonder you all are so thin!"

"Oh, I couldn't have done all this without Abigail and Eden's help." Of course, Janie was basically very modest about her talents, no matter what her daughters thought. She saw her opportunity. "My daughters all have their talents, Mr. Alexander. Eden is the trained chef, but the other three can cook the basics. They sew, keep house well, and can manage a household. The twins are still at that silly teenybopper stage, but I'm pleased to say that they would all make wonderful wives."

Mortified by her mother's pointed hints, Eden looked down at her lap. Abby rolled her eyes. "Mother, how you do go on! Perhaps our guests would like to try Eden's Almond Float." The men were duly impressed, Ben especially. He could hardly believe that the ragamuffin-turned-swan had prepared this delicate concoction. It was light as air and the perfect finale to a grand meal.

The good food, pleasant talk, not to mention the two lovely young women at their sides, gratified the men's hearts, and Mrs. Andres could hardly keep her expectations hidden. She looked from Abigail to Ray and from Eden to Ben. Her maternal pride was at its peak. True, Ray was a bit older than Abigail, but then she was born an old soul. She liked him tremendously, and after an altered first impression, felt she could grow to like Ben also. His perfect manners at the table had redeemed him in her eyes. Both would do magnificently for her two older daughters. She felt a stab of pity for all the girls' nameless beaux.

Ben was rapidly beginning to believe that he didn't know anything at all anymore, so quickly was this family opening his eyes to a new way of living. Ray had been right after all; he had been away from the islands too long and had forgotten all about island hospitality. The Andres family had limited means, and yet they had put on a repast fit for a king. It must have cost them a pretty penny!

Seeing that Eden had been seated opposite him next to Ray, he could only stare at her from time to time. She didn't do much better and refused to look at him at all. Abby was tickled pink at her young sister's conquest. A great talker, she was able to converse with Ben on a variety of topics, so that his opinion of simple folk was quickly amended.

After lunch, the men gathered in the parlor to talk shop. The girls helped their mom clean up and presently brought in tea. Ray was the first to speak.

"The Almond Float was amazingly refreshing, Eden. Jane, Gracie brought a piece of your scrumptious purple sweet potato cheesecake for me this week, and I don't know which I like better."

Mrs. Andres positively bloomed. "Thank you, Ray, but credit must go to Eden. She helped me with the cheesecakes too." Eden, unused to being complimented so freely, just nodded, but it was Janie who smiled as she poured more tea. Yes indeed, Ray would make an excellent choice for Abigail, if only she could get the girl to agree.

"Gracie tells me that the bake sale did very well for the 4-H-ers!" Janie continued.

"Yes," Ray answered, holding his teacup in his hand, "she seemed greatly pleased with the results. They plan to do a cookbook this year, you know! Perhaps, you could share some recipes with them. Please give these two recipes to Consuelo, my cook. She's always looking for new dishes. I must confess that I have a sweet tooth! She's a blessing, that one. Keeps house for me . . .. Well, it's the old manager's house, as you know. Too big for one person rattling around in there. Hopefully, when I marry, it won't always be so lonesome for me. At any rate, Consuelo has been with me for years. Wouldn't know what I'd do without her."

The subject of Maui was brought up at last, and Eden, glad for something to do besides avoid Ben's gaze, shifted her attention to Ray. She was pleased that Ray knew Maui rather well and shared her fervor for the island's attractions. It gave Ben a chance to watch her expressive face. "I love Oʻahu. It's gentler somehow, but then Maui has mystery. Have you been to Hāna or Lahaina recently?"

Ray took his cue. "I can't say that I have, my dear, but did you know that Ben's grandmother Marguerite has a beach house in Spreckelsville? Ben mentioned she was on a river cruise in France and is due home, today, is it?" All eyes turned to Ben.

"Yes, this afternoon. The old girl is pretty feisty and independent for her age. When mother passed on, I was still in grade school, so O-ma, Grandmother that is, had to help raise Brigitte, my sister, and me because father was so busy with the plan . . . with work. It's difficult sometimes to see her as a grandmother. She's been a mother to us for so long."

As he talked, Eden had a good look at him. How could she have thought of him to be arrogant, no, not with the new short haircut which showed off his beautiful ears. How wrong could she have been? How awful to lose his mother at such a tender age.

The conversation continued in this friendly fashion. The newly painted walls of the old house surely brightened up the place and warmed by the afternoon sun and with cups of hot Chinese tea, Ben felt contentment seep in. He had had trouble concentrating on what Ray and Gil had been discussing in earnest for the last few minutes, as his eyes had frequently strayed to where Eden was now sitting so prettily on a pouf next to her mother. Both were crocheting. Abby was seated at the old upright and attempting to play a Chopin prelude. The music was so relaxing that Ben grew thoughtful.

He was hoping to get to talk to Eden personally, but the chance never availed itself. Not once during the meal had she looked at him, and he couldn't imagine why. Had he misinterpreted her warmhearted vibrations the other day at the shopping center? Perhaps there had been something to what Sylvia had intimated about the girl and young Castro. They were certainly a good match, she had said. At the thought of Sylvia, he felt bothered again. Maybe he had led her a merry dance. He hadn't known what to think at the time. She was attractive, he was forced to admit, but the way she fawned over him had only made him feel smothered. She succeeded in turning him off completely when she had tried to coerce him into making their friendship a permanent one by suggesting a business merger of sorts. He had politely and not kindly refused. It bewildered him to see a different side of her when the claws had come out. Losing her temper, yelling at the top of her voice, she had flown off in a huff. Later, he felt mostly annoyed and used and blocked the memory out of his head. He hadn't really given her a thought in the last few days. He'd completely forgotten to heed the advice he'd so freely given to Ray that day of the house inspection. With a look at his Rolex, he motioned to Ray that he had to go. The matriarch of the clan was due to arrive in the early evening by ship, and he had to meet her at the dock in Honolulu.

At the sound of his voice, Eden stopped her crocheting. Working hard at the cafe the last few days, she hadn't had the time, really, to examine her heart. She couldn't stop the growing liking she had for the blond gentleman sitting opposite her, but she felt like an outsider to his world. Their lifestyles were too contrasting, and the fact had been brought home by the encounter with Sylvia. Not being privy to the uproar between the Alexander heir and the hot-headed heiress, she only relied on Camp rumor. She heard that they had met at some fancy shindig, at a winery in Sonoma, where Sylvia's parents owned a home. Ben had checked into the Sonoma Inn Spa on the advice of his doctor, and mutual friends had introduced them.

"Yes," she said realistically to herself, "he looks princely sitting there in that battered old chair." The tailor-made clothing, though casual, made him look elegant, calling to her mind a line from her favorite poetess, Elizabeth Barrett Browning, '. . . he belongs in a king's palace . . .' "Ben Alexander certainly looked like he belonged in a king's palace," she conceded with a sigh, "not here at 199 Hau'oli Way." Getting him to smile was one thing, but to contemplate anything more seemed futile.

The men rose to take their leave. After shaking hands warmly, Ray reminded Gil of the annual Summer **Fête** that was sponsored by the Alexander Trust and held at the mansion on the hill. Invitations were being issued and Gil's family was included on the prestigious guest list. With a grave look, Gil thanked Ray and before they took off, Ray gave the okay sign to Abby. The Range Rover with Ben at the helm sped away. Eden watched them go, not seeing her sister's sympathizing look. Gil took his wife by the hand, "I need to talk to you my dear." It was his cue to his girls that he had something to share with his wife and needed privacy.

"It's about time we had our heart-to-heart talk, sister of mine. Let's grab some snacks and go sit at the picnic table and enjoy the rest of the afternoon," Abby suggested. Armed with their mom's famous shortbread cookies, fresh fruit and homemade lemonade, they made their way out of the old house and to the backyard, giggling all the way like they did as children.

"How can we still be so hungry after that lunch?" Eden asked in mock seriousness.

"Better yet, can anyone resist Mom's shortbread? There goes my diet," Abby replied, throwing caution to the wind.

They stayed outside, talking about everything under the sun, until they came to the subject of Mr. Alexander. Eden grew quiet under her sister's scrutiny.

"Well?" Abby probed.

"Well, what? The guy has a girlfriend, sort of." Abby laughed.

"Eden, for a guy who supposedly is dating someone else, he sure looks at you a lot and I must say, with admiration. Plus, little sister, it is obvious that you like him, too. It shows all over your sweet face."

"Oh no, is it that obvious?" Eden frowned, scrunching her nose then sighing deeply. "How can it work, Abby, we come from different worlds?"

"Take it one step at a time. In my humble opinion, you guys are a perfect match!"

The sun hid behind the Wai'anae Range, turning the sky into soft pastels. It was a lovely and familiar soothing sight. Both girls felt good to be home together and got up instantly when they heard their mother calling them from the kitchen door. They both knew that whatever it was that their parents discussed privately would surely be shared at the dinner table that evening. What could it be all about, they wondered, as they hurried arm in arm into "the old house" they called home.

CHAPTER 9
The Summer Fête

Gil Andres made his decision a few days later. He wasn't in a quandary at what to do, nor overly concerned about what others would think about the new job offer from Ray Mulroney. He considered everything very carefully and felt it best to stick to his calling, that is, to work with the Union.

"I can't do it, Janie," he said. "I feel I would be forsaking my Union roots if I accept Mulroney's offer." He watched her face fall. He knew she was so much looking forward to what would be Gil's salary increase and perhaps to be moving to one of the newer homes built for management. She also knew he didn't make the decision lightly.

"I'm a union man," Gill continued, "and can't see myself crossing over the line now." Janie gave him a hug, mumbled that she would stand with his decision. The girls fretted when they saw the disappointment on their mother's face, but in the end accepted his answer. Gil always stood up for what he believed in, and somehow, they would make do. Ray was not surprised nor sorely disappointed, but Ben's admiration for the man increased ten-fold.

Janie and Gil, however, saw no harm in allowing the girls to attend the fête though they themselves would not. "Just think, dear, how much fun it will be for them to have a 'new experience,'" Janie contended, and Gil had braced himself for another flurry in his household as preparations got under way. Janie, a self-taught seamstress with a flair for the unusual, helped the girls fashion their dresses. Abbey's hot pink 1950's style chiffon dress only needed new accessories and suited her short bob. Eden did not own anything so remotely feminine and was persuaded into wearing a remake of one of her big sister's evening dresses. It was a lovely fitted, white lace affair that fell off the shoulders, exposing the bones of her slim neck. The bottom set of ruffles had been removed to give it an up-to-date look and the result showed off her almost boyish figure to perfection. Never having attended a society function before, Eden wasn't comfortable with the idea. She gladly accepted her sister's advice to go to the local salon. Her luxuriant hair, once curled and sparkling with red highlights from a henna rinse, gave her a modern sophisticated look. At the last minute, Janie added a **haku lei po'o** of bright red flowers and placed it on her head. "There, don't you look a dream!" Janie beamed with satisfaction. Naturally modest, Eden had to agree with her own reflection in the bathroom mirror. Abby's expertise in the makeup department enhanced her already good looks and the total effect was so pleasing that she had given both her mother and sister hugs.

Kimo, the Alexander's property manager, sped the huge estate car toward the mansion on the hill. An hour before the annual Summer Fête, he had appeared at the Andres' door looking very much like the Hawaiian chauffeur, clad in white slacks, a particularly loud aloha shirt and a stunning black **kukui nut** lei. He handed Gil a note from Ray, offering the girls a ride to the mansion. Making small talk with Gil, he waited patiently in the parlor and happily accepted a glass of homemade pineapple cordial and a piece of Janie's famous **haupia**. Gil, always glad to visit with friends, welcomed the chance to catch up on plantation news and their favorite teams. He and Kimo were both rabid Yankee fans.

When daughters number one and two appeared in the parlor looking like debutantes, their parents were extremely gratified. Kimo stood at attention. He had known the girls since they were children and was very proud that they were well turned out. He could see the paternal pride in Gil's eyes.

"Don't worry Gil, I'll have them home at a decent hour."

"There now, dear," Janie sighed as they watched Kimo bear their daughters away, "at the fête there's bound to be any number of eligible young bachelors looking for wives." Gil shook his head. Janie never gave up.

Eden was a bundle of nerves. As the distance between the speeding car and the mansion on the hill shortened, she began to fidget with her mother's heirloom, a beaded red jade necklace, and kept her face to the window. Abby, accustomed to these types of soirees, sought to distract her by doing a perfect imitation of their matchmaking mother.

"Did you notice the gleam in Mother's eye, Eden? I feel like we're up on the auction block." She cleared her throat, and in Janie's voice announced, "And now gentlemen, we present to you, daughter number one. Abigail is 5' – 8", weighs ll0 lbs., with dark brown hair and brown eyes. Her hobbies include reading, tennis and ikebana. Do I hear a bid? Going once, going twice.

Sold to the tall, dark and handsome stranger in the Armani tuxedo." They held back the laughter until they couldn't stand it and fell against the seat into a fit of giggles. Kimo couldn't help but laugh with them.

"Be nice Abigail, your mother means well. And isn't it high time one of you girls got married? Why, my Malia got married right after high school, and has already given me two mo'opuna! You should see how big the boys are now."

"We know, Kimo," Abby cried, wrinkling up her nose, "Malia was born to be married. We can see that she's a wonderful mother to those boys, and she adores her Edwin."

Kimo loved to talk about the joys of grandparenthood. He babbled on happily until the great car slowed down and turned into the vine covered stone entry. He followed the long drive flanked with tall **royal palms**. The mansion stood on the crest of a hill, looking out on the beautiful Wai'anae Range. Eden had passed by it many times and had always dreamed of viewing its stately rooms and its famous botanical garden. She had never given thought to the family who resided there until just recently and wondered if she would get the chance to see one member that night. The object of her thoughts was presently escorting his dear grandmother, Marguerite Alexander, from her cabana near the pool, to the ballroom.

Kimo smiled broadly at his charges. "Here we are, girls. Have fun you two, and remember, . . . behave yourselves." The sisters looked at each other out of the corner of their eyes and kept straight faces.

Valets in red and black uniforms greeted them and opened the doors while a jubilant Ray Mulroney hurried down the steps to meet them and lead them to the great hall. He cut a dashing figure in his gray tuxedo, and as he admired their finery, he knew an instant of regret that he was not so young anymore. Taking on the role of matchmaker had added a few more strands of gray to his auburn head. Eden was spoken for, but Abby, what was a body to do with Abby? He needed to mastermind a plan for that young beauty. In the meantime, that gut feeling was present, and he knew he had done the right thing in inviting the family to this annual event. It presented a united front between the company and the union. The thought pleased him greatly.

"Abigail, Eden," he greeted them suavely, "what a pleasure to have you here. I hope you don't think it high handed of me to send the car for you. But why not, it's great fun to arrive in style. Allow me to escort you inside." As it was his aim to gain their appreciation, he beamed triumphantly when the girls thanked him profusely.

Walking with him into the elegant foyer, Eden couldn't help but feel awed by her surroundings. The house, like a grande dame, spoke of the splendor of bygone days. Her head bent back so she could take in the painted mural on the vaulted ceiling. A great Waterford glass chandelier hung from its center. Swags of greenery and flowers bedecked the walls and arched doorways. Soft classical music was streaming through large speakers everywhere. Eden secretly longed to dawdle and have a look around, but Ray urged them on. Steering them towards the ballroom, he commissioned the first guest on the horizon to take them in for refreshments.

"Ah, here's Anthony. I'll leave you in his capable hands. Enjoy yourselves, my dears. I'm officially on the welcoming committee and must get back to my post." If Abby had noticed Ray's careful orchestration, she didn't let it show. She didn't have a hint as to what was running through Ray's mind now, or did she?

Tony, who had anticipated a dull evening, couldn't believe his good fortune. Accompanied by two gorgeous birds, he escorted them proudly toward the refreshment table. In the middle of the black and white checkerboard marble floor, the trio got waylaid by one of Abby's professional friends, and

Tony reluctantly let her go. He steered the high-strung Eden to the punch table and plied her with drink. Feeling a bit out of her depth, Eden drank deeply to quench her thirst, and was thankful to have something to do besides gawk at everyone. Presently, mellow from punch and Tony's carefree chatter, she relaxed.

Studying the varying expressions on Eden's animated face, Tony felt an immediate attraction to her. To his parents' concern, his predilection for falling in love but never settling down had caused them much unnecessary woe. "Mum, stop fussing! You know I like to date lots of girls!" he would always grumble whenever she got on his case. At their last heated discussion, his mother had muttered **sotto voce** to his father, "You date many, but you marry only one." Mr. Robertson had merely shrugged his shoulders. "Anthony will meet his match someday," he insisted. Tall, lanky Tony with straight, sun-bleached brown hair and light brown eyes that bored into hers, looked more like a surfer than the sheep station heir he was purported to be. Eden envied his tan and fell instantly for his New Zealand accent. He seemed uncomplicated enough, and somehow, she felt remarkably safe with him.

"Call me Tony," he had said. "Everybody does." Captivated by her unusual facial bone structure, he began unreservedly, "Miss Andres, Eden, I mean. I would love the chance to take photographs of you. Would you consider sitting for me? You have a very arresting face." It was the perfect line, delivered so smoothly that Eden choked on her punch and coughed. Tony was taken aback and slapped her on the back a few times, until tears sprang into her eyes. "Say, old girl, are you alright?" His concern was so truly genuine that Eden couldn't take offense at him, and instead burst out laughing. He laughed along with her.

She dabbed her eyes with her napkin. "Sorry Tony . . ."

"Anthony Sebastian Charles Robertson, for my sins actually, at your service," he interrupted and bowed low to the floor. Was this guy for real? Eden had to wonder. She had never entertained anyone in tails before and she couldn't help but be tickled at the picture he presented to her.

"Well, Mr. Anthony Sebastian Charles Robertson," she reproved him boldly, "that was the classic come-on line if ever I heard one. Are you always so forward?"

"Tsk, tsk," Tony defended himself unabashedly. "Take heed to whom you choose to give a set down, young lady. You see before you Lord Snowdon's latest competitor in the flesh. However, I shall forgive you for your wee impertinence. Wouldn't do, you know, to be seen through so easily."

Eden's eyes grew wide. Oh dear, something was amiss here. Lord Snowdon? Set down? She had no earthly idea what he was talking about. Was it she, or was it because the New Zealander was rambling on in the King's English at ninety miles a minute? She was always putting her foot in her mouth. Searching her brain wildly for any recollection of British protocol, she tried to remember something she had read about addressing a member of the nobility. Her mind blank and sufficiently chastened, she entreated, "Forgive me, sir, or Milord, but you're the first blueblood I've ever had the privilege to meet!" At Tony's odd look, she stumbled on, "I mean you don't get to meet many lords in Hawai'i, you know. Well, except for Jack Lord." She laughed at her own joke. She looked so sincere that Tony cracked up.

"I think we're talking at cross purposes here. Lord, did you say? No, doll, that's not what I mean. I'm not that kind of Lord,

I'm a photographer, as one who takes pictures! Lord Snowdon was a photographer. Comprende?"

For a moment Eden was confused, and then greatly relieved. "You are a nut, you know that!"

"Well, my dear," he countered, "so are you!" Relaxed together, they enjoyed each other's company and attacked the punch with gusto. Presently, Tony put all joking aside, and talked in a more serious vein.

"I do mean it when I say I want to photograph you. Being here has been wonderful so far. There is so much to see and capture on film. I'm afraid though, Daddy is not too keen on my ambition. He wants me at home to run the farm, but I've never been into that. My younger brother Kit is the gentleman yeoman of the family. Call me the black sheep, right-e-o. I've been sent here to Aunt Marguerite to straighten things out."

"Aunt Marguerite?"

"Alexander, my cousin's grandmother."

"Cousin?"

"Must you repeat everything I say, old girl? Ben and I aren't cousins really, but Mum and Daddy are good friends with his grandmother and of course, his father, Barnes Alexander. Therefore, I've always called her Aunt Marguerite and him, Uncle Barnes." He fixed his gaze into the garden. "I love it here. It's a photographer's paradise. The physical beauty of the islands, the wonderful ethnic mix, the sky . . . even the light is different here."

"What about New Zealand," Eden asked, "isn't it beautiful there, too?"

"Oh yes," Tony replied, "it is profoundly beautiful, but I've never been to a place quite like Hawai'i. There is something different, almost magical in the islands. I really want to stay here."

Eden nodded. "I think I do understand your plight. Dad is the same with us kids. He wanted us all to become schoolteachers. Abby did and hated it. My brothers both joined the Air Force, and the twins, well, the only thing they're interested in right now is being teenagers. By the way, Abby works for a modeling agency in Honolulu, both as a stylist and a model. When she can, she does freelance modeling. Why don't you get her to sit for you? I'm sure she'd be happy to oblige. "They both looked over hopefully at Abby, who was surrounded by several male guests. "That is, if you get the chance to talk to her." They laughed at the sheer improbability.

Feeling more at ease, Eden continued, "All I've wanted to do is train to become a professional chef. I guess we must follow our own hearts and do what we think is best for our own happiness." Tony looked down at her. She looked up at him earnestly with kindness in her eyes. Here was a girl after his own heart and he was smitten.

It was at this precise moment that Ben Alexander stepped onto the dance floor with his grandmother on his arm. He gave a quick survey around the crowded room and spied the young couple in the corner. What he saw was Tony chatting up a young butterfly, as he called all his cousin's lady loves, and strained to see which one it was. The pair looked mighty cozy together. Putting on his glasses, his jaw dropped. The butterfly in white was the Andres girl! It annoyed him a little to see her looking so young and intense, and paying close attention to his frivolous cousin. He frowned. For some reason, he knew she had been avoiding him, and he wanted to know why. His quest to discover who she reminded him of was at a standstill, and he was determined to talk to her this evening. She couldn't possibly hide herself here, tonight, unless she was deliberately rude, and he knew from experience that she couldn't be that. He escorted his grandmother across the room to sit with some friends.

"Benjamin, darling," his grandmother called up softly to him. He lowered his head to hear her over the din. "I left my shawl in my cabana. Would you be so kind as to fetch it for me?" He bussed her cheek and disappeared from the great room.

Laughing at one of Tony's antics, Eden finally consented to be photographed in the garden. She was feeling a little lightheaded and wanted a breath of fresh air. Tony pointed out the spot where the koi pond was located and instructed her to wait for him there.

"It's going to take me a few minutes to get my equipment together," he called out as he strode in the direction of the guest wing.

The girl in white headed for the French doors which were opened to the **lanai**. She passed Abby, who had an earnest suitor in tow and looked like she didn't need any assistance. Stepping onto the lawn, she felt the change in temperature. The grass offered cool comfort and was soft as a plush carpet. A gentle breeze blew the wisps of her hair away from her heated face. Crickets chirped. The sun was ready to say goodbye and make way for the night. As she progressed across the lawn, she received admiring glances from several guests. The chink of glasses, and the sound of laughter and music floated out from the doors she had just exited and followed her into the gardens. She turned to examine the graceful old mansion now ablaze with lights. The scene before her looked quite mythical and dreamlike. Continuing, she came to the little wooden bridge over the koi pond, removed her shoes, and left them at the last steppingstone. She could hear the gentle ripple in the water made by the brightly colored koi and her eyes slowly swept over the entire garden.

"What a profusion of flowers!" she exclaimed to herself, "this is truly a paradise!" There were gingers of all varieties, every color of **plumeria** imaginable, gardenias, roses, orchids, bougainvilleas, blossoms of **cup of gold**, hibiscus, **heliconia**, ferns, rhododendron vines that covered tall trees and lastly, there was the luscious **night blooming cereus**. The riot of colors and the heady fragrances hanging heavy in the air began to weave an intoxicating spell over her. Eyes aglow, she watched hypnotized as the late afternoon sunlight filtered through the trees, like beacons from some other plane. Time was forgotten and she was completely entranced. That is, until the tall figure in a white coat made haste across the wide lawn and approached her from the other end of the bridge. With her eyelids fluttering, Ben Alexander came into her view, an elegant woman's shawl draped over one arm. Recognition hit Eden, breaking her reverie, and she turned to dash away. Her shoes momentarily forgotten, she stumbled over them.

"Darn these shoes," she muttered and attempted to slip them back on. An iron grip restrained her and rooted her to the spot.

"Wait, don't go," Ben Alexander pleaded softly. He turned her to face him and without her shoes she felt at a disadvantage. Her eyes met the third button of his pleated shirt. What was it about a tuxedo that made a man look bigger than life? She had to look up, and he looked down. Dark eyes met green ones and held.

The man in the white tuxedo looked so studious and scholarly with his dark rimmed glasses, but it was the eyes that held her spellbound. They looked hazel in the fading light and were filled with tenderness. She felt like melting under his penetrating gaze. He felt like raining kisses all over that adoring face. Despite all the reservations they had about one another, they both smiled, Eden shyly and Ben unashamedly. Eden swallowed nervously. After what seemed like an eternity, they both spoke at the same time, stopped and started up simultaneously again, causing Ben to laugh self-consciously.

"Come, let's go for a walk around the grounds." He waited while she slipped on her shoes and guided her onto the path to the gazebo, which was situated next to a large banyan tree. At dusk, the birds that nestled in that wondrous tree were making a cacophony of sound. Eden felt as if they were being serenaded.

"O-ma, my grandmother," Ben began, "turned this place into a sanctuary after Grandfather passed on and Brigitte and I went off to college. She doesn't live here anymore. She divides her time between her family's estate in Wahiawā and her beach home on Maui. This house is quite old, my great-grandfather built it when he settled here in the 1920s. Of course, it's been added on to and remodeled over the years. We have a guest wing that was built more recently and is used on occasions like this. Our private quarters are upstairs except for mine which is on the ground floor, and O-ma has her own cabana next to the pool. All the staff are permanent."

They reached the gingerbread gazebo. It was made of wood and painted white, with a seat all the way around its interior perimeter. A Makai Glass sculpture in the Dale Chihuly style hung from its ceiling.

"Oh, how perfect!" Eden gasped with delight. "Now this is where I would spend all my time if I lived here!" Her outburst pleased Ben.

"Actually, it's one of my favorite refuges on the property. When I was a youngster, this was my sanctuary from our governess. I don't know why it never occurred to her to look for me here."

Sensing Ben's need to unburden himself, Eden let him talk, content just to be standing next to him. She listened thoughtfully as he recounted his recuperation from malaria and his gentle plea for her help to solve this mystery of partial amnesia. She didn't quite grasp why he needed her help, but she knew what he really needed. Perhaps in time she could tell him, and he would listen.

She watched him remove his glasses and place them in his breast pocket. He looked sternly handsome in the filtering light. Out went all her preconceived ideas and plans. How could she avoid the inevitable? No, it wasn't possible anymore to deny what she felt for this enigmatic golden man. By the minute, his soft caressing voice was weakening her resolve to remain aloof.

New to all this, she felt scared and excited as he stood behind her and put his arms around her, pulling her close to him. She smelled like orange blossoms in the Spring, and he bent to kiss the top of her head. Her heart pounded when she felt his lips upon her hair and took in the scent of his spicy aftershave. It felt so safe to be within the bulwark of his arms. How she wished the exquisite moment would last forever.

In his haste, Tony jammed the lever that advanced the film on his old Leica. He struggled with it futilely for a few minutes, then grabbed his digital camera, the A F Nikon with its long lens attached. Anxious to catch the last of the daylight, he hurried through the grass. After reaching the koi pond and not finding Eden there, he scratched his head and decided to search the extensive grounds. Spotting someone in the gazebo, he was about to call out when he noticed Eden wasn't alone. He stopped in his tracks. The couple in the gazebo appeared to be suspended in time and were totally unaware of the lone figure standing a short distance away. As the sun's last rays found their way through the trees to the gazebo, Tony aimed and snapped several shots in quick succession. The timing was perfect. Among those shots he knew he'd captured a prize-winning photo. For a few seconds, he regarded the couple in the gazebo wistfully, replaced the cover over the camera's lens, and slipped unobserved into the guest wing of the great house.

CHAPTER 10
The Midnight Feast

It was the sound of the orchestra tuning up that awakened Ben and Eden from their dreamlike state. "Good Lord, I just lost track of the time," Ben quipped. "Come on, it's tradition at this fête that an Alexander leads off the first waltz." Laughing as he pulled her along, they raced towards the ballroom. In their haste, Eden lost her balance when her shoe caught on a steppingstone, the haku lei poʻo fell out of her hair, and once they crossed the French doors leading into the ballroom, she was hit with a bad case of stage fright.

This unorthodox entrance caused every eye in the place to fall on them. As the emcee announced the official opening of the fête, Ben handed the shawl to his startled grandmother, and promised to introduce Eden after the first dance. The heir to the Alexander Corporation led his partner onto the dance floor. A soft hush spread throughout the ballroom. Ben was a familiar face, but who was the lovely young lady with him? The gentlemen approved of his choice, the ladies admired her dress, and O-ma Alexander nodded her silver head to the emcee. The beautiful strains of "The Blue Danube Waltz" propelled the couple forward, and after a few moments of them dancing solo, other couples joined in. Abby twirled by with her partner, but Eden missed her sister's playful wink. Seeing the furrowed little brow, Ben squeezed her hand to reassure her.

"If you hold your mouth right," he said, not able to resist teasing her, "it would be easier to remember your steps!"

"Please, don't," Eden entreated, looking up at him, "it was difficult enough learning to waltz in grade school. You'd be petrified too if this was your first waltz!" To show him, she lost her concentration and stepped on his toes. Ben regained his composure and started them off again.

"Are you telling me that you've never danced the waltz before?" he asked surprised, and then chuckled. "Well, well, well, this must be the night for firsts. May I say that you waltz beautifully, Eden."

"Well, thanks. You're looking at the mashed potato queen of Leilehua High."

"Mashed potato?" Ben's tawny brows arched.

"Yep, a fellow classmate, Roger T and I won first place. Didn't you ever rock 'n' roll when you were a teenager? The Mashed Potato came into vogue again when I was in high school." The gentleman in question shook his head. At the shock on her expressive face, he maneuvered them around the great room and led a breathless and unsuspecting Eden to his grandmother.

Marguerite Alexander was not the typical stereotype of a grandmother. In her seventies, she was statuesque, silver haired and had inherited her family's aquiline nose. Her Monique Lhuillier dress, covered with silver sequins and tiny pearl beads, and her bejeweled person commanded immediate obeisance. She instantly reminded Eden of an aging dowager queen who was not ready to relinquish her crown to the succeeding heir.

"Benjamin," O-ma dictated imperiously, "you will be forgiven, if you . . . well, don't just stand there looking sappy. Whom do we have here? Introduce this lovely creature to me at once!" Ben grinned unrepentantly and pulled Eden around. Alarmed at being introduced to a member of Ben's family without much preamble, Eden clutched onto Ben's life-saving arm.

"Grandmother, this is Eden, Gil Andres' daughter," he answered all too casually, his arm around her tiny waist. He added with pride in his voice, "Eden, this is my adorable O-ma."

The compliment disarmed O-ma completely. Lifting a gloved hand, she took Eden's trembling one into her own. When his grandmother got a good look at the girl, her tone softened. She quickly forgot her minor annoyance and decided to receive her royally.

"I'm charmed, my dear. What a lovely dress. You must tell me the name of your dressmaker."

Eden couldn't have been more wrong in her assumptions. Ben's eyes looked back at her, though Marguerite Alexander's had lost their brilliant emerald color and were tinged more with yellow. They were genuinely kind. She involuntarily bent to curtsey, but Ben's restraining arm held her in check, amused at her gesture. At such a warm welcome from his grandmother, Eden bent to kiss the dear woman's cheek. A camera's flash caught her eye. Finally, remembering her appointment with Tony, Eden quickly excused herself, and rushed up to him.

"Tony, will you forgive me, I . . . " Another flash went off, and before Eden could offer more apologies, he rewarded her by snapping yet another picture. Each time she protested, he snapped several more, until finally, she gave up. Tony, in photographer's heaven, wasn't going to let the opportunity pass him by. Folks were falling all over themselves to pose for him.

The evening took on a hazy blur, and many eyebrows were raised as Ben stayed constant by Eden's side. Was there romance in the air? They could only guess. When the bold young cub of an old family friend claimed her hand, Ben reluctantly let her go. Chatting amiably with his grandmother, he watched as Eden and her partner twirled away. When Eden caught the eyes of several available young men in the room, and they began to vie for her attention, Ben became increasingly edgy waiting for each dance to be completed. Finally, catching the trend, he decided to act and cut in. His distinctive glare at potential dancing partners and his possessive arm discouraged others less fortunate and kept them at bay. Ray Mulroney, observing from across the room, thoroughly savored the success of his plan and generously patted himself on the back.

Dinner was served on the front lawn, which was dotted with round wooden tables surrounded by white wooden chairs. The tables were covered with the palest pink damask, each with a centerpiece of pink and blue hydrangeas in blue and white porcelain vases. Tiny white lights inside paper lanterns were hung everywhere, giving the place a fairy tale look. Abby was in her element. It was as if the decorator had her in mind when she planned the color scheme for the occasion. Never lacking for admirers, the beauty in pink waved gaily from her coterie of admirers.

As they shared the midnight feast together, Ben's grandmother covertly observed her grandson and Eden from her table. The sight of them sitting close together, so obviously in their own world, comforted her heart. She watched as Ben smiled down at Eden. She couldn't remember the last time she had seen her solemn grandson give his smile so easily. Yes, when he was a child, that devastating smile always got him what he wanted, and from her vantage point, she could see what he wanted.

It had baffled her when Ben had phoned her the other day, sounding so boyishly exuberant.

What a striking contrast to the solemn moody hermit he had become after returning from Thailand. Has true love finally come to her grandson? Growing up in wealth had exposed him, as debutante after debutante had paraded before him. Never really knowing if he was truly liked for himself or for his fortune, he had voiced this disenchantment to her many times, and she had seen him grow cynical toward love. For a short period of time, she thought he had found the girl of his dreams, but when it was discovered that she too was interested mainly in his wealth, Ben had hardened and grown despondent --which was a destructive combination.

It was time for him to begin anew, put the past behind him. For heaven's sake, he deserved a second chance after the distressing events of the last two years. Eden's open face upturned to his own showed her heart. She had liked the girl on the spot. Instinctively, she knew her grandson could safely trust her with his life.

As Marguerite Alexander pondered these things in her heart, Ben tore his gaze from Eden and glanced up at his grandmother. She shook her head. She was not ready to leave the party. Beaming at her grandson and Eden with affection, they had her blessings.

Never in her life had Eden seen so many kinds of hors d'oeuvres all in one setting. She had read about feasts like these, but up until now had only dreamed of ever seeing such a sumptuous display. She had eaten so many canapes that Ben was greatly diverted by her enthusiasm.

"Do you always eat this much?" he asked laughingly.

Before answering, Eden watched as he skillfully handled his fork and knife. She had never seen a gentleman dine with such perfect table manners. In comparison, she felt klutzy, and she was making a hog out of herself. How could he expect her to contain her wonder and enthusiasm when she was enjoying everything to the hilt?

"You know, Mr. Alexander," she said as she picked up a tiny **blini** topped with golden **Osetra** caviar, "this is the ultimate taste trip for any aspiring chef!"

"You can drop the Mr. part. The name is Ben, remember."

"Hmmm, is it short for Benedict?" she asked as she popped the delicious morsel into her mouth.

"No, as a matter of fact, it is not. It's plain old Benjamin, nothing as exotic as Eden Sabina. I was named after my grandfather, Benjamin Harry Alexander. Alan was my mother's maiden name and became my middle name. Benjamin Alan Alexander. Pretty dull if you ask me, but then we go back a long way, we Alexanders do."

"Exotic? Moi?" Eden laughed and rolled her eyes. "I was named after my dad's mom, Sabina and I love that, but Eden has had its challenges. Hmmm, I think I like your name better. Well then, with your long list of illustrious forebears and busy social calendar, I expect you're used to this sort of thing! Is it like this every year?"

Benjamin Alan Alexander had to wonder at her comment. He was accustomed to having to attend social functions and up until now, they had bored him stiff. He was seeing afresh with Eden's young eyes.

"Actually, I haven't been to this particular event in a few years. I'm standing in for Dad." He took a sip from his glass, eyeing her speculatively, as she gulped down yet another glass of punch. "Let's say I had incentive this year," he continued, "and no, it's never the same."

Eden wondered how Ben could sound so casual. She meant to enjoy every minute of her 'experience.' It seemed to her that no cost had been spared, even to the point of decadence, for this lavish function. She eyed the mini fresh fruit tarts. They sparkled like fabulous jewels.

"It was nice of you to include us. I'm sorry the folks wouldn't come. Mom would have loved this!"

"Ray's idea really. You must thank him for that, but don't let the thanks go to his head. He rather fancies himself a dandy, that one. As for me, I'd rather be out doing something more civilized. You can't imagine the duty dances I've had to partake in for the company's sake!" The thought was particularly endearing to Eden. Ben Alexander didn't look the type. What did he mean by something more civilized?

A cool breeze swept through the dining area, shaking the paper lanterns. Eden shivered and Ben insisted she put his coat around her tiny shoulders. It swallowed her and came down to her knees.

"Would you care to go for another walk around the garden?" he suggested, "I feel the need to stretch my legs."

Eden brightened up. "Well, to tell you the truth I would love to, but my feet won't take any more from these shoes. I hate high heels." She looked at him out of the corners of her eyes. "I do have a favor to ask of you, though."

"Favor? Name it and I'll do my level best to accommodate you."

"I would love to have a peek inside your magnificent ancestral home. I especially want to see the inside of the kitchen and the guest bedrooms." Ben was justly proud of his family home, but for a moment he was taken aback at her request. He could understand the kitchen, but the guest bedrooms? Surprise, and then satisfaction, showed on his handsome face as she continued unperturbed. "Someone had to be very creative to have produced all this," pointing to the display of food, "and I have heard that the guest suites contain a most unusual collection of Plantation photographs. I'd love to see them."

"Oh, now where did you get that piece of enlightened information?" Ben inquired, relieved she hadn't guessed his thoughts.

"Your cousin Tony told me, silly."

"Ah yes, my estimable cousin Tony. You can see he's mad about photography. However, we've all been banned from the kitchen and the guest rooms are occupied now, so I'll give you a tour at a more convenient date. I'll take you to the library instead."

He led her to heavy double doors that opened into a long hall which showed off paintings of the Alexander ancestors. Opening the ornately carved koa doors to the library, he reached to turn up the lights that were on low. Immediately the large room was bathed in light streaming from glass chandeliers hanging from the embossed copper ceiling. Eden shaded her eyes from the brightness. The room was grand in a stuffy way. Any minute now, she expected the king, whoever he was, to walk in. Windows that afforded a view of the extensive lawns and the mountains covered one entire wall. The other walls were interspaced with a gold velvet wallpaper and rows and rows of exotic wood shelves filled with leather bound books. A red Persian rug covered the **'ohi'a lehua** floor. The room's opulence dizzied her, and she swayed.

"Are you feeling alright, Eden?" Ben asked gently, holding her steady.

"I . . . I feel like I'm made of lead. I think I ate too much." She removed his coat and placed it on the back of a Queen Anne's chair, done up in lovely crewel embroidery.

"That's rich," Ben chuckled. "Most of the women I know are on these perpetual diets. I think, more likely, the lady has had too much punch." He added mysteriously, "This will make a great story to tell our grandchildren!"

"Gr ... grandchildren???" Eden croaked. What did he mean about too much punch? She didn't suppress the giggle this time. The tawny eyebrows went up with mock gravity in his handsome face. She swiftly begged his pardon and when he excused her like she was a naughty child, she bristled. Up went the tiny chin. She had to enunciate her words slowly, "Don't talk to me like I'm a child. I am not . . ." She hiccupped, then blushed.

Ben wasn't at all sure how to handle this girl-woman. She had spark, and this was a side to her personality that constantly surprised and delighted him. It amazed him that it hadn't sunk into her that he thought she was wonderful.

"Ohhh, would you mind if I sit down?"

Ben gave an exultant laugh. "Remind me to keep tabs on your liquid intake in the future. Didn't you know the punch was mixed with champagne?"

"Champagne?" Eden shook her head. Why, she never touches the stuff.

He led her to a red velvet couch. It was luxurious beyond imagination. Eden melted into its softness. The room, furnished lavishly in red and yellow gold, the colors of Hawaiian royalty, made her feel like a royal.

"Hmmm, I guess this is how the other half lives," she thought dreamily to herself. Presently, Ben lit a cigarette. He drew on it and stubbed it out in a Lalique ashtray.

Eden opened one eye and commented, "I didn't know you smoked!"

"I've quit! If you can understand what that means." Never having smoked, she didn't understand, but she knew that sitting there near Ben in this extravagant setting was doing crazy things to her equilibrium. She closed her eyes once more. She felt like she was floating on a magic carpet.

Ben observed her indulgently. The girl looked young and tremulous in that white dress which showed off lovely shoulders and her beautiful, tanned legs. Her once neatly styled hair, slightly disheveled, was tangled with the jade necklace. Straightening the red beads, his gaze lingered on them, following them up to her tilting head. Her skin was so perfect, he was finding it impossible to take his eyes off her. He took in the finely arched eyebrows and those lashes too long to be real. When he found himself staring at her soft mouth, he couldn't tear his eyes away. He bent his head and took possession of her lips with his own. Taken by surprise, Eden was overwhelmed by the onslaught of kisses that followed. The trail of sweet kisses went from her mouth, over her nose, up to either side of her forehead, down over both eyelids, to her throat and back again to her bruised lips. She could feel the heavy thud of his heart and his spicy aftershave was driving her to distraction. Up went her arms around his neck. Ben held her close to him for the longest time and then pulled away and touched her face with his hands.

"You're quite beautiful, you know."

"Don't say that." Eden rolled her eyes. "Abby's the beauty in our family."

Ben laughed. "Your sister is sensational looking, yes, but you also have a 'beautiful spirit.' I think that's what attracted me in the first place."

"A beautiful spirit?"

"Uh huh. Besides, your gorgeous legs are a bonus."

"I, what do you mean by that?" Eden turned red at that comment. This was just too much for her. She had always been called 'Bones' by her family.

"Eden, hasn't anyone ever told you this?" She shook her head. No one had ever told her this. "Well, get used to being praised, my beauty."

Suddenly, Eden did feel beautiful and ridiculously happy. Neither heard the passing footsteps pause in the hall, nor saw the dejected fellow with the camera in tow walk silently away.

Ben put her from him and studied her face. Eden's eyes with their promise of love pouring out to him sobered him up. What was he doing? She was still a child, and he was in danger of losing his heart to her. He would have to tread lightly and do the thinking for them both.

Shaken by his revelation, he stood up abruptly, walked to the window seat and lit another cigarette. He needed to think. He had known that the spark between them could lead to this. His mind had reasoned against having any further acquaintance with her. How could it work? He had fought his attraction for her with all his might, but his heart was pulling him irresistibly toward her. Where others had failed so miserably, this mere slip of a girl had ingenuously succeeded in winning his trust. So young, yet in the odd moment, she sometimes sounded wise beyond her years, and did she make him feel like laughing!

Eden walked to Ben and rested her cheek against his back. Something flared within him. Fraught with emotion he knew she wouldn't understand, he wrestled inwardly for control. When he did speak, his voice was soft and tender. "Eden, do you know what you're doing?"

Closing her eyes, she murmured, "Doing? What do you mean by that?"

He turned around and held her at arm's length. "I think it's better if we go back to the dance floor, little one!"

Eden had protested, but dancing with Ben had been heavenly. Even though her feet hurt like crazy the next day, it had been worth every blister!

CHAPTER 11
The Courtship

As June meshed into July, the days grew long and lazy. Luscious fruit hanging from trees began to ripen in abundance. The smell of guavas and mangoes dominated the air. In people's gardens in the camp, tropical fruits of all varieties were tended with devotion. The pineapple fields, pregnant with fruit ready to be picked, took center stage. Work gangs composed mostly of eager college kids were wildly harvesting the bumper crop. The steady hum of the harvesters could be heard day and night. Tourists stopped by in droves to watch their progress and to take endless amounts of photos.

The Andres family settled back into routine. Abby, back to her apartment in Honolulu, was busy with assignments. A rosy haze enveloped Eden and Ben as their friendship deepened. They were frequently seen taking walks around the plantation. Despite the cultural differences, they found they could talk to each other like old friends.

Previously, Eden felt she knew almost everything there was to know about pineapple and plantation life, but she was now seeing it from Ben's perspective. "I know that the pineapple, the Ananas Comosus, was first cultivated in the southern part of inland Brazil," she told him.

"Well, the general consensus is that" he responded as he took to enlightening her on the introduction of the King of Fruit to the world, "the pineapple made its way to the Caribbean. When Christopher Columbus got there, he brought plants back to Spain. From Spain it went around the globe to the Philippines, Guam and India and as far away as Zimbabwe. The "Smooth Cayenne" variety was introduced into the Hawaiian Islands in the 1800s and by 1892, the plants did so well in the Hawaiian climate that they could be grown commercially and shipped. About the same time as James Dole started his famous plantation, the Alexander Corporation started theirs," Ben informed her with pride in his voice.

"The Hawaiians called it **hala kahiki** or foreign fruit, because of its resemblance to the fruit of the **hala** trees," Eden added.

"Why yes, you're right. Then you must know that the pineapple was given its English name because of its resemblance to a pinecone!" Eden nodded. Ben added. "Did you know that the pineapple made it to New England and George Washington grew them in Mount Vernon?"

"Oh really, I didn't know that, but I do know that the pineapple was and still is a symbol of hospitality, and continues to be so in New England, especially in Williamsburg. I've made a couple of colonial style centerpieces for our Christmas parties, using apples and oranges and greenery on a wooden cone with spikes and topped with a fresh pineapple, crown and all."

"Hmmm, I'd like to see that," Ben continued, secretly pleased at Eden's interest. "You know, I have a vague memory of my mother making something like that one Christmas when I was little." He went on, "Pineapple in Hawai'i is grown mostly on the wide inland plains between mountain ranges, at about the 3,000 feet elevation. The plant needs cool nights and lots of sunshine, ideally with day temperatures ranging from 70 to 80 degrees F. Wahiawa, on the **Leilehua Plateau**, between the Wai'anae and Ko'olau Ranges, is perfect and meets all these conditions."

"Your great-grandfather must have been a brilliant man to have discovered this place and to have foreseen its great importance to agriculture."

"Well, I think he mostly was following the trend, business wise, with James Dole and other companies founding plantations. He was impressed with the value of pineapple to Hawai'i and saw an opportunity. So, my grandfather, my dad and I were all raised with pineapple. It's in our blood, if you can understand that. Now that I'm back here on the plantation, I can appreciate the intricacies of growing the best pineapple in Hawai'i.

"Oh, and the sweetest," Eden interjected. She was rewarded with a big smile.

"You want to hear something wild? We, as a family, love pineapple upside-down cake. O-ma has made it for me at almost every birthday celebration I can remember."

"Hmmm, remind me to make one for you on your birthday this year," she teased. "I'm sorry I didn't get to meet your grandfather. O-ma must miss him."

Ben turned thoughtful at this comment. He looked down at Eden and could see what a good wife she would make: accomplished, interested in his work, and compassionate.

As she was not the kind of person to hide her feelings, and because Ben was a just man, he put her mind to rest about a certain Miss Reardon. He felt like he'd had a major escape from disaster when he compared the two women. Though young, Eden was true blue, and her compassion reached deep into his heart.

Behind the scenes, O-ma was secretly pleased. Having this chance at love again was having a good effect on her grandson. He was at once lighter at heart and happier than he'd been in a long time. Benjamin was and always would be her favorite. His happiness was paramount in her mind and heart, and she was thankful that for once in his life, the tide had changed for his benefit. She lengthened her stay at her family's estate in Wahiawa for a few weeks and counted her blessings.

A great peace began to settle over Ben. It was no longer imperative for his physical welfare, he confided to his grandmother, to keep on delving into his past to recover the pages of lost memory. He was content to live in the present, and for the first time since his return from Asia, he started to look to the future with bright hope.

Eden introduced him to her tree, and to her surprise, he hadn't laugh at her, but very solemnly confessed to her that he had found her napping there one morning and had figured out that the place was special to her. They met at her favorite spot often, shaded by that giant of a friend. Between her job cooking at the cafe and time spent with Ben, she was engulfed with happiness, and unaware of the mounting tension between the opposite sides within the plantation.

Barnes Alexander, O-ma's only son, and his young bride had not yet returned from their extended honeymoon, but Ben had talked to them twice. Through Eden's gentle urges he had sought to be reconciled with his father and had finally accepted without demur a stepmother just a few years older than himself. His father was an extremely happy man and so was his son. At a safe distance, Ray, secretly pleased for his younger friend, kept a benevolent eye on the objects of his pet project. The troubles brewing within the plantation seemed trivial compared to the future happiness of the son of an old friend.

It was Eden's day off and the perfect day to go to the beach. Ben was free for the day, and they were on their way to Ashley Beach near **Hale'iwa**. They left early in the morning to avoid the heavy traffic to the North Shore. With his Range Rover parked alongside the highway, and their picnic basket stowed under a **sea grape** bush, they made their way to a small outcropping of rock about a hundred yards away. It was a familiar spot to Eden, and Ben decided to go for a short dive. The ocean was calm and perfect for spearfishing.

Ben got ready for his dive. He stripped off his shirt, revealing a muscular physique. Extraordinarily wide shoulders and broad chest tapered into a trim waist. The hair on his chest, arms and legs was sun bleached, and when Eden told him he looked golden, Ben dropped his eyes and turned his head. She added that she liked the dents on either side of his gorgeous mouth, his 'smile dents,' she called them. She was surprised when he turned red in the face. Doesn't he know how handsome he is? she asked herself. Hmmm. She watched as he put in his contact lenses and blinked several times.

"Why don't you have prescription lenses made for your mask? It would save the hassle of having to wear contacts in the water."

"Haven't had the time really, to look into it. Besides, this works just as well." It always pleased Eden that Ben never wore his wealth on his sleeve. He bent to examine his spear gun. It was fashioned out of two pieces of mahogany that had been laminated together. Ben sanded both three prong spears with black sandpaper and, after slipping one in place, attached the spare one to one side of the gun. Having done that, he shrugged into his black wetsuit and strapped on lead weights around his waist. Walking to the water's edge with the rest of his dive gear, he called out to Eden, "Care to join me?"

"I want to sunbathe," Eden shook her head decidedly and evaded his eyes. "I'll go for a walk along the reef in a little bit." She watched him wet his mask with sea water, secure his snorkel onto it, and place it on his head. Stuffing his feet into his Plana flippers, he moved to the reef's edge, secured the snorkel into his mouth and jumped in. Eden watched his progress as he swam along the reef. The orange floater with his stringer attached bobbed in the aquamarine water. Spreading out her beach mat under the shade of an ironwood tree, she removed her tee shirt, showing off a bright blue San Lorenzo bikini, a gift from Franny. Slathering herself with sunscreen, she stretched out full length. Yikes. The sun felt good on her back. Within a few minutes she dozed off into dreamland.

Cold water trickling down her neck woke her with a start! "What the . . .!" She jumped up just in time to have Ben baptize her with a handful of ocean water.

"Wake up, sleeping beauty."

With her eye on revenge, Eden raced him to the water's edge and started splashing water at him in wild abandon. He dodged her efforts neatly and dunked her several times before she surrendered in a panic. Spluttering, she grasped at him, and they tumbled over onto the sand with Ben taking the brunt of the fall.

"Hey, take it easy sweetie, I was only playing." Seeing Eden's pale face, he cuddled her and kissed her cheeks, as the water gently lapped against them. Cupping her face with his hands, he saw her eyes fill with tears. Putting two and two together he said gently, "You should have told me you don't swim, Eden."

Feeling humiliated, she turned her face away. He urged her up and walked her to their beach bag and pulled out a white handkerchief. Eden blew her nose like a good kid. Then, wrapping her in his beach towel, he picked her up and carried her to sit under the ironwood tree. She felt silly. How could anyone who lived in Hawai'i not know how to swim? This was all new to Ben.

He lit a cigarette and proceeded with caution.

"Want to tell me all about it?" Eden frowned and then bit her lip.

"Oh Ben, promise you won't laugh at me!" He nodded. "Well, it all happened so long ago. I was about six or seven years old. We had to take swimming lessons at the old pool in Wahiawā. One of my brother's friends was acting up and he pushed me into the deep end. I went all the way to the bottom before the instructor realized I couldn't swim. After that, you couldn't get me into water more than three feet deep for anything. I know it sounds stupid, but I panic every time I get under water."

It's not stupid, sweetie. Someone should have helped you overcome this trauma." He pulled her onto his lap and cradled her in his arms. "I can teach you; you know. It's just a matter of getting used to being in the water and realizing that it will hold you up. I taught my sister how to swim."

Eden shivered. "I would love to learn." He hugged her and there they stayed until she added quite innocently, "In fact, it's one of my New Year's Resolutions!"

"What is, my beauty?" he asked, kissing her brow.

"Why, to learn how to swim, of course!" Ben had to think a minute for it to register. Her naive optimism always took him by surprise.

"Come on kid, let's eat, I'm hungry." While he peeled out of his wetsuit, Eden unpacked their lunch which she had prepared so diligently the night before. Ben's hair was plastered to his head, and he still smelled of his wetsuit when he sat down to lunch. Eden told him so as she spread out their lunch. He chuckled, showing off the crinkles under his eyes. Looking over their lunch, he appreciated how well she could cook. The chicken was fried tender crisp, the way he liked it, and she had included sushi, homemade pickles, Cole slaw, and mango bread lavished with guava jam. When she pulled out the sliced pineapple, he was tickled.

"Don't you ever get tired of eating pineapple?"

"Never. I can eat pineapple every day! Dad says I'm **buang** because I love it so much."

"Buang?"

"It can mean idiotic or in slang, a little bit crazy. He says it jokingly, you know! Besides, I've been on Maui. The pineapple there is very good but is not the same as this. Don't you ever get tired of eating pineapple upside-down cake?"

"Touché!" Ben quipped, amused as she chomped happily.

He liked hearing about her easy and happy relationship with her dad. Yes, he was also beginning to enjoy the simpler things in life. Ray had just commented that week about Ben's new hearty appetite. He had even gained a few pounds. Since meeting Eden, he couldn't understand why he had never paid any attention to food before. Leaning back on the ironwood tree, he felt gratified to know that she had the makings of becoming a fine hostess, a job she would have to fill in the future as his wife. Marriage? Oh yes, it had crossed his mind several times already. No, maybe he was pushing it, because she was much too young. Perhaps she needed more time before he could even mention anything permanent to her. Possibly, he was a bit too old for her, well, maybe. Yet, he wanted her badly. How true that the spirit is willing, but the flesh is weak.

"Eden am I too old for you?" he asked unguardedly.

"What?" She grinned and answered mischievously. "You, old? Would you rather I call you uncle? I have one who is five years younger than you, you know." Ben wasn't sure what to make of that statement until he saw her shoulders shake.

"Uncle, huh? Well, let's see what you think of this?" He grabbed her and tickled her unmercifully, until she pleaded between laughter and tears for him to be kind.

"Ben, please, please, don't tickle me anymore. I'm laughing already. I . . . promise I won't call you uncle, ever." Ben Alexander relented.

Replete from their meal, Ben got up to clean the fish he had caught. Eden stashed away the leftovers. She shrugged into her T-shirt, jammed the straw hat over her head, slipped into rubber zori and followed Ben to the tide pool. Clambering onto the rocks, she sat close to where he was scaling a kūmū, her favorite red fish. She watched with contentment and dangled her bare feet in the cool water.

"Don't keep your feet there, Eden," Ben warned. "An eel might come out and mistake you for a fish. They'll pick up the scent from this one I'm cleaning and try to get a free meal." Eden ignored him. She didn't know how to swim, but she knew there were no eels here. She looked down into the clear water. Idly chewing some gum, she dangled her feet some more, until Ben, in slight exasperation said, "Eden . . . I told you. Get your feet out of the water. There are eels under the rock formations!"

"The Hawaiians call them **puhi**, you know," she said airily, "and don't be so bossy. I've been here a thousand times and I've never seen one." Her eyes glinted. "I betcha ten bucks," she challenged smugly, "there aren't any eels. Why, it's a swimming hole!"

"Alright," Ben said matter-of-factly, "if that's the way you want it, it's a bet. Don't say I didn't warn you." Eden gave him a cheeky smile.

She watched in fascination as he scaled and gutted all the fish. Ben was sure good at catching fish. Aside from the kūmū, he had caught a good-sized **kala**, some **manini**, a nice **weke** and a small red **uhu** that would be just right for steaming. As she sat there on the huge sun-heated rock, her mind wandered while her feet dipped in the cool water.

Then, it happened. In a split second, a huge moray eel, bigger around than her leg, slipped out from under the rock she was sitting on. It glided over her feet, attacked the kūmū, and dragged it back to its hiding place. Eden screamed, lifted her legs out of the water, and scrambled up the rocks.

In her fright, she swallowed her gum and tripped over Ben's stringer. Her hat was lost to the breeze, and she landed with a thud on her rear. Caught off guard, Ben quickly dropped the fish scaler and grabbed his spear gun. He pulled the rubbers and aimed at the spot where the eel had disappeared.

The kumu surfaced, a piece gone from it, and drifted to where Eden's feet had been in the water a few seconds before. Agitated, Ben waited but the eel didn't show its face again. He glanced up at Eden.

"You, okay?" Eden nodded dumbly, looking at the kumu that could have been her foot. Ben shook his head and stifled a laugh. "I told you! Now, will you listen to me?" Eden was relieved he didn't scold this time. He could be so kind, and she had learned her lesson. It would be quite a while before she could look a kūmū in the eye without thinking about her close call.

With the fish packed in the ice chest, Ben decided to give Eden a swimming lesson. He had to coax her to go back to the pool and reassure her that the eel wasn't going to come out a second time. Succeeding in that, he had her hang on to him while he gave her instructions on how to float on her back. Each time she tried, she freaked out, and Ben was slightly alarmed at how a girl who could swing with such grace and rhythm on a dance floor, could be reduced to a screaming ninny in the water.

"Eden, it's alright. Calm down, I'm not going to let go of you. Now, take a deep breath. Relax. There's a good girl." Presently, under his patient tutoring, she relaxed and learned to float.

"This is fun," Eden exclaimed after successfully adding arm strokes and kicks. She was looking forward to more swimming lessons. The afternoon passed by quickly as they lazed in the sun, content just to have each other for company.

They stopped at Haleʻiwa Beach to watch the orange sunset at **Kaʻena Point**. It was one of Eden's favorite sights on the island. Well, that and the blond prince beside her. They walked hand in hand along the white sandy beach. The gentle lapping of the water and the slight stir of the palm fronds in the breeze was the perfect end to a lovely day. "I wish we could stay here forever," she sighed.

"Unfortunately, Eden, no work would get done if everyone did exactly that." Ben called a judicial halt to this pleasant interlude when the sun slid below the horizon.

The Range Rover roared to life. They were crossing the **Rainbow Bridge** to Hale'iwa when Eden insisted on stopping at **Matsumoto Store**. Ben pulled over into the small parking area.

"I want to get **shave ice**!" When Ben didn't know what she was talking about, she exclaimed, "I can't believe you've never had shave ice! You've been culturally deprived, my good man." They sat on the bench outside the store and watched the traffic go by. He marveled at her child-like enthusiasm, as she dug into the large rainbow-colored treat that turned her lips all colors. He savored his cup of coffee while Eden periodically fed him a spoonful of her icy treat.

The sky, now a deep orange and dark blue, made the perfect backdrop for the silver clouds that resembled kangaroos jumping along the horizon, and the air cooled considerably. Bundling Eden into the Range Rover, Ben instructed her to put on his Yale sweatshirt while he wrapped her with his beach towel. Feeling coddled and secure, she leaned her head on his shoulder and closed her eyes. The vehicle slowly headed up Kamehameha Highway towards the plantation.

CHAPTER 12
La Mer

It didn't rain most of July. With no trade winds and several days of record-breaking temperatures, the black pineapple bugs were having a field day. No one could stand the heat, and what a time for the air conditioning to break down again. Ben Alexander had lost his taste for paperwork over an hour ago. Feeling mentally fatigued, he placed the files on his desk and turned off his computer. Perspiring at the temples, he ran his fingers through his limp hair, and decided to call it quits for the day. He buzzed his secretary.

"Yes, Mr. Alexander."

"Reschedule my afternoon appointment, Chloe, and make reservations for two at **La Mer**, at the Halekūlani for 7:00."

"La Mer, did you say, sir?" she asked incredulously.

"Yes, Chloe, I did say La Mer. Please call Eden for me, will you. Tell her I'll pick her up within the hour." Miss Chloe wasn't surprised at her boss's impulsiveness of late, but La Mer? It would take her whole week's pay to have dinner for two at that famed restaurant! She wondered if Eden was up to such luxury. Shaking her head and chuckling, she dialed the number for the hotel.

Lately, Chloe's boss had taken to daydreaming. The changes in the plantation owner's son had not gone unnoticed by the office staff. He was friendlier and more approachable. His spontaneous laughter, which could be heard throughout the work week, became infectious. The girls would stop a while and gossip, and sometimes dream a little. They all agreed that Mr. Alexander deserved a big measure of happiness.

Eden was having a relaxing day off from work. Her just shampooed hair was wrapped in a towel. After the call from Chloe, she scrambled like crazy to get ready. The old house reminded her of a burning furnace. She dried her hair and pinned it tightly into a French roll, but as soon as she got into his car, Ben pulled the pins out. Down went the lovely hair in one fell swoop.

"Ben, it's too hot. I'd rather . . ."

"Sweetie, I love to see you with your hair down. You have gorgeous hair. Don't you know that men prefer women with long hair?"

"Well, not really." She remained unconvinced. What was Ben talking about? All the females in her family – herself excluded, of course – had short hair. Her lower lip stuck out, and Ben's mouth twitched with amusement. He could always tell when Eden's feathers were ruffled.

"Alright," he answered in a conciliatory tone, "if you're that uncomfy, I'll let the top down." He had the top down in no time at all, removed his coat and carelessly threw it over the seat. He looked at her dark teal brocade **cheongsam** which clashed wildly with the gold-colored car. "By the way," he said, "I like that dress on you. It's very becoming." Eden, unused to being complimented so openly, smiled shyly in response.

Ben handled the car with ease and slipped onto the freeway. The tropic sun beat down on them and the breeze proved to be delectable. As the car gained speed, to her utter dismay, Eden's hair flew every which way. With one hand on the door handle and the other frantically trying to hold on to her hair, she reminded Ben of the outraged maiden. He threw back his head and laughed. Eden loved his laugh, and come to think of it, she was truly falling for the man who did the laughing. If this was love, then she was all for it!

He dropped in a CD of Hawaiian songs. The man behind the wheel began to sing along at the top of his voice. "It's Aloha Friday, No Work till Monday." Eden couldn't believe her ears. What had gotten into Ben? He was acting wild and carefree, so out of character. She decided to sing as loud as she could. The car sped along, defying the speed limit, Eden hanging on for dear life, secretly loving every minute of it!

The freeway to **Honolulu** was light of traffic as it was not quite rush hour. "Honolulu means calm harbor, you know," she informed Ben as she relished the environs, which included Pearl Harbor, Chinatown, and Aloha Tower. What a pretty city, she thought to herself, when she took note of the new ritzy glass buildings interspersed between the very old stone ones around downtown. Nimitz turned into Ala Moana Boulevard, and they whizzed past the newly remodeled Ala Moana Shopping Center and headed for Kalākaua Avenue, the entrance to the famed **Waikīkī**. In the late afternoon, the place was teeming with tourists. Never having spent much time there, delight spread over Eden's face as she took in the sights. They passed the Ala Wai Yacht Harbor and the new Hawai'i Prince Hotel. Canlis, the old, famous restaurant in Waikīkī, caught her eye, as well as the International Market Place. There was Lau Yee Chai, the first Chinese restaurant in Hawai'i, the **Duke Kahanamoku** statue, and the graceful and old wooden Moana Surfrider Hotel. The traffic cleared as they headed toward **Diamond Head** and approached the Waikīkī

Shell, the Honolulu Zoo, Kapiʻolani Park and finally, a break from hotels lining the ocean, Waikīkī Beach.

"There she is," Ben pointed out, "probably the most famous beach in the world!"

With a couple of hours to spare before dinner, Ben decided on a whim to take Eden to the Waikīkī Aquarium. He parked right in front of the building and allowed her a few minutes to tidy her hair. The minimally dressed tourists gawked at the couple decked out in their evening duds. Eden had visited the aquarium many times while in grade school and was surprised that it was only recently that Ben had discovered it.

"Didn't you have any fun when you were a child?"

"Oh, we had fun alright, but from the beginning we had our governess, Miss Bishop, who kept us on a tight leash. And as soon as we were old enough, we were shipped off to boarding school in California. Not all of us have the freedom to choose our own paths in life, Eden." She felt a stab of pity for the young Ben, but what did he mean? He was full of wonderful contradictions. If today wasn't choosing his own path, what was?

Eden patiently followed him down every row of tanks filled with marine life. There were so many colorful fish. She watched as he studied them and scrutinized every detail. She read all the signs and information posted on the walls, and occasionally, would look up at Ben's face. He was completely absorbed. When he asked questions about certain fish, she felt slightly embarrassed at her ignorance. Ben knew more about them than she did. 'Professor,' she called him. 'For pshaw,' he replied, and laughed when she could only think of ways to cook them. They lingered at the aquarium and by the time they walked out of the darkened viewing rooms, it was early evening, and the marine biologists were feeding the dolphins.

Arriving at the Halekūlani, House Befitting Heaven, where La Mer was located, Eden was awed by the valets in their military navy and white outfits. Designed by C. W. Dickey, the hotel had been recently remodeled. It was lovely, so Old Hawai'i that she fell in love with it immediately. She admired the open tropical style and the wood-framed sliding glass doors. The muted elegance of the large lobby with its white and gold decor, the gorgeous floor made of the 'ohi'a lehua wood and the furnishings of natural fabrics and orchid plants took her breath away.

Yes, she had heard about the Halekūlani, who hadn't? The internationally acclaimed hotel with its understated luxury was visited by tourists who came from all corners of the world. Her cooking instructor had once been invited by Gourmet World to attend a cooking demonstration held at La Mer in honor of several well-known European chefs. What she omitted to tell Ben was that the opportunity of dining at such a fine restaurant, especially one that was known for serving the best French cuisine in the islands, had never availed itself to her before this day.

With a few minutes to spare, Ben suggested they take a brief tour of the shops in the lobby. Eden's eyes popped out when she saw those gorgeous Chanel suits displayed in a store window. "**Après le Fête**," a large portrait hanging over the fireplace in the lounge, brought a smile to her face. The reclining young woman with shoes in her hand reminded her of how she felt the morning after the Summer Fête. They stood under the flowering vines hanging over the trellis next to the miniature falls and presently they climbed the stairs to the restaurant.

La Mer overlooked Waïkïkï Beach. Nowhere before had Eden experienced such a blend of Polynesia and Asia, all in one setting. The entire restaurant was done in soft white, pale gold and varying shades of brown. The screens, trimmed with dark rattan and resembling tapa cloth, were etchings done in wood. The maître d' seated them at a window with a perfect postcard view of Diamond Head. The ocean breeze was like velvet. Eden leaned towards her companion.

"Ben, this is the kind of place that one would have found Ernest Hemingway or Jack London dining," she whispered dreamily. Her companion merely nodded and admired the enthusiasm that lit up her lovely eyes. A handsome, well-groomed waiter handed them menus and hovered over them until Eden finally told him, "You can relax and come back in a few minutes, ok?" About to intervene, Ben hesitated, then changed his mind. Eden was full of surprises and always came up with something original to say. The menu's offerings were so impressive that Eden was quite awed. Her chef's heart was excited just looking at the names of dishes that she'd only heard about in cooking school. Ben was thoroughly amused. This was the first time he'd seen 'the kid,' as he often called her, so bereft of speech.

The waiter returned. He filled their glasses with Voss sparkling water. Before she could say anything, Ben promptly took the menu from her, ordered the special dinners, with two entrees.

"Ben, I don't know if I can eat fish after looking at them from a scientific point of view." Her words came out louder than she intended, and heads turned. La Mer was also famous for its excellent seafood. Ben Alexander flushed to the roots of his golden hair.

"Hush Eden, not so loud, there are a lot of people here besides us, you know!" She looked around and smiled sweetly at the guests rudely staring at them. She fidgeted with her napkin and after a while drank all the sparkling water.

The food came in succession. Of course, Eden was delighted with the **'ōpakapaka** baked in parchment paper and served with a creamy **velouté sauce**, steamed California organic brown basmati rice, and barely cooked steamed baby root vegetables, just the way she liked them. Ben indulged in grass fed steak **au poivre** in a cream sauce, **bouillabaisse**, served with a crisp wild caught **Moi**, delicious French bread and a **salade niçoise** with fingerling blue potatoes. Every morsel was like a gift from heaven, and Eden tried to figure out the ingredients of the delectable sauces. Finally, after finishing her dinner, she leaned over and in a subdued voice asked Ben to tell the waiter to skip dessert. His eye fell onto her cleaned plate.

"Eden, you didn't have to eat everything."

"Ben," she whispered, "this is costing a mint. How can you be so casual? Why, the cost of one meal here is enough to feed a whole army at the cafe!"

It took Ben a few minutes before he was sufficiently composed and able to speak. "I'm sure you know the desserts are included with the entree." Eden rolled her eyes. "You mean, waste not, want not?" he asked incredulously. "Sweetie, you're incorrigible! What am I going to do with you?" She smiled at him weakly. In a playful mood, he insisted on enjoying dessert, with Eden groaning every time he deliberately smacked his lips. Never had **Baba au Rum** and Chocolate Mousse seemed so unappealing to the chef apprentice.

"Wait, who can really say no to dessert, especially to chocolate?" she quipped as Ben gave her a taste of his goodies.

It was still early when they ventured out of the hotel lobby and floated along Kālia Road and Lewers Street. Waikīkī was even more crowded at night.

"There must be other places in the world just as exciting as Waikīkī is at night!" Eden enthused. Ben favored Bangkok and they agreed to disagree as to which place was the most intriguing. Arm in arm they strolled in a desultory fashion until they stumbled upon the Royal Hawaiian Shopping Plaza on Kalākaua Avenue. For fun, they pretended to be tourists and Ben showered her with trinkets and flowers. When she had gone to the Ginseng King to inquire about the American ginseng for sale, he excused himself for a few minutes and zipped back to Tiffany's where Eden had lingered over the display cabinet filled with pearls, her birthstone. The clerk assured him that his tiny parcel would be sent to the mansion at Aloha Nui Loa. Ben had decided to save its contents for the right moment!

The right time arrived sooner than expected because the inevitable happened and love bloomed. Who can explain why we love the one we love? All Ben knew was that he wanted Eden to be with him all the time. He felt more at peace, released from a lonely and difficult past. He was amazed at how short a time it had taken Eden to change his whole outlook on life. Her zest for living was rubbing off on him. Antisocial before, he now found himself interested in people. He wanted to marry her, and although he didn't want to rush her, he didn't want to wait longer than was necessary. He had to tell her soon, at least before she had to return to Maui to complete her last semester at school, and he did.

On the day they visited the botanical garden in Wahiawā, he took the plunge. He had heard that the garden boasted a **powder puff tree** with pink blossoms from Brazil which he was eager to see. Eden had been oohing and aahing over the flowers, and on a whim, he had surprised her by buying her the pot of red roses she had admired in the plant shop. She had carried it on her lap, sitting primly in the Mercedes, still not accustomed to such luxury. With Ben, would she ever stop feeling like a princess?

Pulling off to the side of Kamehameha Highway at the pineapple garden above the plantation, he took the plant from her, and placed it next to her dainty feet. Eden looked at him with questioning eyes. He reached for her left hand, kissed it, then placed two packages in her palm.

Eden opened the bigger of the two and chuckled when she saw the newest edition of a Samsung cell phone. She thanked him properly. He was always busy with phone calls, and this was a perfect gift.

"Now you can reach me whenever you need to," he said indulgently.

With heart pounding, she opened the smaller package that contained a blue velvet box. Why was she so nervous? The blue pearl, set in white gold and surrounded by several diamonds, dazzled in the afternoon light. For a few seconds, Eden couldn't speak. She was overcome with emotion over his thoughtfulness. How had he known that she loved blue pearls? He lifted her left hand and slipped on the ring. They admired it together, silently. Ben cleared his throat.

"Eden, I'm not one for fancy speeches and such," he began with rich emotion in his voice, "but I want you to know that these last few months have been the finest of my life." She looked into his glowing eyes, fringed with those ridiculously long eyelashes, and her own eyes misted.

"Oh Benjamin, I . . ."

"Shhh, it's my turn." He placed a finger over her lips. "I, I want you to know that I love you, Eden, as I have loved no other. Will you accept this ring and do me the honor of becoming my wife?" Ben meant every word with all his heart.

"Yes."

It was barely a whisper, but her answer was all he needed. His heart swelled with love for her, but much to his surprise, his betrothed burst into tears "Sweetheart, what's wrong? This is supposed to be a happy occasion. Why are you crying?"

"I always cry when I'm happy." Through her tears, Eden managed a smile. Up went her arms around his neck. Ben crushed her to him.

"Cry all you want, my beauty. You've just made me a very happy man!" He had so much to give. She had grown up with so little. He wanted more than anything to take care of her and shower her with everything she'd never had. She was content just to have his love. They sat close to each other and watched as the rays of the sun peeked through **Kolekole Pass**, turning the sky into a rosy haze. As the sun slid behind the Wai'anae Range, Ben headed for Aloha Nui Loa.

Janie was ecstatic. She could see the **hapa haole** grandchildren already bouncing on her knees. Gil, not ready to give up his number two daughter just yet, asked only that they wait until Eden was twenty-one. At this request, Eden boo-hooed, for her twenty-first birthday was almost a year away. "It will give us time to arrange things properly," Ben comforted her.

In their present happiness, the couple decided to wait until Ben's father and his new bride returned home, to break the news to them. Through the coconut wireless around the plantation, everyone was buzzing about their engagement. Despite his initial reservations, Phil offered his congratulations. Taking pen and paper in hand, Eden wrote a letter to Franny which was received with deep satisfaction and joy. Her saucy reply arrived the following week. Playfully reminding Eden of her declaration a few months ago about her favorite author Jack London's taste for **mountain apples**, that she hoped to find a man like him, she wrote, "Does Benjamin think that mountain apples make excellent eating?" That was all she asked. It was just like her, Eden thought affectionately.

A postcard was sent post haste to Hāna. Scribbled in Eden's flowing hand was this note: "I can't wait to see what he says about mountain apples!"

CHAPTER 13
Filipino Wedding

The Range Rover, heading to and from the old house on Hau'oli Way, became a familiar sight on the plantation. Neighbors would smile and wave at the passing vehicle and speculate about the date of the Alexander-Andres wedding. It was sure to be the event of the year, they predicted, and they all expected to be invited to the celebration. Yes, it appeared to most that the match was one of those storybook romances. Some even went so far as to say it was made in heaven. Who would have believed something like this could happen right in their own hometown? The upright Ben Alexander was doing the noble thing in taking his time to woo the lovely plantation girl. Congratulations kept pouring in and Gil and Janie Andres were slightly overwhelmed by the good sentiments. "How fortunate could they get," their friends remarked, "Eden snagged the most eligible bachelor in town."

Much has been said about opposites attracting, but who can really explain it? Both Ben and Eden were intrigued with each other's cultural backgrounds. Their mutual tutoring developed into a friendly game that started the day he talked her into attending a Vivaldi concert with the Honolulu Chamber Orchestra. Eden surprised him one Saturday by dragging him to the Swap Meet at Aloha Stadium. He in turn, took her education seriously, and she was given a tour of the Bishop Museum. Meanwhile, she decided to teach him the fine art of eating **saimin** and treated him to lunch at the famous Shiro's Saimin Haven in Waimalu. After taking him to Walmart in

Waipahu, she had him try the Hawaiian plate lunch at the Highway Inn. It surprised her how much Ben enjoyed the **poi** and **poke**. They both began to see each other's Hawai'i.

Oftentimes, Ben picked her up at the cafe after work. She would get glimpses of him from behind the kitchen counter, while he waited for her to close shop. It seemed to her that he spent a lot of time doing research, and seeing his blond head engrossed in some technical tome had become a familiar sight at the cafe. When asked about it, he mumbled something about possibly working towards an MBA, and when no one else was around, those plastic black rimmed glasses would be slipped onto his often-sunburned nose. Eden and Mrs. Chang, the cafe owner, loved to josh him about that. That little smile always tugged at the corners of his mouth and transformed the stern face into something magical. Mrs. Chang, a believer in happy endings, was extremely delighted for the couple. The handsome serious Ben would be good for the lively Eden. She often expressed to her own family that Gil and Janie Andres were going to be blessed with beautiful grandchildren.

After work early one Friday evening, an unsuspecting Ben accompanied Eden to a wedding reception on the plantation. A friend of the family, Miguel Garcia, had married Maria Dela Cruz earlier that afternoon. Ben had never attended a camp festivity before and was looking forward to mingling with the guests. His desire to blend in with the crowd tickled Eden. He was a head taller than everyone else.

They arrived after the new couple had been introduced and dinner was under way. The Clubhouse was transformed into a pink palace. Pink balloons, pink crepe paper, and pink paper hearts hung from the ceiling. The three-tiered wedding cake was also decorated with pink flowers. In one corner, a band of

Filipino musicians, with Phil's dad on mandolin, were tuning various instruments.

Eden led her fiancé to the food serving table that was conveniently placed under a makeshift tent next to the clubhouse. She was secretly pleased to be giving Ben "the experience," instead of vice versa. He, in turn, appeared to be genuinely intrigued with the customs attached to a Filipino wedding.

"**Mabuhay**, Bones, Mr. Alexander. Are you enjoying yourselves?" It was Magdalena, Phil's Mom. The plucky, brown-skinned woman heaped liberal servings of rice onto their paper plates and asked if they wanted some **dinuguan**. Ben eyed the contents of the pot suspiciously. "This is good stuff, you know. My father-in-law made it. He added some mint. Here, taste. . ." Ben hesitated then followed Eden's example and held his plate out for Magdalena to cover the scoops of rice with the "good stuff." It was chocolate in color and had a peculiar smell. His face whitened visibly.

"This all looks great, Mrs. Castro," Eden enthused. "I hope you ladies weren't up all night preparing the food!"

"Nah, we had plenty of help, Bones." Magdalena's sly glance fell onto Eden's ring. "By the way, have you seen Phil and Michiko?" she asked innocently. "They were supposed to be here over an hour ago." Eden's finely arched brows knit together. Was she missing something here?

"No, I haven't seen them. They're together, as in dating?" She didn't mean to sound so surprised, and her expression caused Magdalena to sparkle.

"Oh, I hope so, and I'm relieved. That girl is the right one for my boy." Eden made a mental note to give Phil a call. Why hadn't he told her the news?

Down the line they continued until their plates were filled. By that time, most of the guests had arrived. Nothing escaped Ben's all-seeing eyes. The wooden tables were covered with thick white paper that had been stapled on. Ti leaves and flowers with pineapples as centerpieces were attractively displayed on each one. They got their cups of punch and waited while a family with big smiles vacated a spot for them and they sat down. By this time, Eden was starved. She told him, "You really haven't lived until you've tried Filipino food!" Ben watched Eden offer a small blessing and start on the succulent chicken and he did likewise. The combination of vinegar and soy sauce and the **umami** of the dish surprised and pleased him.

"Wow," he let out with gusto, "this is very tasty! I've never had chicken cooked like this before. So, Bones, this is the famous Chicken **Adobo**?"

"Oh shoot . . . please don't call me that. I was hoping you wouldn't notice. It's a childhood nickname I haven't been able to get rid of." Ben kept a straight face, and she wasn't sure whether he was laughing at her or not. Eden proceeded to give him a lesson on how to eat rice Filipino style, with his fingers. He was not adept at all, and after several tries, rice covered his right hand. Feeling quite helpless, he looked to Eden for aid. This time it was her turn to laugh. She had to go back to the food table for more paper napkins. With her eyes full of glee and amongst the sea of Filipinos, he saw again how much she resembled her dad.

The food was delicious, quite unlike anything Ben ever had, but the "good stuff" still looked strange. He cautiously took a bite ... the sauce was chalky, with odd tasting bits. He watched Eden down a spoonful smoothly. He tried again, this time with some rice mixed with it. He had to force himself to get it down, trying not to gag. Finally, he couldn't stand it any longer and asked politely, "Eden, just what is the 'good stuff' made of anyway?"

"Blood and guts," Eden replied matter-of-factly. Perhaps the noise in the food tent was too loud. Ben wasn't sure if he had heard her right.

"I beg your pardon!" Eden's 'sweet look,' which he was beginning to recognize, should have warned him.

"The "good stuff" is made of pig intestines and blood." At the mention of those words, Ben paled and, feeling the stirrings of nausea, discreetly scraped the good stuff off the rice.

"Eden," he whispered into her ear, "I like everything else, but this 'good stuff' is awful." The girl who resembled her dad almost choked on her food.

"How about the **pinakbet**," she offered kindly. "It's a veggie stew, sort of like a ratatouille."

Ben tried the eggplant. Hmmm. It was very different but exceptionally good. He speared a piece of what looked like an anemic lumpy cucumber and popped it into his mouth. Horrors. It was terrifyingly bitter. He spat it out.

"That's the most horrible thing I've ever tasted! In fact, it's downright inedible!"

"Gee, for a guy with an educated palate, you sure protest a lot. It's an acquired taste, but very healthy!" Eden quipped.

Ben feigned a look of hurt. Eden repented quickly. "Alright, I'm sorry. I shouldn't tease. . . Try that dessert. It's called **bibingka**. That will disguise both the blood and guts and the bitterness of the **bitter melon**." Eden was being very graphic, and he knew he was at her mercy.

After their meal, Ben watched in amazement as guests bore away plates piled high with food. "I hate to sound ignorant, Eden, but aren't those people being rude?" Eden's brow furrowed.

"Oh Ben, it's customary for guests to take food home with them," she explained. He nodded his head and wondered what O-ma would think of the guests making away with the leftovers.

The band started up and they got up to join the wedding party in the clubhouse, passing a group of men seated around a small table. Unable to curb his curiosity any longer, Ben queried, "What are those men doing? It looks like serious business to me."

Eden pulled him along without a backward glance. Once inside the clubhouse she put a finger to her mouth. "Shhh. They're selling jiggers of whiskey for two bucks a shot!"

"Whisky? Good Lord, isn't that against the law?" He turned to give them a lengthy inspection.

"Ben, please don't stare at them. They're making money for the bride and groom." Ben could only look at Eden's face blankly.

The sound of the mandolin, with its Spanish influence, pleased him. A group of young children performed several Filipino folk dances. Their colorful costumes, made with bright plaid fabrics or embroidered **Piña Cloth** were enchanting. The pounding of the bamboo poles of the **Tinikling** folk dance completely captivated him. Watching the dancers jump in and out of the poles, Ben inquired softly, "Can you do that, Eden?" She nodded. Gratified with her answer, he held her tighter. "You'll have to teach our daughter these folk dances. They're lovely."

The dancers cleared the area as the emcee called the bride and groom to the dance floor.

"They're going to do the traditional money dance, called the **Sabitan ng pera**," Eden whispered. "It's the Hawaiian version, of course." Ben had never witnessed such cheering done by wedding guests! He watched in amazement as they walked, one by one, up to the dancing couple. Each guest placed money into the bride's mouth, for good fortune, Eden explained. The groom was then required to take the money from his bride with his mouth. Each time their lips met, the guests whooped and hollered. Once the groom had the money secured in his mouth, he quickly dropped it to the floor, and the flower girl picked it up and placed it in a beribboned pink basket.

"Good gosh, I don't think I've ever seen anything like that before. I guess it provides a nest egg for the happy couple, huh!" Eden nodded, eyes aglow. The emcee's laughing voice urged the guests to join in with the dancing, and although Ben was unused to dancing to the music of the mandolin, he willingly agreed. There was always a first time for everything. As they whiled away the next couple of hours, Eden wondered from time to time, how her fiancé would fare if her parents insisted on a Filipino wedding. She just had a feeling that life with him would certainly never be dull.

CHAPTER 14
Trouble

Eden followed Ben faithfully as he explored an old book shop in Chinatown. Of all the places they frequented, Chinatown was one place that absolutely captured her attention. It happened every time she stepped foot onto the main thoroughfare. Mingling with the mostly Chinese populace, it brought out the Chinese side of her. Tuning into the singsong voices of the people as they hustled and bustled through the open marketplace, Eden asked out of the blue, "Do I seem Asian to you, Ben?"

"Asian? Sweetheart, you are Asian!"

"Yes, no, that's not what I meant!" Ben rolled his eyes.

"Explain then. I'm curious." She paused for a moment.

"Well, do I seem more Asian than American? After all, Hawai'i is a state, part of the U.S.A, we've been thoroughly westernized. Yet, you must take into consideration that I've been raised by my Chinese mother."

Ben looked down at her lovingly and gave her hand a squeeze. "Sweetheart, you are my sweet Asian flower!" Eden sighed and hoped Ben would always think of her that way.

They decided on **Hakka** food for lunch. Eden explained to Ben about her Hakka heritage. It was all new to him but so interesting and he valiantly tried all the dishes. She remembered to ask for an extra container of **Jook** to take home for Janie.

They later toured Chinatown, holding hands and every few minutes gazing into each other's eyes, bringing smiles to the faces of the passing shoppers. Eden couldn't resist and had to stop at a bakery to select her family's favorites. Ben was again slightly taken aback that his tiny fiancée could eat so much. He watched as she polished off a huge 5-inch cookie after all that lunch.

At his look, Eden said, "What? It's a Chinese Wedding cookie and it tastes like an almond cookie. I can't resist! Plus, I have to fill up my Hakka feet!"

"What do you mean by that?"

"Oh Ben, as I said at lunch, Mom is part Hakka and she is forever teasing me for having big feet!"

"Big feet?" He always thought she had tiny feet.

"Well, the Hakka are a minority people in China who never bound the feet of their women. So, they had big feet. Mom and my sisters are all a size 5 and I wear a size 6. Not bad for a preemie, I'm told. But I got the biggest feet among the women in my family."

"Eden, Brigitte wears a size 10!"

"Wow, that's humongous, but she's still very gorgeous. You know what I mean. I read that Jackie Kennedy Onassis wore a size 10, too!"

Ben knew that feet binding in its day was very popular, but it was very painful and caused health problems. However, the comment about the famous first lady was too much to take in and made him chuckle all the way home.

The traffic on the way out of Honolulu to Wahiawa in mid-afternoon was normally stressful to the everyday commuter, but not so to the young couple in love. In fact, they savored every minute they had together and took their sweet old time getting back to the plantation. Whenever they went out together, Ben purposely left his cell phone home and asked her to do the same.

Hankering for a cup of coffee, Ben stopped at Dot's Inn in Wahiawā before heading back to Aloha Nui Loa. It was dark when they eventually reached the plantation. They found the old house lit up like a Christmas tree. Cars were parked all over her father's precious lawn. Eden sat at attention.

"Hmmm, I wonder what's up. Ordinarily, Dad would have a royal fit if anyone parked on the newly planted grass."

"Why don't I wait while you go in, and you can let me know if there is a problem." Ben pulled her gently to him.

"Oh no, Benjamin," Eden replied and bussed his cheek, "don't wait. I know you must get home.

When you call tonight, I'll let you know the scoop. Thank you for a wonderful day."

"It's getting cool. In you go, there's a good girl." He gave her a chaste kiss on her forehead. "I'll call you after eight, as usual. Goodnight sweetheart!" Ben waited, as he always did to make sure she was safely inside before starting up the Range Rover. His head began to throb, but he grinned at her as she waved while she made her way to the door.

The porch was covered with a myriad of footwear. Eden tried to avoid squishing them and took pains walking around the pile. Noticing a movement in the shadows, she looked up and saw Lefty Shimizu at the other end of the porch. He was puffing on a cigar.

"Oh, hi Mr. Shimizu. Pardon, I didn't see you there, trying to get around all these slippers, you know. Why are there so many cars here" she remarked with a short laugh, "are you having a meeting?"

"Yeah kid, we're in the middle of a meeting." The shifty eyes narrowed. Lefty Shimizu always looked like he needed a shave, and standing there in the dark, he looked more like a thug than an old friend of her father's. Eden bit her lower lip and opened the screened door.

"Well, I'd best go in and see if my mother needs my help."

She turned to wave one last time to Ben as he honked the horn a couple of times and drove slowly up Hau'oli Way toward the mansion on the hill. The conversation stopped when she entered the parlor. Her father sat on the floor crossed legged and was surrounded by papers. He looked up wearily and gave her the high sign to **hele** out of there. She excused herself politely and quickly headed for the kitchen. As soon as she closed the door behind her, she could hear the buzz of voices once more. Only one voice was missing.

Lefty lingered on the porch and watched Ben Alexander's vehicle disappear into the night. When Gil had shared the news of his daughter's engagement, Shimizu had sneered. He felt a daughter of Gil's was too good for a son of the big boss. Leaning against the porch rail, and planning his revenge, he blew smoke rings into the cool air. He had a score to settle with Ben Alexander.

"Eden," Janie Andres cried out in relief, "I'm so glad you're home! Where's Ben?" Eden found her mom in the kitchen washing up. She looked a bit worse for wear.

"I sent him home, Mom, he has paperwork to catch up on. He'll call me later this evening. I got you some jook and your favorite **moon cakes** and **gin dui**." Placing the bag of goodies on the kitchen table, she saw her mom's eyes spark up, then cloud over. She probed, "What's happening anyway? What are the men doing here? Lefty Shimizu was on the porch when I came in. He said they're having a meeting. What kind of meeting?" She peeked into the pot that was on the stove. It was tinola, her favorite. Serving herself a bowl of soup, she sat down, and swallowed a mouthful of the savory chicken and green papaya. She continued. "I'm sorry I didn't get home earlier to help out, but you never mentioned anything about a gathering tonight."

Mrs. Andres gave her daughter an enigmatic look and dabbed her brow with her dish towel.

Something wasn't right. Her mother would never condescend to wipe her brow with a dish towel. Eden studied her. Yes, she looked worried. In fact, she really looked to be in a state of distress.

"Let's go into Gramps' room," her mother suggested, "he's gone out with Manuel to some party in the camp. We can talk there. You can finish that soup later." Securely inside, she closed the door. "It's been a terrible day. First, Dad and your grandfather got into a terrible disagreement all over again about that white rooster. Then, they took off to some cockfight who knows where. Around noon, trouble flared up at work and since your dad wasn't around to keep things under control, the men walked off the job. Having to answer the phone all day,

I burned our dinner!" Mrs. Andres uttered a short sob over that. "I had to make a quick pot of tinola!" Before Eden could respond, she blubbered, "Gramps wouldn't listen to reason and insisted on going out tonight. I know he was upset earlier, but they did win at the cock fight, and I guess he wanted to celebrate with Manuel. He was so grumpy when I suggested he stay in tonight. Do you think he's out gambling at Paiute again? Oh, and then Jack has disappeared. He may have gone looking for Gramps. Just when I needed to talk to Abigail, I couldn't reach her by phone. I think she's gone to Kaua'i for the weekend."

"Mom, slow down. You're just running off at the mouth." Eden grabbed her mother by the shoulders and shook her gently.

"I feel awful, Eden, and I'm so glad you're home." Tears sprang to Janie's eyes and as she dried them, she sighed deeply. Eden patted her mother on the shoulder until the tears stopped.

"Mom, you're overwrought. Let's get some tea. Listen, Dad's quite capable of smoothing things over. You know how things have always worked out."

"I'm not so sure, Eden. He's been feeling the strain lately. I'm worried about him." She wrung her hands and asked cautiously, "How was your day? Are you planning to see Ben tomorrow?"

"Yes, mother, I'm seeing Ben tomorrow. He wants me to attend church with him. The family pew, you understand." Mrs. Andres couldn't help but giggle. Eden could be so amusing when she chose to be.

Her daughter rambled on dreamily. "Oh Momsy, I'm so outrageously happy. We had a glorious day. I swear, that man can spend hours looking at old books. He's so kind, so good and tenderhearted. How could I have been so blessed to have found him? I love it that he takes the time to explore new restaurants because he knows I'm interested in that sort of thing. We stopped at your favorite restaurant that also had jook on the menu." Mrs. Andres smiled weakly. She was so fond of jook which one could find in every Chinese restaurant these days. She especially loved Hakka food. After all, she was part Hakka on her mother's side.

"I'm glad someone had a good day," her mom commented, keeping her eyes on her hands. "I feel terrible having to tell you this."

"Tell me what? What are you trying to say?"

"It's about Ben." Janie sat her daughter down on Milton's old Lazy Boy recliner.

"Ben? What about Ben?"

"You know how your father is looked up to by the men. He's a man of principle and has always fought for justice. Well, they expect him to fight for them in this situation. It looks like this walkout will turn into a strike for more pay. They have to negotiate the new contract, you know."

"I know that Mom, but what's so different about the contract negotiations this time? We've been through this before. It's always been resolved amicably. What has all this got to do with Ben, for heaven's sake?"

"Don't you see? It's so obvious he's on the other side. Someone questioned your father's loyalty to the union because of your engagement. Dad feels it would be better if you and Ben agree to hold off the engagement until the strike is settled."

The light went out of Eden's lovely brown eyes and her brows knit together.

"You mean, Ben knew all about this?" she asked incredulously. "He didn't breathe a word about it to me! In fact, I can ask him for details when he calls tonight."

"No, no, he . . . of course he didn't know anything. He was gone all day with you. I couldn't reach you by phone. Look at it from our perspective, it just doesn't look good for your father at this time with his daughter engaged to the head honcho's son." At this remark, Eden's shoulders sagged.

"Mom, I can't believe you're telling me this. It's ridiculous. Our personal lives have nothing to do with this strike! How can people be so small-minded? This isn't Victorian England. Ben and I are engaged, as in getting married, remember? Besides, you know for yourself what an honorable man he is. He wouldn't do anything to harm us."

"Oh dear, I can see I have put this very badly. Your father told me he would speak with you about this… Perhaps I should have let him do it himself. It's just that there's been talk, and ever since the Summer Fête, people have been questioning his authority as union rep. They say he's pro-management!"

"Mom, that's bunk and you know it." Every part of Eden wanted to protest. "For heaven's sake, Dad only recently turned down the offer of a management position out of loyalty to the union! How can they talk like that about him, after all the years of hard work he's devoted to the union, just for them? You can't please everyone!" They stopped their talk when a knock sounded at the door.

"Janie, are you in there? Gil wants more refreshments for the men." It was Mike, Phil's Dad.

"I'll be right out, Mike. Give me a minute." They waited until his footsteps retreated down the hall. Janie noted Eden's bent head as her daughter fiddled with her engagement ring. It was so lovely. She could feel the conflict waging within Eden's breast. Perhaps she had been overly eager to have pushed her so soon into this relationship. "Come dear, I need your help in the kitchen for now. We can talk more about this later."

The hour was late and the last of the dishes were washed and stacked neatly in the drainer. Eden took a second look around the shiny kitchen and hung up her apron. She joined her folks in the parlor and waited for her dad to say the inevitable. Earlier, after the men had left, he had explained his position. She had listened but had not made any comment.

Her father, now sitting in his favorite recliner with his head resting against the back of the chair, had his eyes covered with his rough hands. He looked exhausted. Mrs. Andres was back to her crocheting again and every few minutes glanced nervously at Eden and then to her husband.

"Dad," Eden offered after a long moment, "you've had a trying day, and you look beat. Why don't you hit the sack? Come on, I'll give you a back rub."

Gil moaned and placed his right hand onto his chest. That tightness was there again. Eden flew to his side. Mrs. Andres hovered over them. The pain subsided after a few minutes and Gil opened his eyes. The wrinkles under his beautiful eyes were more pronounced and his graying hair seemed whiter than usual.

"You're doing too much lately, Dad. Why don't you take tomorrow off? Go see the doctor and get this checked out."

"Don't fuss, Bones. I'm fine . . . just help me up. What I need is a good night's sleep, that's all." He stood up after much exertion, propped up on either arm by his wife and his daughter. They got him into bed, but he hushed them away. "Janie, I'm alright. A cup of warm milk would be nice just now." Janie was in the kitchen in an instant.

"Well, if you're sure you're okay, Dad, I'll say goodnight for now. I need to shower and get to sleep." She gave her dad a peck on the forehead and turned to leave.

"Eden, you understand my position, don't you? It won't be forever, you know. We should get this settled soon." His daughter nodded. She loved her father and for as long as she could remember, she always heeded his advice. She hoped somehow that Ben would understand.

Her mom took over taking care of her dad, and Eden was left to secure the house for the night. She locked the front door and turned off the lights. A hot shower did wonders for her morale. In her room she debated whether to call Ben again. He hadn't called at his usual hour and his line had been busy all night. Getting ready for bed, her dad's request kept swirling around in her mind. She desperately wanted to talk to Ben. Should she try his number again, or wait until tomorrow? Being sensible, the lateness of the hour decided for her.

As she settled into her bed, crazy thoughts bombarded her mind. Her parents' wish seemed so unreasonable. Dad's burden seemed so unfair. On the other hand, what was Ben facing? What was he thinking? Life was full of unexpected twists alright. Well, at least there was one reprise, she comforted herself, tomorrow was Sunday, the Lord's Day!

CHAPTER 15
A Surprise Proposal

Sunday dragged by without a word from Ben. Eden wracked her brains trying to figure out how her situation could be resolved. She didn't want the whole thing to grow way out of proportion. Really, she was in two minds about what to do. She wanted to honor her parents, but she ached to see Ben. She missed attending church with him and allowed her parents to take her to mass. The one day of waiting turned into a week. August set in.

Inside the old house, the air was so still. She tried to get some sleep, but every time she drifted off, she thought she heard her cell phone ring. Finally, she sat up and glanced at the clock. It was close on to midnight. Wrapped in her **happi coat**, she turned on the lamp in the parlor on low, so as not to disturb her parents and went in search of the thriller she had been reading to get her mind off things.

She saw the door to her grandfather's room slightly ajar. She gently pushed it open and looked in on the snoring man. His bedside lamp was on low, and he was still clutching the evening newspaper in one hand. Eden grinned and slowly removed it from his grip. Her grandfather's snoring stopped. She waited and saw the soft rise and fall of his chest. She placed the paper on his nightstand and turned off the light. She felt a prick of conscience that she hadn't spent much time with him lately. Her grandfather loved the independence he enjoyed staying at his son's home. Since it brought him pleasure going out with his friends, she brushed away the worry. She decided to take in the night sky and stepped onto the porch. It was much cooler outdoors. She made a wish on a shooting star, yawned and after a few minutes of star gazing, went quietly back into the parlor. The book was stashed between the couch cushions. She retrieved it and opened it up to where she had dogeared it and headed for her room. She adjusted her reading lamp and made herself comfy. Looking at her cell phone, she debated whether to try calling Ben again, and decided not to. It was late. After a few pages, she dropped off to sleep. In the last watch of the night, her cell phone rang sharply. Eden awoke at once. It was Ben.

"Hello," she answered cautiously.

"Eden, sweetheart," Ben's low voice, a bit raspy after days of talking, came over the line, "I was hoping you'd pick up. Can you meet me at our tree as soon as possible? We need to talk."

"Ben, what's happening? I've been calling you for days. I . . ."

"Let's talk face to face. Just do as I ask."

"Do you think it's wise for us to meet at this hour? It's quite late. How about tomorrow?"

"It is tomorrow," he answered dryly. "Look, it would be odd to show up at your place at this hour. I need to see you. We need to talk. Be a good girl and meet me in twenty minutes!" The phone clicked. Ben had sounded so strange. That old commanding tone was back in his voice, and she hadn't liked the sound of it. She fumed as she crept stealthily to her closet, then rebuked herself for being so silly. If she was upset with this strike business, she could well imagine how he felt.

From the light of the streetlamp, she changed swiftly into jeans and a sweatshirt with a big pocket in front, pulled on her sneakers, and tied her hair back with a scarf. Walking quietly past her parents' bedroom, she stopped and listened. She could hear her father snoring. On the way out of the banyo, she grabbed a flashlight, and went out into the dark. The damp grass wet the bottoms of her jeans. She scurried along as fast as she could, glancing over her shoulder every few minutes. The trees that were so familiar in the daytime looked horribly eerie at night. She shouldn't have started on that paperback mystery, she mumbled to herself, as she walked on at a rather fast pace, her mind racing a mile a minute. What madness this was. Ben must be feeling the pressure to ask her to consent to a clandestine meeting. This wasn't like him at all. If it weren't for the awkwardness of the situation, she would think the whole thing highly romantic. She made it to the tree in record time and got there before Ben did. Dimming the flashlight, she waited for what seemed an eternity. Where was he? The air cooled considerably. She heard a vehicle come up the road and stop nearby. It had to be Ben. The gentleman in question appeared out of nowhere, Mag-Lite in hand.

"Ben, is that you?" Eden called out quite unnecessarily. She ran into his open arms and kissed him until she felt slightly dizzy.

"Careful there, sweetheart," he said as he eased them down to the base of the great tree.

"Oh," she shuddered, "it's damp out here. Ben, what are we doing? I've had a nerve-racking week. Everyone at home is so keyed up. I don't know what to think anymore . . ."

"Hush, little one. I'm worn out from all the talking. Just hold on to me. I haven't been able to sleep much since I last saw you." Warmth stole back into her bones as she grasped Ben wrapped in his hoodie. In his arms again, she felt safe and comforted. "The Board called an emergency meeting tonight," Ben began, his voice quite hoarse. "Like the one before," he continued, clearing his throat, "I had to preside in Dad's absence. It doesn't look good, Eden. They're up in arms. The consensus is to shut down the entire operation after the harvest. Even Ray couldn't perform his magic tonight," he reported wearily. "I can't do much until Dad gets back. I was able to reach him by phone in Tahiti. He was mighty upset at the news. Anyway, I expect him back sometime within the next forty-eight hours."

Eden merely listened, outwardly showing more calm than she felt. The sky was getting light, and she could see the planes of his face. Ben closed his eyes. Even under so much duress he looked dangerously handsome. Several days of beard growth made him look older, a bit distinguished and she could well imagine what he would look like in old age. The excitement of being with him was there all over again. She lifted her chin until her lips met his. Ben's eyes flipped open, and his arms tightened around her as if he would never let her go.

"Oh Ben, what are we to do?"

Presently, his arms relaxed. His voice was a whisper and he mumbled as if to himself, "I can't take much more of this. Why don't we just get married? You know I want you with me all the time. How about eloping? We can please the folks and have a reception after the fact. Once Dad is here, he'll relieve me of my duties. I'll go back to my freelance work. . ." He stopped mid-sentence. After a few minutes, Eden saw that he was asleep. She propped his perspiring head against the tree's wide trunk and got up to stretch. Thank God she had snatched a short nap today, or rather yesterday.

She turned and touched the tree. "What now my good friend? I've never felt this way about anyone before."

Was it God who had smiled down upon her and brought him into her life? Her heart told her so, yet somehow, she felt uneasy. Lately, she had been so torn between pleasing both her father and Ben. Life had gotten complicated overnight. Ben seemed so different tonight from the man he usually was, and what of herself? She felt like she had aged overnight. What was he thinking of to suggest an elopement? What would her parents say? The Eden of yesterday would have jumped at the chance of doing something so impulsive. "The man doesn't know what he's saying at the moment and we're in a fix for sure." The great tree smiled down on her as if in silent agreement.

The sun was going to be up soon, and Eden knew she needed to get back home. She glanced down at the sleeping Ben, looking boyish with his head flopped to one side. He must be exhausted to fall asleep just like that. Bending to scrutinize his long lashes, she took in his tousled hair. She leaned over to brush back the golden strands away from his high forehead and was astonished to find that he was burning up. She opened his hoodie. His shirt was soaking wet. Rousing him gently didn't get a response. She shook him harder.

"Ben, wake up."

When he didn't budge, she pulled the scarf off her head, wet it in the stream and bathed his forehead. He started to shiver and opened glazed eyes briefly. His mouth formed words that Eden couldn't decipher. Then in English he muttered, "Tai, please, we must do what is right. I promised . . ."

Eden stuffed the scarf into her back pocket. "Ben, please get up," she pleaded. "You're feverish. We have to get you home." He opened his eyes again, this time recognizing her. He struggled for voice.

"Eden, help me up, will you, sweetheart. I, I need my medication." Leaning on her tiny frame, they stumbled along the path. "Do you think you can drive the Range Rover to my home?" he asked under labored breathing.

"I'll try, Ben. Take it slowly. I'll get you home somehow." She stuffed the flashlights into her sweatshirt pocket and felt thankful that her brother Albert had insisted she learn how to drive her dad's truck. "You need to know how to drive different types of vehicles," he had said.

The Range Rover was parked at the edge of the grove. Getting Ben into it was another story. By that time, he was shaking uncontrollably, and couldn't lift himself up into the passenger's seat without her help. He leaned his great bulk against the seat while Eden pushed to get him in it. Then she got in on the driver's side and tugged until he was secure in the passenger's seat. She strapped on his seat belt and covered him with the beach towel that was on the back seat. She looked at the keys in the ignition, said a little prayer and pulled the seat closer to the steering wheel. Snapping on her seat belt, she started up with a jerk. She turned on the headlights, and moving slowly at first, she edged the vehicle onto the road. With as much speed as she could muster courage for, she drove to the mansion on the hill. Parking in the drive, she helped Ben out and then walked him to the side entrance and towards the large kitchen. They made slow progress. "Thank God," she thought, "the lights are on. Amo'o must be up."

"Which way is your medicine, Ben?"

"Down the hall," he got out with much effort. His shivering had subsided, but she stumbled along while Ben's ancestors on the canvases looked down at them with genteel faces. They came to his room at the rear of the building. The lamp at the bedside was on. There was a four poster koa bed with its antique red and yellow breadfruit patterned Hawaiian quilt pulled back. Ben fell into the bed. Eden bent quickly to examine him.

"Ben, why don't I wake someone? You need help. I'm not sure what's wrong with you."

With even greater effort, he turned over and restrained her arm. "No, it's nothing serious, Eden, just the after-effects from a tropical bug . . . Don't wake anyone. Just get my medication on top of that koa tall boy over there." He indicated with a wave of his hand.

She followed his direction and spotted the bottle. Reading the instructions, she picked up a glass in the bath and filled it with tap water. Taking one pill out, she handed it to Ben and urged him to swallow it. She had to help hold the glass. With unsteady hands, he drank greedily, then fell back onto the pillows taking Eden with him. Most of the water spilled all over the front of her sweatshirt. She took out his Mag-Lite and left it on the chair beside his bed.

The whole scene was beginning to take on an absurd dimension, or more likely, the sense of the ridiculous was finally getting to her. Instead of being upset, Eden wanted to laugh out loud. What was the matter with her anyway? She had to stifle her laughter when he relaxed his hold on her. Easing herself away from him, Eden found a washcloth in the bath, moistened it and bathed his face. Thank God, he wasn't burning up anymore. She looked around the very masculine room. This would never do, she thought. What would her parents think?

"Oh my gosh," she muttered. She had completely forgotten about them. Eden checked her watch. The sun would be up any minute. She had to get home fast. Looking at Ben, she removed his hoodie and damp shirt, pulled off his sneakers, and covered him with the top sheet. She bent to rain kisses on his now cooled face. How she loved him! He looked innocent in his sleep. She hated to leave him like this, but the time would come when she would be able to stay with him forever.

Reaching to turn the lamp to its lowest setting, her hand brushed against a tattered Bible, causing it to fall onto the carpet. Eden picked it up. She opened the cover and saw the inscription. It had been a gift from Amelia Grace Alan Alexander to her darling son Benjamin Alan with a date showing Ben had been twelve at the time. Out dropped a photograph. Its edges were worn, and a tear had been scotch taped back in place. Three people stood in front of a Thai restaurant: a pretty Asian girl with straight long hair with her arms around Ben and another man with curly red hair.

She blinked and looked again. She felt disturbed to see Ben with another girl, especially another Asian like herself. Turning the photo over, she saw written in Ben's bold handwriting, "With George and Tai."

Someone was walking in the hall. Eden stuffed the photo back in the Bible, placed it on the nightstand and stood very still. The strangeness of the scene was unnerving her. To her relief, it was Amoʻo, the housekeeper, heading for the kitchen and humming a song. Eden followed her and called out softly.

"Missy Eden! You here early? Master Ben, he don't get up at this time in the morning."

"Thank heavens, it's you, Amoʻo. Something is terribly wrong with Ben. He asked me to meet him tonight, and he got the shakes and fever. I just brought him home and tried to put him to bed. Come help me." Amo'o followed her into Ben's room, with concern on her face.

"Oooooh, he no look so good, Missy Eden. He was plenty sick last year, you know. He say it not serious. Gotta make sure, yeah. **Mo betta** I call the doctor and Mrs. Maggie. She know what to do for Master Ben." Eden was relieved to hear that.

"That's a good idea, Amo'o. I'd feel better if the doctor looked at him. I must get home." She stifled a yawn. "Will you watch over him until the doctor comes and let me know later how he is? His fever seems to have gone down a bit."

"You leave that boy to me. I take care of him until the doctor come here… You let Kimo drive you home?"

"No, no. I'll just walk home. It's not too long a way and I'm used to it!"

"Up to you, Missy Eden. I tell Mrs. Maggie to call you later." Eden hugged her, looked longingly at the sleeping man, and then made her way out of the mansion. She latched the side door quietly behind her.

Once outside, she rationalized that there would be time to talk later. With a quick look down the long drive, she began walking at a brisk pace. The sun popped up. At the end of the drive, Eden opened into a run and skedaddled home. Her mind was too beset with questions to notice the dark form smoking his telltale cigar. He was leaning against a tree across the road from the mansion and had watched her leave the big house. His spying efforts had finally paid off!

To her surprise, no one at home was up. She slipped into her room, changed back into her pjs and fell straight into bed. Her mind was in a jumble. The whole experience had taken on a surreal quality. What was wrong with Ben? Who were the other two people in that photo? The timing was all wrong for a strike. She was too tired, too numb to reason anymore. Ben always kidded her that she spent too much time thinking. Everything will look better in the morning, she told herself, as sleep overtook her.

CHAPTER 16
The Photo Contest

Morning came soon enough. Mrs. Andres, looking in on her daughter and finding her sleeping like a log, decided to let her have a lay in. Feeling remorseful about their talk the week before, she left a note for Eden. She had persuaded Gil to see the doctor, and, with his father's help, he had gone docilely.

Eden slept until noon. She found her mother's note taped to the frig. The message told her they were going to the doctor's and were going to stop at Tamura's Market before they got home after lunch. Eden was to water the plants and start dinner. In the sink was a chicken thawing. Her mom thought of everything.

After a bowl of oatmeal and a cup of tea, Eden got started on the dinner menu. She baked an apple pie. While that was in the oven, she prepared veggies to go with the roast chicken. The apple pie came out perfect, thank goodness. She placed it on a wire rack to cool, popped the chicken into the oven, and went out to water the plants. She could hear the mail truck coming up the street. Charlie, at the helm, waved to her. Turning the water off, she ran to greet him and heard the phone in the parlor ring insistently. Eden shot into the house to answer its sharp shrill.

"Eden, it's Marguerite Alexander. Thank goodness, you're home. Are you busy at the moment?"

"Oh, O-ma, what a relief to hear from you. I'm holding down the fort while my folks are in town. How's Ben doing? Is he alright?"

"Yes, thank God, he's alright. His fever comes and goes and he's feeling slightly weak. Being exhausted all week didn't help. Not to worry, though, he's holding his own. I'm so sorry to have taken so long to call you. Ben's father arrived home in the middle of the day, causing a minor upheaval in the household, and it took time to reach Ben's physician, Dr. Miller, who is vacationing on the mainland. He recommended a colleague in Honolulu, a brilliant specialist named Dr. Alohi Kaumea who has him confined to his room. He's been asking for you for the last hour or so. Between his mumbles and Amo'o's explanation, I gathered you had to bring him home in that condition." She paused to catch her breath. "I think seeing you would cheer him up tremendously. Is there any chance of you coming over when he's feeling better?"

"Truthfully," Eden answered, remaining calm, "I'm not sure what I'm to do with this strike business and all. My parents have asked that we hold off the engagement plans until the strike is settled. I'd have to talk with them first and see what they think. I haven't had the chance to talk with them today. They left for town while I was still asleep. Is it really bad with Ben?"

"No, not like it was initially, but Dr. Miller had hoped he had gotten over that bug he contracted while he was in Thailand. Seems it's flared up again. Very distressing with everything else happening. He'll have to catch up on his rest. However, he's on new medication and we are reassured that he will regain his strength. Thank God for medical advances. But my dear, how are you holding up? I'm sure in this case, your parents will understand."

"Actually, I'm waiting for Dad and Mom to get home. Perhaps, I can come over after I talk with them. I don't know what they're going to say. My folks wanted me to keep a low profile until this strike blows over. I must work this week, but Wednesday is my night off. If it's okay with them, I'll come after dinner if that's fine with you."

"Any time is a good time, my dear, though I don't know what I'll do to keep Ben occupied. He's not the world's best patient."

"Tell him I do love him, and I'll see him soon."

"Oh, that I will, my dear, that I will. However, I won't be here on Wednesday. I have guests flying in from Vancouver. I'll call when I can." She rang off.

Eden heard her parents pull into the drive just as the roast chicken was done and the rice cooker clicked off. Her father looked weary, and Eden watched silently from the kitchen doorway as her mom made him comfy in front of the television. Her mother was a bit frazzled. A cup of tea would revive her. She joined her daughter at the kitchen table.

"I see you've gotten dinner prepared, dear," Janie began, her demeanor somewhat subdued. "I do appreciate your help, Eden." She drank her tea in deep swallows. "I left your grandfather at the chicken coop. Thank God he is here to help your dad feed the chickens," she continued and then dropped her bomb. "Dr. Kim says Dad suffered a mild heart attack and wants him to see a heart specialist as soon as possible."

"A heart attack? A heart specialist?" Her mom's words pierced her soul.

"Dad may need heart surgery," her mom went on, "and it's going to be expensive. We'll need to talk to someone about what our medical insurance covers."

Eden overcame her shock, immediately reaching out to her mom. She placed her hands on Janie's shoulders saying as if she was also talking to herself, "Mom, I don't want you worrying. We'll manage. Dad's health is most important of all. I'll call Abby tonight and see what we can come up with."

At Eden's comforting words, Janie's shoulders slumped. For the first time since Eden was a teen, Janie saw how precious her second daughter was to her.

"You're a comfort, Eden," she got out, her voice choking up. "We'll see what Abigail has to say. As soon as Gramps gets back from feeding the chickens, we'll have dinner."

On Wednesday, after getting dinner ready for her folks, Eden drove to the mansion. It was a relief to have an evening off. All week her father's condition took priority, and only late at night did she allow herself to think of Ben. Anxious to see him, she had called him several times, but there was always no answer. On the way, she noticed Tony's blue Triumph parked at the cafe. "This would be a good time to see how he's faring," she thought, and pulled over to the curb. She popped into the cafe and found him having an early dinner or, probably, a late lunch, knowing his erratic schedule.

"Tony, what a surprise. When did you get back? Ben told me that you've been island hopping."

"Yes, I got back from Kaua'i this morning. It's been a mite tense at the house with Ben not feeling well and Uncle Barnes back. I've been waiting for you. Are you on tonight?" Tony pushed his plate aside for the waitress to clear away.

"No, my schedule has been changed. By the way, are you headed home? I'm on my way to see Ben."

Watching her face turn luminous at the mention of Ben's name, Tony hid his feelings. He knew he was out of the picture even before he was in it. Unlucky in love seemed to be his theme song lately. Seeing Eden and Ben come hand in hand into the ballroom after the scene in the gazebo had told him everything. He had kept discreetly out of the way since that time. Now, he looked at Eden with secret longing and felt a rush of envy for Ben. Ben had everything, he thought bittersweetly. Sensing his woebegone mood, Eden grabbed his hands.

"Hey, why so glum? You look like you've lost your best friend." He almost told her then, but he refrained from temptation admirably. The years of experience in amateur theater came in handy at the oddest moments.

"Ben's in good hands, Eden doll. You don't have to worry on that score. I'm glad you came in. I wasn't sure if you would be working, but I took a chance. I need to talk to someone." He waited as she ordered a lemonade and took a few sips.

"Alright, my friend, what's up?"

"My old man will be out in a few weeks. He's given me the ultimatum: either I get a job or go back home. Aunt Maggie is sore about the whole deal and I'm on her blacklist lately. With this strike, and now my dad, I'm sort of in limbo." Sensing Eden's concern he added, "Look, I don't like to dwell on unpleasantries. Thank God I have my photography to keep me busy." He took a few gulps of coffee. "Is this **Kona coffee**?" Eden nodded. "It's lovely coffee. I'm going to have to take some home with me. Don't think I can go back to tea after this."

"That will be the day. I've yet to see a **Kiwi** switch from tea to coffee." The girl looked at him affectionately. Tony beamed.

"I have one venture I've been working on, and I wanted your opinion." He pulled out a manila folder from his briefcase. Tony watched Eden's face glow with pleasure at the glossies he showed her. The picture of her with Ben in the gazebo was perfect and dreamlike.

"Why, this is beautiful, Tony. I'd love to have a copy of it." Tony looked at her small, neat head bent over the gazebo shot.

"Well, doll, you can have as many copies as you want, but you must give me your word to keep mum about it all. There's a surprise in store for us!"

"Surprise? Why shouldn't you share this photo? After all, it is art. I think you captured that late afternoon light so wonderfully."

"Eden I . . . I'm thinking of entering it in the Hawaiian Perfumes Photo Contest in the Fall."

"A photo contest?"

"Not just a photo contest, doll. It's the photo contest of the year! The competition is stiff, you know. Wouldn't want someone to steal my idea." Eden wasn't sure of all that. She thought of Ben and how he guarded his family's privacy. She looked at Tony, who needed her approval. Ben was the stronger of the two. At the vulnerable look on Tony's face, she gave in generously.

"It's alright with me, but perhaps you should ask Ben about it first." That was all the encouragement Tony needed.

"Ben won't mind. You'll see." He looked at his watch. "I have a friend back home who owns galleries in Auckland and Christchurch. He wants me to put on a show as soon as I get back. Thing is, Dad is not convinced. He's right in a way, I'm running low on money, and I need to get a break or go home. Sometimes, I truly feel like throwing in the towel and going back to the farm. At least I can make a good living farming in New Zealand."

"So, what's wrong with that? There's lots of time to develop your art, you know!"

"Girl, you don't know what you're saying. Once I'm back on the farm, that's it. Besides, my younger brother Kit is off to **Uni**, and he's too young to run the farm. It wouldn't be fair to him anyway. He must sow a few wild oats. Dad needs my help, and I guess I should do my duty. He did give me this time off to sort things out. Heavens, all I've thought of is photography . . . and you," he added silently.

"Alright, quit feeling sorry for yourself, it's not the end of the world. Has your father seen any of your work? These are fantastic," she exclaimed, as she viewed the other photos. "You've got talent. I can see that for myself. There's got to be a way that you can make a living doing this." Eden was thoughtful for a few minutes. "I have a great idea, why don't you approach a gallery here in town? Perhaps Abby could give you advice. It's her business to know the photographers. Give her a call or come and see her. She'll be home this weekend. Dad hasn't been feeling well."

"I think I'll take you up on that. Anyway, what's wrong with your dad? Too much stress from the strike?"

"Yes, that too, but we were shocked to discover that he has heart trouble." Her voice caught in her throat as she continued,

"He suffered a mild heart attack a few days ago and will consult with a heart specialist next week. We don't know yet what he needs, so it's been distressing not knowing what to expect. The strike has put a strain on our finances."

Tony gingerly placed his photos back into the folder. He knew only too well just what Eden was talking about, being in financial need himself.

"Wow, I'm sorry to hear that. Look, is there anything I can do? I can help around the yard, anything. Just say the word, and I'll be there!" He glanced at his watch again. "Oops. I must get back. I'm expecting a phone call from that mate in New Zealand and I've inadvertently left my cell phone at home. How did you get here? Do you need a ride to the mansion?"

"No, I drove. You go on, I'll see you later. You can show off your farming talents later."

"Will do and thanks for listening, Eden. Ben's a lucky man. I must warn you though, Uncle Barnes and Ben have been at it again. Ethel has stayed out of it, thank God."

"Yes, Ben's grandmother called me and told me how it's been. What's Ethel like, anyway?"

"Oh, she's very proper. Petite and pretty, and clearly adores her husband. Caters to Barnes, but she and Ben don't talk much. Just take this advice from Uncle Tony and tread carefully, doll, and you'll be okay. Please tell your folks that my thoughts are with them. And remember what I said, I'm ready to help in any way. Just let me know." Eden, grateful for his concern, gave him a peck on the cheek and watched him rush out of the cafe.

It was closing time, so Eden collected her paycheck, stashed it into her purse, and bid Mrs. Chang a pleasant goodnight.

The old woman looked up from the cash register and shook her head.

Dusk was settling in. That gorgeous time of day when the sky turns a dark blue. Eden drove slowly to the mansion, taking in the scenery. She parked the aged blue Dodge and walked to the kitchen, opening the door and knocking. Amo'o was cleaning up.

"Oh, hello Missy Eden, thank goodness you finally made it. Mrs. Maggie say you were coming today."

"Hello, Amo'o." She gave the plump woman a hug, Hawaiian style, and kissed her on each cheek. "I sure appreciate your help last week. Is Ben up and able to see me?"

"Yeah, he in the library with Mr. Barnes. I'm glad you here. Whew! Master Ben ask for you all the time. He not one easy patient, let me tell you. Maybe, you can make him listen. He gotta rest and get well, you know. He looks much better now than when you brought him home. Just go in. He is expecting you. Go on, I bring in refreshments later."

Eden found her way to the library easily. She recognized Ben's voice, and the other, she assumed, was his father's. They were speaking rather heatedly, and she hesitated. About to knock and herald her appearance, she heard her name come up loud and clear. She pulled back, heart thumping, and listened. Father and son were arguing about her!

"Why can't you just listen to reason? The girl is too young. Furthermore, what kind of match do you think she will make? She has no fortune, no connections. Consider the cultural differences. Someday, the business will be all yours. What then?"

"Ha! Don't make me laugh, Dad," Ben retorted, but with effort. "You should be the one to talk. Eden is only eleven years my junior while Ethyl could be your daughter. You've been on my case for years about my getting married and taking over the business. And what better candidate for a wife could you find? Eden was raised on the plantation." The senior Alexander flushed.

"Don't bring my wife into this. We're talking about you and that girl."

"Dad, so far you haven't given me one good reason why you're so opposed to our engagement."

Barnes Alexander folded his hands neatly. He took his time. Finally, he looked away from his son and said rather lamely, "She's not our kind."

Ben turned white at his words. He slammed his fist on the writing desk and stood up. His father had angered him in the past, but this was the limit.

"Look here son, sit down. You look peaky. Let me get Amoʻo to bring some refreshments." He buzzed the intercom and after giving his housekeeper-cook his message, he looked guiltily at his son and walked to the window.

Amoʻo came at once bearing a tray of coffee and a coconut cream pie. She found Eden, a stricken look on her face, leaning against the library door. She beckoned the girl to follow her. As Amoʻo entered the library, Barnes Alexander with his back to her, didn't notice Eden slip into the room and headed straight for his coffee and pie. Ben's pale face brightened when he saw his beloved following in the bold housekeeper's wake. The tray was placed on the sofa table. Amoʻo could feel the tension in the room and rolled her eyes at Eden. She closed the door behind her, and Ben stood up shakily and extended his arms.

"Eden, sweetheart," he let out with relief in his voice.

Eden rushed immediately to his side and tried to push him back into his chair. He looked thinner and so incredibly pale in his kimono-style robe. His long arms wove around her and held her firmly, while he drank in the very scent of her.

Barnes Alexander lifted his head, and looking askance at his son and the girl, he frowned. When he got a proper look at Eden, for a moment he was at a loss for words. No wonder his son was in a lather of late. The girl had the look of an angel. Yes, the dress she wore was homemade, but somehow its very simplicity emphasized her exotic looks. The skin was faultless, and the sight of her glorious hair startled him. Also, there was adoration in her lovely eyes for his only son. Obviously, she wasn't the gold-digger type he had imagined. Observing his son's heightened complexion, he shook his head. The lad was obsessed with the young beauty, and he realized that Ben was serious about giving Eden the family name. He shook his head. He had come home in the nick of time. Better to nip the romance in the bud. His was a nasty business, he reminded himself. If it weren't for her lack of fortune, maybe he felt he could be persuaded to approve of the match. As it stood, it was going to be even harder than he thought to convince Benjamin to give her up. He cleared his throat.

"I beg your pardon, my dear, you must be Eden. I'm Barnes Alexander, Ben's dad." Eden shook his hand, but Ben wouldn't let go of her. "For heaven sakes, Benjamin, do allow the girl to sit down!"

"Not on your life, Dad. She stays by my side." Ben gave his father a challenging look. The older man had the grace to look uncomfortable.

"Well, you look considerably improved." Feeling like an intruder on the young lovers, he decided to make himself scarce. "I'm looking forward to getting to know you better, Eden. I'll leave you two to talk. I'm retiring for the night. Goodnight."

They watched him pick up his cup of coffee and a piece of the pie. As soon as they heard his step on the stairs, Ben instructed Eden to shut the door. His eyes followed her every move and he motioned to her to sit next to him on the red velvet sofa. For a few minutes not a word could be said because he held her so tightly and then kissed her over and over. They sat back, with Eden's head fitting into the crook of his shoulder. She fit so perfectly. Ben could feel at ease again now that he had his little one with him.

"You can't imagine what a wretched week I've had." Eden looked at the lines under his green eyes.

"You look like you need more rest."

"Heck no, I've had enough of that. This isn't serious, but my body is taking its sweet old time kicking this bug. You'd think I was going to break the way the family cossets me. I'd rather go to the dentist than go through another week like this one. I guess it comes from being an only child. You should have seen the way they were when I was a kid."

"Hmmm," Eden chuckled, "you must be getting better. Back to your autocratic ways I see. I didn't know that you were an only child. What about Brigitte?"

"Well, I come by it honestly. Despite our hassles, I'm glad the old man is back. I've had enough of all this strike hullaboo. It's not public knowledge that my sister is adopted. She's a trooper, that one. I think you'll really like her. Not to change the subject, but what's this nonsense that O-ma tells me about your parents not wanting us to see each other."

"No, it's not like that. Dad is being unreasonably persecuted by several members of the union. He feels it would be better if we didn't see each other in public while the strike is on. Eden couldn't keep it in any longer. "Oh, Ben," she sobbed, "Dad had a mild heart attack last week after the meeting at our house. Dr. Kim confirmed it. He has an appointment with a heart specialist next week. Mom and I have been worried, of course. We're going to have to figure out a way to pool our resources if Dad needs heart surgery."

"Oh my God, heart surgery? Are you certain?" The news shook Ben, and he tightened his hold on Eden.

"It looks like it. He has to take tests first!"

"Eden, sweetheart, I don't want you or your parents to worry. I can easily give them the money . . ."

"No, Ben, don't you see? They would never accept a loan. We'll work it out, somehow." He was unconvinced.

"Sweetheart, it's not a loan. My intentions are honorable. As their future son-in-law, I'm happy to help them."

"Oh Ben, you're so good and big-hearted, but I can't let you. It would look like I was taking advantage of you. Besides, it just wouldn't be right or fair to you." This time she kissed him. "Let's don't talk about it. I just want to concentrate on you while I'm here. It's a relief to know you're okay. You had me worried."

He gave up trying and held onto Eden, kissing her every few minutes just to make sure she was real, unaware that his father was upstairs with a troubled mind, pondering his next move. They shared a piece of the delicious pie and felt rather comforted.

"Amo'o is something else. I wonder why she served this particular pie. It's Dad's favorite, you know."

"Hmmm, being Hawaiian, I think she's filled with the aloha spirit. She knows exactly how to handle your dad."

They talked, content to be together, both keeping their fathers out of the conversation, until Ben got weary and reluctantly sent his beloved home.

CHAPTER 17
Remembrances of Things Past

While she washed the lunch dishes, Eden happened to look out the kitchen window. She could see her father's figure, shoulders slumped, as he walked slowly around their yard. What a picture of fatigue he projected these days. He wasn't unusual in this. Everyone in the plantation began to take on that same drained look. The strike was taking its toll. After each mediation meeting, Gil would wait patiently at home for the results from Mike Castro and shake his head when Janie looked at him expectantly. With both sides refusing to budge, it looked like this particular strike was going to last forever. For the first time in his work life, Gil felt like he was being useless. Under the doctor's strict orders, he had to take it easy. Usually very active physically, it was a first for him.

The dishes were done; Eden attacked the stove. It was her least favorite job, but, what the heck, she thought, today was one of those funky days anyway. She believed that a good workout with elbow grease would shoo away the blahs. As she scrubbed, she thought of the tension between her grandfather and father that had mounted since the strike's inception. The relationship between father and son has always been a loving one, but they heartily agree to disagree on many things. The strain created by the strike was only exacerbating an already stressful situation. Something had to change soon. It was getting on her nerves to always play the peacemaker in the family, what with the double concerns about her dad and Ben.

Her grandfather didn't fail her. Sharp as a tack, he had seen the handwriting on the wall, and had made his decision to return to Waialua earlier than anticipated. He realized that he was adding to the already tough situation at home and wanted only the best for his son's health. He was firm in his stand, and no amount of dissuasion on Eden's part would avail. If there was anything Gramps was famous for, it was for his stubbornness. Anyway, she conceded, the old man was retired and did not need this extra stress in his life.

Gil had stoically accepted his father's decision to return to his sister Michelle's home, but Janie was secretly relieved when Milton announced that he was leaving the next day. She couldn't cope with two firebrands, even though one was old, and the other wasn't in the best of health. Eden, relinquishing her responsibility of taking care of silly Jack, held back the tears as she bid aloha to her beloved grandparent.

"Now Gramps," Eden coaxed with a cheer that wasn't true to her real feelings, "don't forget to take your medications every morning. You know Dr. Santos' orders." Milton Andres grunted. His doctor bugged him, and he disliked goodbyes. Eden saw her grandfather into his small Valiant. It was silver colored and nicknamed the Silver Bullet. The red seats were faded, and the back seat was pushed down to make it comfy for Jack. Somehow, the seriousness of the moment had transformed the silly mutt into a dog of quiet submission. He jumped into the back when Eden called him and sniffed the rug that she had laid out for him. She stowed his bowls and the remainder of his dog food and locked up the back. Jack stood solemnly behind his master's seat. As Eden gave her grandfather a final hug and kiss, he playfully pinched her cheek.

"Chin up, Sabina," he said resolutely. "The strike will be settled in its time. Being apart from Ben won't last forever, you know, and your dad is in good hands. Things have a way of working out for good, you wait and see!" He saluted, gunned the motor a bit, only to drive slowly down the road. The silver car grew smaller and smaller until it was just a small speck on the horizon.

An **anuenue** appeared in the sky, and Eden felt the beginnings of a light sprinkle. "Hello, **liquid sunshine**," she called out as she ran to the back of the house to take the laundry off the line. Perhaps it was a good sign, she didn't really know, but the sight of the rainbow chased away the blues. She felt encouraged for some reason.

She needed the boost, for when Charlie delivered the mail, she was to find the electric bill among the lot of junk mail and letters from her young sisters. What a shock it was to her system. She had just gotten rid of the water bill and now this. At first, she felt defeated. All this scraping to make ends meet was humiliating. She wondered how the others on the plantation were coping. No need to wonder, she concluded, it was evident that people were beginning to feel desperate. Talk of starting a soup kitchen had been brought up at the last union meeting. For the first time in her life, Eden had to question the validity of the union's stand and evaluate the problem from the management's point of view. Hadn't she always sided with her father in the past, and didn't she feel proud that he was a man of principle? This one time, however, she had to admit that perhaps the union was taking the wrong tack.

She consulted with her mother and together they juggled the family budget. Janie gave up after several tries and went to fortify her brain with a cup of tea. Eden sat at her makeshift desk, chewing thoughtfully on her pencil eraser. Thank goodness they had the food in the extra freezer to count on. What a brainstorm! A big smile spread across her face.

Brooking no argument from anyone, she sold the white rooster that very afternoon. Gramps would have been proud of her! They both disliked that white bird. Not one word of protest slipped past her parents' lips. They were too surprised by her bold move. What mattered most to them in a time like this was that the electric bill was paid on time. Their pride on being prompt settlers of their various accounts was salvaged.

Finally, after two trips to Honolulu and several tests later, Dr. Chen, the heart specialist, strongly recommended heart surgery for Gil Andres. He concurred with Dr. Kim, that his patient had clogged coronary arteries and had suffered a mild heart attack. Triple bypass surgery was recommended as soon as possible. The news stunned everyone as Mr. Andres had always been the picture of health. He was relieved of his official union duties, and oddly enough, Lefty Shimizu volunteered in his stead. The whole plantation buzzed with the news. Not only was the waiting for the strike settlement wearing thin, but it was also proving to be costly for everyone involved, particularly the Andres family. Dr. Miyamoto, the heart surgeon who was to do the operation was the best in the Hawaiian Islands, but as a non-preferred provider, his fee had to be paid up front, and the amount seemed completely out of reach for them. Surely, their medical would cover a large percentage of the hospital costs. That was a blessing. However, it would take a while to process the papers for the reimbursement of the surgeon's fees. "Oh, the injustice of the system," their relatives and friends had wailed.

Thoroughly shaken, Janie Andres worried and fretted during most of her waking hours and would wake up in the middle of the night in a cold sweat. Where were they going to get such a large sum of money? The Andres kids with Abby contributing the largest amount had scraped together all their savings, and several thousand had been pooled. Without the extra hand to help around the place and with her mom's preoccupation with her dad, the brunt of keeping the household together fell more and more upon Eden's shoulders. Mike Castro was kind enough to offer to take care of her father's chickens for them. She was beginning to waiver on her decision not to accept Ben's help. It would be so simple just to hand over the responsibility to him. With any problem, the real battle begins in the mind. Back and forth, forth and back she argued within herself. Finally, after wrestling with her indecision, she vowed to follow her first inclination. She knew instinctively that it would be the best solution not to ask Ben for help. Something would work out. Something always did, reassured Phil when she asked him for advice. Phil stepped up his efforts in praying for his best friend's family!

In the meantime, Eden lived on nervous energy. She never complained, but the strain of having to work at the cafe and to cope at home was making her edgy. She wished that Abby could somehow be back living at home, but she knew that her sister's job almost necessitated that she live close to her work. Abby was a trooper: she never grumbled about working extra hours. Also, with the cost of gasoline in Hawai'i the highest in the nation, commuting would add one more financial burden --something they didn't need. She came home every few days to help out and made sure she called home often to keep abreast of the situation. The two sisters spent a long time on the phone whenever they could, and Eden was always comforted after their talks.

Some days when she was on break, Eden would daydream of Maui, of that incredible fresh ocean breeze off the North Shore. She longed to be away from Oahu's fast pace and the oppressive atmosphere at the plantation. Just a short time ago, she had been a happy-go-lucky college student. Today, she felt like a middle-aged frump burdened with domestic problems. If only her school chums, especially Francesca, could see her like this. She wondered what they all would say if they saw her now, dressed in old clothes and scrubbing the floor. She was so close, just two courses away from obtaining her two-year degree. Yet, she had willingly given up her plans to return to school for the Fall semester. Franny had been disappointed but understanding. It was the easiest decision Eden had ever made. The ever-increasing pressure of making ends meet had made the decision for her. For once she was truly glad she could be home to give her mom all the support she needed.

Today was a day for mulling things over in her already burdened mind. Her family's financial situation constantly reminded her of the great gulf between her family's social position and Ben's. While they struggled along, the Alexanders didn't have to rely on the plantation for their livelihood. She could very well understand why the Bible says, that "you have the poor with you always." Doubts plagued her. How were they going to deal with their differences once she and Ben were married? The thought brought her some measure of anxiety, but today, as most days, she shoved it to the back burner. After all, she was an extreme optimist at heart. She was convinced that nothing could be stronger than the bond of love and that differences could always be resolved.

Phil kept reminding her constantly that tough situations usually get resolved in the most surprising ways. Eden was grateful that her father was so well-loved and respected that everyone wanted to help and breathed a sigh of relief when a group of friends from the plantation acted. A fund was started, and monetary gifts began to flow in from friends and family from all over the island. Michiko, Lefty's younger sister, was the first to bring her offering. It was her egg money in an old cigar box. Janie, sitting on her old rattan chair, received it graciously and cried when the two women embraced. Gracie came too, this time with a gift from the 4-H-ers. It was the total from their bake sale that summer. Eden couldn't help but feel a sense of pride at the sacrificial giving of her father's friends. One of the privileges of plantation living was the fact that people stuck together through thick and thin.

It hurt Eden though, to see her father so resigned to his fate. It was a big change to see him, once so athletic, spend most of his time quietly at home with her mother fussing over him. He didn't talk much, but occasionally would smile bleakly at her.

It rained the last of August, which boded well for the pineapple crop, but not for the striking workers. With nothing much to do but picket, or sit around at home, the men grew restless and aggressive. Nerves were frayed, tempers often flared, and Ray Mulroney had his hands full acting as a mediator between the Alexander Corporation and the union officials. He missed Gil's presence in the negotiations. Another meeting between the two factions had ended in stalemate, much to the frustration of everyone involved.

Ben's health improved considerably, but not his disposition. Eden knew something was agitating him. Although he was as persistent as ever in strengthening their relationship, he seemed preoccupied with the family's business matters and didn't have much free time. When they were together, it was brief and oftentimes he would be faraway in thought. He wasn't as carefree or garrulous as he was during the summer months. He became moody and sometimes almost melancholy. Some of the junior office clerks were given temporary leave, and his secretary Chloe was the only one who noticed how troubled

Ben looked these days when he thought no one was looking. She would shake her head and get back to her work.

Whenever he could, Ben would meet Eden at their tree for a few precious stolen moments together. They were always happy in each other's company until that hated subject of the money was brought up. It became such a bone of contention between them that Eden simply refused to talk about it any further. Ben alternated between extreme gentleness and utter impatience. Eden, however, remained unmoved about accepting his help.

On one afternoon, Ben had gotten to the tree a few minutes before she did. He sat for a few minutes just soaking in the heat and the quiet of the late afternoon. He'd been bothered with more headaches lately and it affected his mood.

Eden saw Ben before he saw her. His blond head was pushed back against the tree and his eyes were closed tightly. It was her favorite picture of him. Her heartbeat quickened. Chemistry, he had told her once, was an inexplicable thing. She would always feel the same mad JOY whenever she looked at him. Today, he looked vulnerable and weary. Eden approached shyly. Ben's eyes flipped open, and he turned his head when he heard her footsteps on the leaves. Their eyes met. They exchanged a tender look that only lovers possess. Eden bent to kiss him on the cheek and slid next to him on the grass. "Hi!" she said cheerily, her smile wide. The green eyes lit up.

"Hi, yourself, smiley," Ben quipped, giving Eden a hard kiss on the lips.

"You look bushed," Eden replied as she took in his tired look. "Had a hard day?"

"Well, I guess you could say that I did." Ben hunched his shoulders and rested his chin on his knees. "Lord, I wish this strike business were over," he continued, "I don't know how you all can bear it. Dad's always getting on my back for something or other." He was silent for a few minutes as he chewed on some grass and brooded. The peaceful moment passed when he asked suddenly, "How's Gil?"

Eden's smile disappeared. She had learned not to bring up the subject of her father at their meetings, but as always Ben asked.

"He's, you know. . . waiting for the surgery date." Eden knew what was coming. It happened every time they got together lately, and she braced herself for his argument.

"Eden," he said in exasperation, "why won't your family accept my help?" This time he sounded hurt. "It's the most natural thing in the world for me to do. For heaven's sake, I'm your fiancé. It's not like I'm struggling or you're taking advantage." He sat in moody silence and stared into the distance. She trembled as she always did when Ben seemed to remove himself mentally from her presence and she positively hated it when he used that disappointed tone of voice with her. He sounded so much like his father.

"Ben," she sighed, "please, let's not talk about that again. You know how we all feel. Just understand."

"How can I understand when you won't even give me a chance? You just say no to me, but you accept help from friends. Don't I count as a friend?" That hurt little boy look was all over his face. Eden turned away. How could she make him understand? He grabbed her tiny hands. The nails were clipped short, and the skin was rough. "She's been doing her dad's yard work," he thought. He kissed them anyway and looked imploringly into her eyes. "Sweetheart, look at it from my point of view. You're going to be my wife. It's my prerogative to want to provide for you. I can't stand to see you so overworked all the time. Why should you struggle when I can so easily remove the obstacle? Time is of the essence for your dad. Let me help!" He hugged her tightly. They sat for a few moments just savoring being in each other's arms. He smelled like he had been working hard. Eden stirred, taking in his scent.

"Ben."

"Hmmm," he murmured.

"What would your father think?"

"About what?"

"About you wanting to help us out financially." Ben stiffened. Eden sensed his withdrawal again. He reached for another cigarette and Eden watched him light up. She wished he would quit smoking. After a few drags, he put it out in the dirt. "Eden, my father has got nothing to do with my decisions." Eden wondered but didn't comment. "When my mother passed on, she left the bulk of her father's estate to me. Brigitte is well provided for. I can do pretty much what I want to do with it. Dad has no say whatsoever. Besides, why should he?" Ben looked at his watch. "Look sweetheart, I must go. At least promise me this time, you'll think about my offer." Eden was about to protest, but Ben wouldn't give her a chance. He stood her up, hugged her, and let go of her promptly. Up the path he strode. She sat down with her back against her tree, feeling jangled up inside.

Muttering to himself, Ben reached his vehicle and started it up. He hated it when Eden was being unnecessarily stubborn.

He could change her present circumstance so easily and yet she remained adamant. It made him feel helpless, but on the other hand, it irritated him tremendously. He took off burning rubber. Eden pouted as she heard the noise. She loved him with all her heart, but his changing moods bewildered her. Why couldn't he just understand? She understood, didn't she? Why did she feel that accepting his help wasn't the thing to do? Anyone looking in would see that they both loathed the situations they were enmeshed in. As much as she adored the son, she admitted to herself, she avoided contact with the senior Alexander whenever she could. After their initial encounter in the library, she couldn't help but feel that things weren't all what they seemed on the surface between herself and Barnes Alexander. He was polite, way too polite. Ben didn't seem to pay attention, and Eden wondered if he was blind to his father's condescending attitude towards her or was just being indifferent. Ben's stepmother, the diminutive well-dressed Ethel, stayed close to her husband's side and never said much. Eden felt quite sorry for her. Barnes Alexander dominated his wife, and in Eden's eyes, Ethel seemed almost like a nonentity. The thought gave her the shivers. She ardently hoped that Ben hadn't inherited his father's peremptory ways. She got up and headed home.

As she walked slowly towards the old house, she recalled the time she had been invited to dinner at the mansion soon after Barnes' return. She wasn't so overawed by the grand old estate or by the wealth of the Alexanders anymore, but she was bothered by their insensitivity to each other.

Amo'o had done herself proud and the place was overflowing with flowers from the garden. O-ma had begged off at the last moment, pleading a sore throat, and Eden had faced the dreaded ordeal without her staunch ally. She had sensed a deep foreboding in the air. Barnes' verbal jabs at Ben were efficiently and neatly warded off. Though Ethel was friendly enough, Eden could see that she tended to side with her husband on most things. She couldn't help but compare the unpleasant atmosphere, elegant as it was, to the conviviality that surrounded her family's mealtimes. It made her wonder why it didn't seem to bother Ben. She had even felt a little sorry for Amo'o. That bosomy creature who had been tutored under the Alexander family chef, recently retired, had prepared a gastronomic feast. Eden couldn't get over it! With the strained atmosphere at dinner, she hadn't done justice to the succulent Duck a l'Orange, served with **black forbidden rice**, but the creamy macadamia soup had at least contributed to soothing her nerves. The **Okinawan Sweet Potato Haupia Pie** was superb, but she was relieved when the meal ended and couldn't wait to escape from that temporary prison. Ben had wisely suggested a walk around the grounds after dinner and only then did she relax.

"You're awfully quiet this evening. Tired?" Eden shook her head. She had washed her hair and perfumed it with **Monoi Tiki Tahiti oil**. He looked at her with open admiration in his eyes.

"Ben, what do you think of your father?"

"My father? Sweetheart, you ask the oddest questions sometimes."

"You know . . . every time I see you two together, it seems like you're at loggerheads with one another. What was it like growing up with him?" Ben was silent for a moment. He peered up at the night sky.

"Is that how we seem to you, always at loggerheads with each other? Hmmm. That's interesting. Well, we have our differences, but we do have what you would call a typical father-son relationship." He looked down at Eden. Her forehead was wrinkled with concern. "We have been at odds with each other lately, you mean?" She nodded. "You know Dad, he's rather opinionated, a control freak, if you will. I don't remember much of what it was like before my mother passed on. He was away at work a lot. I know he must have loved her very much. He grieved for her for such a long time. In fact, I don't think he's fully gotten over her death. You may not know it, but my mother was quite religious. When she died suddenly, Dad went off the deep end, and of course, he blamed God and became embittered. That's why I'm surprised he married Ethel the way he did."

Ben reached out to Eden, cupped the back of her neck in his hand and pulled her gently to him. Winding his hand around her scented hair, he put his lips to it. She smelled like a thousand gardenias. They listened to the crickets chirping in the brush.

"Eden," he said softly, "I don't want you worrying about my family. We're like characters in a Tennessee Williams play. Tragic, if you know what I mean. It's just the way we are with each other. You can't really change that. As long as I can remember, Dad and I have been at odds with each other. He wants me to continue with the plantation, which is only natural. I think that when he lost mother, he became slightly fearful that he would lose his children, too. By the time we were in college, his manipulations were the norm, and we don't pay heed to them anymore. I've learned to survive independently of him. Brigitte and he don't get on at all. She refuses to come home. Anyway, let's not dwell on my family. You're my family now. We have each other, we're together and that's what really matters." Eden hadn't wanted the conversation to end, but Ben had made up his mind.

"Hush, the subject is closed," he'd said firmly, and then had smiled, looking down at Eden's fluttering eyelashes. "Come on." He pulled her along and said in a lighter vein, "I'll show you those plantation photographs you've wanted to see!"

CHAPTER 18
A Day for Visitors

Marguerite Alexander resolutely made up her mind. It was time to intervene. The situation between her son and grandson had reached an impasse and their constant bickering about the engagement had to end. She was weary of being a stop gap between the two persons she loved most. She blamed herself chiefly. If she had only proceeded with caution, maybe all of this wouldn't have happened. Benjamin was besotted with the girl, and it was only natural for her to want to see him happy. She should have known Barnes would have objections. She had lived with both men a long time. They were Alexanders, headstrong and accustomed to giving orders and having their own way. Perhaps, she sighed, there would be peace in the household once more if Eden would consider Barnes' condition to the engagement. The girl was of a more tractable nature and, she hoped, more approachable about the situation than either Barnes or Ben. She set out for the cafe that very afternoon. Unfortunately, she arrived unannounced and found Tony in attendance to Eden, who was on a break. She eyed Tony disapprovingly.

"Aunt Marguerite" Tony blurted out and stood up abruptly. "How nice to see you . . . I'll talk to you later, Eden." He left without paying his check, bumping into a chair before he got to the swinging doors. He reminded Eden of the errant schoolboy caught playing hooky. She suppressed her laugh and graciously had Mrs. Chang put his tab on her bill.

"My dear, it's not wise for you to allow that young man to take advantage of you," Marguerite Alexander said with slight exasperation in her voice. She sat down and removed her gloves. She was a bit overdressed for the homestyle cafe though the magenta Vittadini outfit did wonders for her silver hair. "I'm certain Ben would have something to say about that!" she continued. "How his father puts up with Anthony is beyond me. All the while he's been here, he has't given a thought to anyone else but himself. Why, the lad has no sense of family obligation and only lives and breathes his hobby. His father plans to be out in just a few weeks. I just hope he comes to his senses and returns home with him." Tony had his wild moments, but somehow he had Eden's sympathies.

"O-ma, I hope you're feeling more at ease now that Ben is doing better. Chamomile tea is soothing and comforting. Would you care for a cup?" O-ma said she would. Eden called for Mrs. Chang to pour them some tea. The woman approached her august guest with awe and some trepidation. Mrs. Chang had been acting a little snippy lately, but Eden decided she could afford to be kind to her boss. She guessed the strike had everyone on edge. Business at the cafe had noticeably dropped off and their hours had been cut back.

Marguerite Alexander collected herself as she sipped her tea. She studied the composed figure sitting in front of her. What she saw didn't surprise her. Eden was more complex than she looked, showing a side of herself that was quite capable of handling difficult situations. She faltered for a second and wondered if it was wise to proceed with her plan. Then she looked quickly at Eden's mouth, which was a trifle too large for that narrow face, but the eyes were exquisite and the look so tender. The girl was surely without guile and almost too good to be true. "The best thing that has ever happened to

Benjamin," she comforted herself. The older woman decided to stick to her plan. The strike had posed some restraints on the relationship between her grandson and this lovely plantation girl. Dark shadows under Eden's eyes told their tale, and O-ma forced herself to carry out what she had come to propose.

The cafe emptied out. Marguerite steadied herself. "Ray was out to see us today. The Union has refused to negotiate any further. The Board is considering shutting down Aloha Nui Loa and phasing out before the year's end. Unless there is a settlement soon, everyone will be forced to take early retirement and to move out of the plantation." She took a deep breath. The wrinkles on her face looked more pronounced than ever. "I might warn you that Barnes intends to send Ben to the Philippines to assist the new manager on the Luzon plantation."

"The Philippines!" The news came as a complete surprise. It took Eden a moment to digest the information. She stirred her tea.

"Ben hasn't mentioned anything to me about the Philippines."

"I fear that's not all there is to it, my dear. Barnes is very much against the idea of . . . well," Marguerite halted, embarrassed. "They simply haven't been getting along since Barnes' return." At her words, a certain weariness crept over Eden.

"You don't have to spare my feelings, O-ma, I know how Ben's father feels about our engagement. This has nothing to do with Ben. It's about me, isn't it? Is this why Ben has been so preoccupied lately?" Marguerite Alexander could not look her in the eye.

"My dear," she finally said, "how I wish it were all so simple. If it were only your and Ben's happiness that was paramount, perhaps I would have kept quiet. I have tried to reason with my son, but he feels, as he always has, that I spoil Benjamin." In one of those rare instances, Marguerite Alexander felt her age. "When Amelia, Ben's mother, passed away," she confided, "Barnes was devastated. It was as if nothing mattered anymore and part of him died with her. He was so overcome with grief that he cut himself off from every living soul and withdrew into himself. He neglected Benjamin, who himself was dreadfully bewildered by the loss of his mother. The boy clung to me as his refuge. Brigitte was much too young to realize what had happened. She doesn't remember her mama. Ben, however, was the apple of her eye. It hurt him tremendously to lose her. His father's seemingly cold attitude towards his children alienated them from him." The hurt was there in her yellow green eyes.

"It's okay, O-ma. You can tell me." She looked so much like Ben that Eden patted her hands.

"Time heals all wounds," O-ma continued, "and for a while it looked like Barnes was making some progress. Much to my dismay, when he finally pulled himself together, he shot in the opposite direction and tried to control the children. By that time, they were older, and it was too late to change the situation. Ben developed a hardness towards his father and Brigitte refused to listen to reason." Marguerite Alexander wrung her hands.

Eden poured her more tea and waited. She could see that O-ma needed comfort, and to unburden herself. Eden felt compassion for her.

"Their relationship with Barnes was further complicated," the older woman continued, "when they became of age and inherited their mother's estate. No longer financially dependent on her father, Brigitte was the first to fly the coop. She went off to college and refused to return home to Hawai'i. Her brother did his father's bidding and excelled at Yale and later at the U. of C. at Davis, but when he got offered an engineering job in Thailand, he took off with no regrets. His father didn't hear from him often until we got word that he was ill. I had hoped that this summer, he would have at long last laid all these struggles to rest. This relapse brought back that old anxiety about his memory loss. He's been very uncommunicative about it. I don't know if he has shared anything with you." Eden shook her head.

"Well, I know something has been on his mind. I've decided to just let him work it out for himself. You know how he dislikes for people who pry into his privacy. Even though I'm not as touchy, I can respect his wishes. When he's ready, I'm certain he'll share it with me."

"I wish I had your confidence, but sometimes it's not so simple with our Ben. He tends to suffer more than he should. Like the verse says, 'he beats the air.'" She sipped her tea and finished off the blueberry muffin, which she said was very good. "This particular strike has been so stressful. Without your father's steady hand, the union has remained unmovable. The company can't go on the way it has been going. It's a no-win situation. The Board is considering bringing in non-union workers just to salvage the pineapple crop. If they lose the pineapple, they must turn to something else, like selling off land to keep the capital flowing." She looked uneasy but proceeded cautiously. "Would you, my dear, be willing to let your fiancé go to the Philippines, for say, six months? Barnes feels it's a good amount of time to test your commitment to each other. I'm not defending my son's behavior, but I think it might be a good way to eliminate any future interference from him. Our boy is doing tremendously well with his new medication."

A customer entered the cafe. Both women turned their heads. It was Phil Castro. He looked troubled. Eden raised her fine eyebrows. Today must be her day for visitors.

"Phil! What's up?"

"Hello Mrs. Alexander, Eden. Eden, I must talk to you at once," he begged in earnest.

"What is it?" she asked quizzically.

Phil looked at Marguerite Alexander warily and shook his head. "Just come now. It's important!"

Eden's elegant visitor shot Phil a tight little smile. Dismissing herself, she stood up and gathered her gloves and handbag. "We shall continue this conversation at a more convenient time, my dear. I'm sure that Ben will discuss all this with you when he's ready. Please give your parents my regards. I'm praying all will go well when Gil has his surgery. Ben hasn't told me any particulars, but I just want to say that he is extremely worried about your dad. Please think about letting him help." They hugged. She promptly called for her check and paid Mrs. Chang. Eden watched her go while Phil made sure the yellow Cadillac was gone before he volunteered to help her close shop. She felt wrung out. It was too much information all at once. She shuddered as if to get a grip on things.

"I'll see you tomorrow, Mrs. Chang. Don't forget to bring the basil for the pesto!" She said goodnight and stepped outside with Phil pushing her along. Mrs. Chang shook her head. Three suitors for one girl were too many. She wondered if Eden could give a few tips to her still single daughter Millicent.

"How did you get here, Phil? I don't see your car."

"Miguel gave me a ride in his Corolla." Phil grabbed her arm and guided her along to the old Dodge. Phil was not himself. Eden knew him too well. He was being rude, and she waited for him to tell her what was on his mind. They got into the car and Eden headed for home.

Once on the main road, she questioned, "Alright, Castro, what's with this cloak and dagger stuff? Why did you have to come and get me at the cafe? You could have called, you know. What's so important that you had to drag me away from my job?"

Phil, her self-appointed watchdog, was holding his temper in check. "Eden, I've kept my mouth shut long enough. I told you before to take it easy with Ben Alexander. Why didn't you listen to me? You're in trouble and you don't even know it."

"Phil, if you don't tell me right now, I'm stopping the car and you can walk home."

"Look knucklehead, why did you have to go and do it?"

After bottling up all her troubles for days on end, Eden lost her cool. She pulled the car over to the side of the road. "Don't you dare raise your voice at me. I'm not impressed one bit with your big brother act. So quit it. I don't have the foggiest notion what you're talking about!"

"Girl," he let out in exasperation, "this is worse than I expected." Phil examined her angry face. If he knew anything about her, he knew that she wasn't the type to tell a lie. "You mean you haven't heard?" he asked incredulously. "Idiot, someone saw you sneaking out of the Alexander house in the wee hours of the morning. Can you imagine what people are saying?"

"Sneaking out! What do you mean by that?" Eden reddened, then defended herself hotly. "I had a very legit reason for being there. Ben wasn't well. Don't you get it? He'd asked me to meet him at a very late hour and so I did. He was feverish and out of it, and I had to get him home."

When Phil eyed her unbelievingly, she cried, "Look, ask Amo'o, she was there to help me. She'll tell you! Ben needed me. No one else was around to help." Eden glowered at Phil indignantly. Finally, it dawned on her. "Are you implying that people are gossiping about me?"

"Implying, my eye. You should know how some plantation folk can be. They're saying you're after Ben's money and since your dad needs this operation, you'd go to any lengths to get it. I don't know what will happen when your folks hear about this," he added on a sour note.

"Oh, shut up. Some friend you are!" Stung by his unfair words, but mostly by his lack of faith in her, Eden punched him in the arm as hard as she could. "I can't believe that you, of all people, would think this of me. What's the matter with you, anyhow? Ben is the noblest man I know. So big deal, I was over at his place early in the morning!" Looking over at Phil she asked cautiously, "You . . . you don't plan on saying anything to Mom and Dad, do you?"

"No, I wouldn't do that! Who do you think I am? I care about your father's health too, you know." Phil rubbed his arm and rolled down his window. After a moment's thought, he added in a gentler tone, "Are you really telling me the truth?"

"Oh you!" Eden turned her face away and fumed. "Look, nobody asked you to be my keeper."

Phil didn't reply right away. She really did look like an injured innocent. Her chest was heaving with anger. He couldn't believe it. They were having their first fight. They had never been at odds with each other before. He scratched his head and did a quick rethink. Perhaps he was wrong. She had always paid heed to his advice in the past. He had hoped that the romance between Eden and Ben would have petered out before the summer was through and she would go back to Maui unscathed. He realized now that Eden had completely made up her mind about Ben Alexander. Trust a woman to be so sure.

"Eden," he said finally, "you're too young to know what love is." Trying to soothe her ruffled feathers, he added, "I mean, you've just turned twenty. You've had crushes on guys before. Why are you so attached to this one, anyway?"

He sounded so patronizing that Eden replied with a snide "Well, I suppose your being just a couple years older makes you an expert on the subject. And how should you know? You've never been in love before!" Phil frowned and pain showed on his open face. For a moment there, Eden softened and felt remorseful for her anger toward him. She was famous for hitting the nail on the head with her off-the-cuff comments.

"I'm off beam, aren't I? Sorry."

"Well, it's not your fault it's hopeless. You can't order a person to fall in love."

"Hey, come on . . . we've known each other since we were kids. At least give me a clue. Who is the lucky lady? . . . . Michiko?" Phil shook his head.

"I'm shocked that you don't already know who it is."

For a moment, Eden froze. Phil couldn't possibly mean her.

"Listen Castro, this isn't a confession thing, is it?" Phil's shoulders drooped.

"Bones, don't you ever pay attention? It's not you, for gosh sakes. It's Abby, always has been."

"Abby?" she cried in amazement. "Oh brother! You might as well try for the moon."

"Hey, knock it off. I've always felt that way about her."

Eden's mind was blown. Phil liked Abby. Yikes. How could she not have guessed it before?

"Do you want me to drop you at home?" Eden asked kindly.

"Yeah, I guess so. Sorry about everything, Eden. I just lost my head when I heard . . . I, I really don't know the source, but I know you're a girl of principle. That doesn't mean I approve of your choice, though. You come from different worlds. I mean, will it work?"

"Phil, what more can I say? We've already discussed this. I love Benjamin. I don't want anyone else. He's the one who offered to help us financially with Dad's surgery. I didn't ask him, and I refused to accept his offer. I keep telling him that it will all work out with my dad. You're the one who keeps reminding me of that. Please try to understand for my sake. Ben's generous, kind, so gentle, so smart . . ."

"Hey, stop it. I get the idea. I know he's a great guy in his own way."

"Oh, what's the use of it? You won't understand until your turn comes. You'll know what I mean sooner or later."

"Pax, Eden. We're friends for life, remember! It's only because I care what happens to you that I've said something. Why don't you come over to our Bible study tonight? It's the last one we're hosting before I go back to school. At least we can pray for your dad and all."

"Thanks Phil, but I'll have to think about it!"

She dropped him off and drove home with her mind in a clutter. Life seemed doubly complicated of late.

After preparing a very early dinner, Eden walked to her tree. As she tramped over the tall grass, she could feel the late afternoon heat rise and hit her in the face. She loved the smell of eucalyptus leaves. She wished she could go back in time, and forget all the troubles of the day, but too many questions arose in her heart. Her father was a good man. Why did this happen to him? Then, there was Ben. Not in her wildest dreams did she think she would ever meet someone like him. It sounded sappy, but he was the most beautiful thing to have ever happened to her. She wondered if he was suffering from the same kind of qualms with his father. Never had she felt so torn up inside. The two men in her life were poles apart and she loved both equally, only with a different kind of love. She had never been so sure of anything in her life as she was of her love for Ben. His love brought her such happiness and a deep feeling of peace in her heart. Yet lately everything seemed to be pulling them apart. How could love to be so good, so simple and yet so complicated? It seemed as if everything was in a tangled mess. Perhaps Phil was right. She needed guidance. She made up her mind to attend the Bible study that night.

She patted the tree's trunk and knew it agreed. The walk home was done in deliberate steps. It had been a long time since she had really paid any attention to the plantation. The houses looked shabby all of a sudden. What had happened to her paradise? Had she been living in a dream world? The sun was going down. She stopped her reverie. Stepping up her pace, she took the shortcut between the hibiscus hedges and hurried home.

Later that evening Eden lay under her covers awhile before she fell asleep. The time at Phil's home had surprised her. She had expected a bunch of goody-two-shoes and instead she had been impressed with the sincerity of the little group. As soon as they started to sing hymns and a few popular worship choruses, a joy, undefinable, emanated from them. Eden felt it so strongly. The woman leading the study was Charlotte MacDougal, whose missionary grandparents had emigrated from Scotland to the islands eons ago. She was thirty-five and single, which surprised Eden because Charlotte was beautiful in a puritanical way. Her jet-black hair contrasted with her white skin and bright blue eyes. When she spoke, wisdom flowed from her lips.

Charlotte had welcomed Eden warmly and had shown genuine concern for her and for the situation in which she found herself. Raised a Catholic, Eden had a new world of praying opened to her. She had come away with a respect born in her heart for Charlotte and Phil. He was to be off to school the next day and she wouldn't see him until Christmas. They had parted on friendly terms once more. Declining Phil's offer of a ride, she instead walked home slowly, stopping here and there to look up at the stars which shone so brightly. She felt as if she could reach out and touch them. How far away yet so close they were, just like the savior himself. Charlotte's glowing face as she read from the Bible had come back to Eden so vividly. "The heavens declare the glory of God, and the firmament shows His handiwork," the missionary had quoted. Eden had been carrying the burden of everything by herself, she was told. Now she knew she wasn't alone in this, and she could leave it all in the Lord's hands and allow him to work it out.

The balmy night air was so soothing that Eden wanted to savor the moment. Her troubles seemed so insignificant compared to the magnitude of the night sky. Presently, she sighed, "Oh Lord, I know you're right here with me. I give my life to you. Please intervene and help me. If there was ever a time I needed your help, I need it now." A peace she had never known before fell over Eden as she walked home, tears filling the lovely eyes that Ben loved.

CHAPTER 19
Parting Is Sweet Sorrow

Lefty Shimizu could hardly believe his luck. For years he felt scorned by the union members and to think that because he volunteered to take Gil's place as temporary rep, he was now their spokesman. By golly, he was going to get their respect, and was diligent in his job as the acting union rep. Without Gil Andres' stable influence, however, the ability to wield so much power over men who had looked down on him in the past turned his head. His volatile leadership brought about bad feelings between the two sides. Ray Mulroney, in his valiant effort to save the pineapple crop, was forced to hire non-union laborers. Lefty was incensed and counterattacked by urging the strikers to be more militant, and the picketing was stepped up. The atmosphere surrounding the strike was becoming one of unyielding hostility. Not to be outdone by a rogue, Ray wisely called upon the Wahiawa Police Department to provide a few officers to keep the strikers from getting out of hand.

In the small community, gossip spread like wildfire. Eden's parents had gotten wind of her early morning escapade through the plantation grapevine, and she was called on the carpet. Her mother politely stayed out of the kitchen while her dad waited for her to settle down at the table. Eden already knew what her father was going to say.

"Eden," he began with effort, "I want you to know that I usually don't listen to this kind of talk. However, this one came from a trusted source. Just tell me what you were up to at the Alexanders so early in the morning." Eden explained, and her father listened and nodded his head from time to time. Her dad was too worn down to get into a hassle with his daughter. They had been at opposite poles over Eden's decision to go to Maui, and he had given in. This time he was adamant. She was not to have any contact with Ben Alexander for the duration of the strike. There was a long silence.

"Dad," she finally answered spiritlessly, "I want to do what is best in this situation. I know that the strike won't last forever, and Ben surely will understand, but I don't think it's fair to tell him over the phone. He is still my fiancé, the man I've promised to marry. You must let me talk to him in person."

Gil sighed. He was very aware of Barnes' treatment of his future daughter-in-law, and he wished he could spare Eden the difficulties he knew she could face in future. She was a good girl and would make any man a good wife, but it wasn't going to be easy with Ben's dad. He understood that the young lovers were crazy about each other. Yet, he still wasn't entirely convinced that Eden would fit in with the Alexander lifestyle. True, they came from good stock, but oil and water didn't mix, and Eden would have to learn for herself.

"Fair enough. Ben's a good man, girl. I'm sure he'll be reasonable." The interview over, Gil walked slowly out to the backyard to water the garden. Eden did the ironing and then went in search of her mother who was in the backyard taking down the laundry.

"Mom, let me help you."

"Now dear, you do enough as it is. How was your talk with Dad?"

"Oh, I can see Dad's point. If you don't mind, I must take the car and go talk to Ben."

"Alright, dear, you get going. I'll get dinner ready tonight." Janie watched as Eden hurried back to the house, carrying the weight of the world upon her shoulders.

They met at the cafe. Ben was livid and said things he didn't really mean. He took off before giving her a chance to explain. Tears streamed down her woeful face. Her parents said nothing because her subdued behavior at dinner spoke for itself. Ben had chosen to be unreasonable. For several days he avoided her like he would the plague. Eden was wretched with misery.

The following week Ben accompanied Ray on a trip to survey the harvesting by the temporary non-union workers. The two men got out of Ray's truck and leaned against the fender. Ray was first to speak.

"I may be going too far this time Ben, old boy, but I guess it's time I said something. I need to get this off my chest anyway."

"Nothing you've ever told me has shocked me much, Ray. I'm only sorry that this strike hasn't been settled yet."

"Oh, I'm not worried about that. This is a personal matter." Ben's face became guarded.

"I don't want to talk about Eden, if that's what you mean."

Ray took his time. "Why are you doing this to her? That girl is the best thing that has ever happened to you, man. I can see that she's pining away for you. If I didn't know she wanted you, and if I were twenty years younger, I wouldn't hesitate."

"Stay away from her, Mulroney," Ben warned. "What do you want me to do, pull the same stunt my father did?"

"I'm not talking about your father, but since you mentioned him, let me ask you, what does he have against the girl? Why are you letting him influence you now? You never let him influence you much in the past."

"Well, what do you suggest that I do? She won't accept my offer to help her father. She's her father's daughter alright. Stubborn to the core. Andres says it's best that we don't see each other until the strike is settled. Can you believe that one? If there is one thing I can't tolerate, it's malicious gossip. Perhaps Dad was right after all. We come from two different worlds. Eden's too young to get married, he says. You know, he suggested I go to the new plantation in the Philippines for six months." Ben's head began to throb, and he rubbed his forehead.

Visibly perturbed, Ray ran out of patience. "The trouble with you, Ben, is that you're hung up on your family. You rant and rave about independence, yet you let your misguided sense of family obligation ruin your judgment!" This time Ray had really gone too far.

"You think I haven't thought this thing through?" Ben exploded. "I hate seeing Eden's face cloud up whenever Dad is condescending towards her. She gets this pained expression on her face. She must toughen up, learn how to guard herself, is all. I keep telling her to leave things as they are. Dad will never change. So much hassle for nothing. It makes me feel all knotted up inside. I don't know why she doesn't let up. When she's like that she reminds me so much of . . ." The scene before him swirled. Ben's head ached, and to steady himself he turned and grabbed at the truck's passenger door but slipped to the ground. Ray reached to catch him, but not before the blond head hit the side of the door. A look of horror came into Ben's face as the older man revived him and guided him back into the vehicle. It was several hours later, after Ben's doctor had been located, that Ray thoughtfully picked up the phone and called Eden.

"Eden, Ray Mulroney here."

"Hello Ray. It's so nice to hear your voice."

"My dear, I'm afraid I have some distressing news. Ben slipped and fell today and hit his head against the door to my work truck."

"What? Is he alright?" Eden responded with alarm in her voice.

"Yes, he's doing ok. We had his doctor in to see him."

"Thank God! Is it possible to visit him? I long to see him."

"I know, my dear, but I think it would be better if we go easy with him for now, give him some space."

"What do you mean?"

"I think he may have regained at least some of his lost memory today."

Eden gasped.

Ray continued, "That, and he's got the weight of the contract renewal and strike on his shoulders. He's feeling pressure from his dad. And he still hasn't totally gotten rid of that tropical bug he contracted in Thailand, which makes him feel weak. Plus, he's stubborn and won't admit how much he misses you. I'm so sorry about that."

"Did he say anything about his memory?"

"No, I just gathered it from the way he acted. If he did, in fact, regain his memory, he's going to have to sort through what he's going to do about it."

"Ok, now I see why you said we need to give him space."

"I'm sure Ben will share everything with you in time."

Eden sighed deeply. She knew Ray was right and it would be better to wait and let Ben come to her.

"Thank you for sharing with me, Ray. Please keep me updated. I'll give O-ma a call."

"Don't worry, I'll be in touch. O-ma would love to hear from you. Have a brave heart."

Ray said good-bye and hung up, feeling a bit uneasy. "I hope this works out," he voiced out loud.

Plan A had gone terribly awry.

Across town, the following week, Tony was on his way to see Eden. He couldn't believe his good fortune. The liberating news had come just in the nick of time when he was ready to chuck the whole photography bag for a ticket back home. He stopped at the cafe but hadn't found Eden at work. He could never keep track of her schedule anyway. When he inquired about her whereabouts, poor Mrs. Chang didn't know what to think. She was beginning to worry about Eden.

He found her at home pulling up cassava in the garden. He couldn't hide his excitement and lifted her up and twirled her in the air.

"Eden, doll, we did it! We did it!" Round and round he spun a laughing Eden.

"Tony, please, please put me down," she squealed for mercy. "I'm getting dizzy!" She let out a breathless, "What's got into you?"

Tony laughed out loud and then calmed the savage beast in him. Gently, he eased her onto her feet.

"Listen Eden, remember those glossies I showed you?"

"Yes, I do."

"Well, I took your advice, and I did call Abby. She referred me to Mark Benton, of Orientale International modeling agency. As a favor to her, he agreed to see me. He was wild about my idea of entering my photos into the Hawaiian Perfumes Poster Contest and gave me the impetus I needed. Listen to this, Eden: out of the hundreds of photographs entered, they've selected our photo!!! We've won, doll. Did you hear me? I said we've won! The advertising rep called a little while ago and wants an interview with me and, of course, with you!!"

"What are you talking about? Which photo, and why me?"

"Remember that photo of you in the gazebo? They've selected that one for their new perfume, 'Paradise!' We'll be rich, my dear, as in one hundred thousand dollars rich. We'll split it 50-50. After all, I couldn't have done it without you! That contract, to be the new spokesperson for 'Paradise,' is the dream of a lifetime. I've always known you'd make a terrific celebrity!"

"A hundred thousand dollars? Contract?" Eden could scarcely take it all in. "Anthony Robertson, what are you talking about? You never told me anything about prize money. What's all this about a contract?" Eden eyed him skeptically. "You're not playing one of your jokes on me again, are you?"

"Good heavens, would I do that?" The photographer shook his head. "How remiss of me not to tell you about all the details. Why, my dear girl, you're the new 'it' girl for 'Paradise,' their latest perfume.'" Eden eyed him, not comprehending his words. "Eden, I'm not joking about the money or the contract! They were so impressed with your photo that you've been chosen to be their new poster girl. That is, with your consent of course. No, no, don't you see, your troubles are over! Your dad will be able to have his operation sooner than you expected. Isn't that a relief? I tell you; we've actually won! I'm to receive the check in just a couple of days!"

"You mean, the money is yours, just like that?"

"Correction! The money is ours. What do you think I've been telling you for the last ten minutes? Yes, yes, yes!"

Eden quickly added up her half of the prize money with the amount they had in the fund for her dad. "Oh Tony, Dad will have more than enough to pay the surgeon! How can I ever thank you?" Released from worry, she threw her arms around the surprised New Zealander and hugged him. Her sudden gesture shook him, and he bent down and kissed her full on the mouth. Taken aback, Eden pushed him gently away. "Tony, don't…"

"Eden doll, please forgive me," he pleaded, instantly chastened. "You know how I am, I'm so impulsive. I really didn't mean to do that!"

"Don't worry Tony, I understand. What's a kiss between friends?" She paused. "Oh, my God," she cried out, placing her hands on her forehead, "Phil was absolutely right. God does answer prayer! I must call him and give him the good news. He'll blow his mind!"

"What are you blathering about? Come on," Tony released her, "let's go and tell your folks."

"Yes, I can hardly wait to see Dad's face. Now, what do I have to do for the interview?"

The Andres were taken aback to see Eden and young Tony walk arm and arm into the kitchen, but the news of the poster contest rocked them even more. Janie promptly burst into tears, while Gil stood there looking quite stupefied.

"Well, I'll be darned," was all he said. Gathering around the kitchen table, he expressed his gratitude and added, "Now Eden, can't have you using up all your prize money on your old dad. I insist that you save some of it for yourself. After all, . . ." He looked at her tenderly, but she just smiled thoughtfully at her father. This time, he didn't have any say in the matter.

Again, news spread around the plantation like wildfire. By noon the next day, everyone was rejoicing with the Andres family. Everyone except for the Alexander family, that is. For some reason, Tony kept the news to himself.

After Gil's next visit with the heart surgeon, the date for the operation was set. Abby came home for a few days to help while Eden accompanied Tony to the interview with Hawaiian Perfumes. Eden was a mass of nerves and quite flabbergasted when Hawaiian Perfumes offered her a lucrative five-year contract to be the spokesperson for the new perfume.

"Paradise," the brainstorm and guarded secret of Julia De Ponte, was an ingenious blend of tropical flowers, and its promotion was to be launched into the Hawaiian Islands during the Christmas season. The fanfare generated from the contest alerted Mark Benton, and Orientale International offered to take Eden under its wing. She could work all her life at the cafe and never come close to earning what she could with those two combined yearly salaries.

Her parents were consulted and although they were not certain that this was the best choice of careers for Eden, they gave their consent. After all, their miracle had come through their daughter. She gave her notice at the cafe, and Mrs. Chang was sad to see her go. Eden asked her parents if she could share the news with Ben. How could she not share her good fortune with the man she loved? Gil couldn't refuse. He could only hope that all was well between the young lovers.

She hadn't seen Ben for days. Ray's phone call had given her food for thought, and she had taken his advice and had given Ben the space he needed to sort things out. The good news of the last week had lifted her spirits. In her naive excitement, she forgot how hurt and upset he had been after their last meeting. She decided to give him a surprise visit. She drove to the mansion late that afternoon. Ben was found lounging in a chaise in the garden, the sunlight glistening in his hair. What pleasure it gave her just to look at him! He looked so much stronger than she anticipated. She approached him boldly. One of the things he truly liked about Eden was that she was constantly surprising him. Taken off guard, he stared at her as if she was an apparition. The little smile finally surfaced. The space between them was covered in two seconds. They embraced, kissed, and embraced again. All was forgiven. She was disappointed when he didn't take her news well.

"I'm glad that solves it, though, for the life of me, I can't understand why you'd accept help from Tony and not from me, Eden."

"Ben, I thought we cleared that up once and for all. It's not from Tony, it's just that he, we, we earned it." When he winced, she covered her slip of tongue. "I mean, it's not as if you don't earn your money, but you know what I mean," she threw out, frustrated. "The salary is fabulous. I don't earn half that much at the cafe. Tony is working on my portfolio. Here, I've brought it with me."

"Look, don't bother. I'm relieved for your father, and glad for Tony for that matter, but is that what you really want? I thought we have something special going here. When we're married, I want my wife at home, not gallivanting all over the creation. You don't know what that lifestyle is all about, anyhow. It couldn't be healthy and seems like a shallow sort of life. What about your schooling? You're so close to graduating with your A.A. Degree. Are you just going to chuck it after all your hard work?"

It was not what Eden expected to hear from her loyal fiancé. In that moment of time, Ben's handsome features contorted and superimposed onto his countenance was his father's mocking face. Something welled up in Eden and she overreacted.

"Stop it! Don't talk like that! How can you be so uncaring? My father's health is at stake here. I happen to love him very much unlike some people I know who don't appreciate their fathers. We weren't all born rich, you know!"

Ben flinched. It was the wrong thing for her to say. "So, it all comes down to that now. Money? Perhaps, I was wrong about you Eden," he said venomously, "You're just a product of your background after all."

His words cut deep, and Eden lost her temper. "Whoa, who's being a product of his background now, The Lord and Mighty B. A. Alexander? Ha! Benjamin Alan was a misnomer. They should have christened you Benedict Arnold. That's more fitting, you impossible . . . traitor! Why don't you tell me what

I have done to deserve this kind of treatment from you? I can't read your mind!" Hot tears filled her eyes. Her body shook with anger. Eden turned away from Ben. How he hated scenes.

"Eden, stop being so melodramatic. You're young and inexperienced and life is simple for you. You want everything to be just so nice. Well, life isn't always simple and nice. The sooner you learn that the better off you'll be. You certainly don't need that kind of fast lifestyle. Listen well, I'm not your knight in shining armor. I'm not the saint you make me out to be. I'm not mistake proof. I can't help it if I was born with money. Can't you understand that? It shouldn't make a difference, but it seems it does." He sounded so forlorn when he muttered, "Maybe Dad is right. I should go to the Philippines. It seems like the best thing to do in the circumstances."

Eden couldn't believe how pitiful he sounded. How could he be so blind? So much for having compassion for the man. He was forever jumping to conclusions and never giving her the chance to speak her mind. A certain resolve rose within her. She wouldn't give Barnes Alexander the satisfaction of seeing her whipped. Recalling Ray's strange phone call, she brushed the tears from her eyes.

"It's that other girl in the photo, isn't it?"

"What photo?"

"Oh, don't play so dumb! The photo in your Bible!"

"Eden, I . . . you don't know the circumstances." Eden's perception had always surprised him, but this time he was startled.

"No, don't Ben, don't patronize me. Don't say another word. I may be young, but I'm not stupid. Go ahead, do what your father has dictated to you. Go to the Philippines. See if it makes a difference to me. At least, I know what I must do." She unceremoniously took off her ring and handed it back to him. When he wouldn't take it, she left it on the lawn chair and ran to her car. Wordlessly, he watched her drive away from the mansion. He fought for control, picked up the ring and threw it into the koi pond. A bewildered Amoʻo watched her beloved master Ben storm into the house and slam the door to his study.

Eden cried her eyes out when O-ma broke the news to her that Ben had left almost immediately for the Philippines. The two women embraced and promised to keep in touch, each with tears in her eyes. Eden's parents were stunned and blamed themselves. Their closest friends couldn't believe the unpredictable rise and fall of the Andres family's good fortune and blessings. Feeling crafty, Lefty Shimizu hid his evil triumph from his good friend, Gil Andres. Suddenly life seemed so unfair, and it was Eden who felt the most desolate. She couldn't make herself write to Franny, let alone talk to Phil. There was no one to share her sorrow except Abby, and for once, her big sister was quite at a loss at what to say or do.

CHAPTER 20
For Everything There Is a Season

How ironic, the strike ended a few days after Ben's departure. Mulroney's genius once again saved the day. His brainstorm was to phase out growing pineapple bound for the cannery, which had been dwindling in profit for years. Instead, the production of fresh fruit would be emphasized, and the cannery was to be sold to the state to be remodeled into rental shops for other businesses. Diversification into other farm produce would be further developed, allowing the plantation to continue as it had been, but on a smaller scale.

There was great rejoicing on the plantation. Facing the reality of the times, the union members agreed to compromise, and the crop had been salvaged. The work force was reduced by the company offering early retirement. Most of the older workers happily accepted the opportunity. Many of the families were able to find moderate income housing and moved away from the plantation into their own homes in Wahiawā and neighboring Mililani. These included several of Gil's closest friends, but his family still needed their plantation home, and so the Andreses stayed on.

Lefty Shimizu, forced to accept the settlement, resigned his temporary post with bitterness, and took off to the mountains for a prolonged hunting trip. With the settlement of the strike, and the return to work of the old head engineer, Matt Campbell, Barnes Alexander and his wife Ethyl left for a brief respite to Kaua'i. Things settled down and Ray Mulroney once again felt he had a grip on his management of Aloha Nui Loa. Life was good.

Thanksgiving turned out to be more memorable than ever. Despite all the hardships leading up to Gil's surgery, the Andreses were feeling more than blessed. No matter that they didn't have their own home yet. They had Gil's health back and their children to be thankful for. What more could they ask for? Abigail and Eden doted on them. Albert and the twins called to wish them a happy day. Their precious older son Robert was enroute home.

Fortunate to be of a strong constitution, Gil Andres recovered more quickly than expected from the surgery. As the family sat at the table to give thanks to the Lord, Eden hid her personal heartache behind a grateful heart. God had given her father a second chance at life. Three months after the operation, Gil could be seen walking around the plantation with his new dog Rusty. Robert, recently returned from his tour of duty in the Air Force, intended to start classes at the U.H. in the Summer. With someone at home to help and her father on the mend, Eden carefully decided to move in with Abby. She didn't relish daily commuting to and from Honolulu and took turns with her big sister to come home for the weekend to help out. Abby, thankfully relinquishing her role as chief cook to her sister, gladly welcomed her company. Greatly challenged by her new job, Eden worked long hours and was still very much overwhelmed with the fact that an aspiring chef had been transformed into a poster girl.

Tony quickly followed suit and rented a studio in Waikīkī. Winning the contest for Paradise brought him the free-lance work he dreamed of, and his father's approval. Reginald Robertson postponed his trip to Hawai'i and instead sent Tony an open plane ticket to come home to New Zealand when the time was right. Tony was flying high these days. He and Eden enjoyed hitting the night spots together in Honolulu and Waikīkī.

"I've finally accepted God's will for my life," Phil said forthrightly when he called at Thanksgiving. Eden, accustomed to Phil's way of talking, waited for him to explain his statement. "Michiko and I are getting married!" There was a gasp on the other end of the line. Phil always managed to come up with something different, but this one was totally unexpected.

"Oh Phil, I'm so happy for you and Michiko." Tears came to her eyes.

"We're not going to wait," he continued with a slight catch in his voice, "and you, my good friend, are invited to the wedding. It will be small, just the family and close friends next week."

After their lengthy talk, Eden didn't know whether to laugh or cry. What a twist of fate, that it would be Phil who was marrying and not her. Ben's name never came up in the conversation. Phil had enough sense to allow Eden her private grief. He may have been slow to get it, but he finally understood what she had meant about committed love. Once he had seen his infatuation with Abby for what it was, he was able to let go of it and see Michiko in a new light. She was beautiful, everything he wanted in a wife. He felt extremely fortunate and happy. Why shouldn't Eden be happy too? He daily bombarded heaven with his prayers for a reconciliation between the union man's daughter and the plantation owner's son.

The "Paradise Girl" was in constant demand. Eden was relieved she could be selective when her phone buzzed with job offers. Keep busy, that's what she told herself. With appearances for Hawai'i Perfumes, she didn't have time to think about Ben and it helped to ease the pain of their broken engagement. She was happy when Sun Hawai'i offered her a lucrative contract to model their new swimsuit line. Pictures of a more streamlined Eden under the trade name Sabina started to appear in various magazines and locations all over the islands. Janie Andres, who loved all her children, was justly proud of Eden and began a scrapbook of her assignments.

With the late autumn rains, Eden's soft heart got the better of her. The weather turned decidedly cooler and one drizzly afternoon, she penned a letter of apology to Ben. When she received no response, she reasoned that it was due to the location it was sent to. The Philippine mail wasn't known for reliability. Not the type to give up hope so easily, she prayed for Ben's return. Feeling optimistic the first week of December, she sent him a gift and another letter of explanation. Surely, he would contact her during Christmas! It was her favorite holiday, a time to celebrate the Lord's birth, a time for forgiveness, love and perhaps reconciliation. She didn't receive a response and didn't know what to do next. "Rest in the Lord," she kept reassuring herself.

Christmas was three weeks away. Douglas fir trees from the Northwest were on sale everywhere, their scent permeating the air. Salvation Army volunteers could be seen and heard on street corners. People were in a frenzy with their last-minute shopping, and with getting boxes of gifts in the mail in time to make the Christmas deadline. The malls were jam-packed, and parking became a big problem. Eden and Abby hit Ala Moana Shopping Center several nights in a row and came home laughing with bags of gifts to wrap. For the first time in her life, Eden was truly able to get into the spirit of the season, of giving, and was grateful she could afford lovely presents for her family. Boxes were sent to Albert in Georgia and to the twins, who were spending Christmas with their host family in California. Every day off was spent making goodies with her mother. There were **plum puddings** and **stollens** to make for friends, cookies to bake and to decorate, and a gingerbread house to set up on the dining table. The old house smelled so Christmassy. Gil's gorgeous poinsettias and the decorated Norfolk pine gave it a festive air.

Orientale International staged a Christmas show for the House of Hawai'i department store and Eden was kept busy until the twenty-third. When on Christmas Eve a mysterious package bearing the Alexander Crest arrived, Eden opened it with anxious hands. A note from O-ma Alexander was tucked inside. Carefully wrapped in beautiful Christmas paper, was a framed print of the old plantation picture she had admired so much. Ben would not be home for Christmas, she read. Disappointed, she shed a few tears when she remembered the time Ben had so proudly showed her the plantation photo collection. Touched at the sweet gesture, but hurt she had not heard from Ben, she gently placed the print on her desk and watched the rain splash against her old bedroom window.

Christmas Eve was celebrated at mass in Wahiawā with her parents and Abby, as Robert had gone to be with Natalie and her folks. It was rather quiet without the twins, and Eden didn't hesitate when her mother suggested she invite Tony to join them for Christmas dinner. He accepted gladly –life was finally going his way.

Early Christmas morning, the Andreses called Al and the twins. After taking turns on the phone, Eden excused herself and slipped away to her tree. She needed some time just to be alone. She had hoped that Ben would at least have called her on this blessed day. Abby shook her lovely head, as she watched her sister pick her way along the path that led to the stream.

O-ma Alexander, bless her heart, kept Eden abreast of Ben's doings with calls and notes from time to time, but Eden couldn't make herself respond with hope. Her brother Robert's gift, the newest CD from Eden's favorite **slack key** guitarist, Keola Beamer, was apropos. His song, "Our Time for Letting Go," played over and over in her mind. Was this the time for letting go? She missed Ben so crazily, but when she didn't hear from him at Christmas, she felt perhaps it would be better to just let go of him.

On New Year's Eve, Eden opened another package from O-ma. It turned out to be a thick letter mailed from Maui. Ben, she learned, was going on to Thailand after his six-month stint in the Philippines. He had fitted the missing puzzles of his lost memory and now needed to search for a Laotian girl he had met in Bangkok. His explanations were sketchy, and she didn't have all the details, but she gathered they had been separated somehow when Ben had taken ill. Tai had disappeared among the thousands at one of the refugee camps after a terrible storm, the same time Ben had been brought home ill. "Take heart, child," she encouraged, "I'm sure all is not what it seems. Ben will be home soon to explain everything. You'll see." Shocked, but not surprised, Eden received the news calmly. She knew in her heart when she found the picture in Ben's Bible that something like this was in the offing. How strange that she didn't shed one single tear. Instead, she kept the information to ponder in her heart. When she called her parents to see what they were up to on New Year's Day, they sensed something was very wrong, but were discreet enough not to press her about it. They had a feeling she was thinking about Ben, and even though they didn't talk about her broken engagement, it didn't stop both from feeling equally sad and remorseful about the whole thing.

During Mr. Andres' recuperation, Mrs. Andres had given up her frivolous matchmaking career and devoted herself to caring for her husband. With her full-time care, his health returned capitally, and in another three months' time he was back at part-time work. The crisis passed and life resumed its normal course. It was planting time and Gil Andres became occupied with the work gangs preparing the way for the plowed fields to be **papered**. His union position was temporarily taken up by Mike Castro, giving Gil the break he desired.

Ray stopped by frequently when the girls were home. Eden began to suspect that his interest in the family centered around her sister, but Abby didn't show any inclination to getting romantically involved with anyone at this time. Though his friendly self, Ray was too close of a connection with Ben, and Eden always felt uneasy in his presence. It didn't bother Ray, for with Abby's cooperation, Plan B was still in effect.

In late January, thrilled with the unprecedented burst of sales of "Paradise" in Hawai'i, the marketing executives of Hawaiian Perfumes decided to promote the new scent all over the South Pacific. As their spokesperson, Eden was due to make appearances and shoots in various venues in Tahiti, Fiji, Australia and New Zealand during March.

"Oh Tony," she informed him, "I'm so excited about this project! I'll be able to see the beauty of New Zealand myself!" Not one to miss out on anything, Tony planned his trip back home to coincide with Eden's schedule. The timing was perfect. He joyfully made plans to take Eden to meet his family on New Zealand's South Island.

Eden was eagerly looking forward to her first trip to the South Pacific. She'd never been out of the islands except for a short trip to California with Gramps, and she was curious about Tony's family. She felt a need to get away from Hawai'i and its strong memories of Ben. Even with her ultra-busy schedule, she still hadn't gotten Ben Alexander completely out of her system. That inner ache was still resident, but she refused to give it ground. Abby would find her brooding on a Saturday night, knowing full well that her sister had turned down yet another date. She didn't think this romance stuff was all it was cracked up to be. As far as she was concerned, Eden could have anyone she wanted, but that's where the difference between the sisters lay. Eden would always be a one-man woman. The phone calls continued, but Eden refused to date anyone but Tony. Abby had observed her sister with the Kiwi but had not seen any signs of reciprocation. Yes, Tony was sweet and charming, but not the one for her younger sister. She could only hope that he would realize soon that Eden only looked at him as a brother. He, on the other hand, optimistically believed it was only a matter of time before Eden would come to reason. He was content to wait.

After successful trips in Papeete, Nandi, Sydney, and Auckland, the "Paradise" crew headed home. Eden stayed on an extra week in New Zealand to meet Tony's family, who lived outside of Nelson, on the South Island.

Recalling the highlights of the visit on the flight back to Honolulu, Eden had felt like a traitor. Tony had declared himself, and she had been too kind to turn him down flat. He had kissed her on the night they had gone into Nelson for dinner. It was more fervent, this second kiss, but still there were no bells, no stars, just the pleasant comfort of his company. She would need time, she said. Full of hope, he made her promise to give him an answer when they got back to Hawai'i. He was staying on for another week to help his father with some farm decisions.

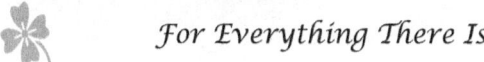

Tony's family had welcomed her warmly. Though well off, they were homey and warm, and had made her feel like one of the family. She was stupefied that their farm stretched out for several thousand acres. She had been given the grand tour via the work **Ute** and had been blown away by the thousands of sheep and deer that roamed the autumnal hills. Kit, Tony's younger brother, had given her riding lessons on his beautiful **Friesian**, Prince Andrei, and Bunty, Tony's mum, had welcomed her help in the kitchen. Under her patient tutoring, Eden was thrilled to use her **AGA** wood burning stove. She herself would love to have one at home! She learned how to make scones the proper New Zealand way, she was told, and a decent Pavlova, a deliciously light meringue dessert named after the famous ballerina, Anna Pavlova. As for jovial Reginald Robertson, well, he was secretly pleased at what a change the Hawaiian girl had wrought in his prodigal son.

One evening the entire community converged on the neighboring The Long White Cloud Farm for a **hangi**. There, Eden met Hillary Mack, the daughter of the owners of the farm. She was all rosy and sweet and genuinely friendly, and Eden noticed how she trembled when Tony introduced her to Eden as his 'old pal.' Tony was as blind as a bat. Anyone could see that Hillary was nursing a broken heart over him. Kit let it slip that everyone assumed that the two would eventually marry someday and their family farms would merge. What a midsummer's night dream the visit turned out to be. Eden made up her mind then and there to refuse Tony's marriage proposal before they returned to Hawai'i. The right moment evaded her, however, and she knew the truth had to be told as soon as Tony returned to Hawai'i. She was not the type to send Dear John letters.

"If only Ben's father had been as open and caring as the Robertsons," she agonized. The thought of Ben made her feel sad and tears fell from her cheeks unto her hands resting on her lap. Never had she cried so much in her whole life as she had in the last six months. What was the use? Ben belonged to someone else, and she was wasting time pining over the man. She dabbed her eyes, dismissed her jumbled thoughts, and slept.

The captain's voice awoke her from her slumber and her eyes opened as he announced they were to land in Honolulu in an hour's time. The flight had been long, over eight hours, and she needed a familiar face and a good soak in Abbie's hot tub.

Eden made her way to the baggage claim area which was teeming with tourists arriving from international destinations. She stopped short. Just a few feet away from her stood a familiar figure. The woman with brilliant red hair turned her head. It was Sylvia Reardon. Eden paled and tried to mix in with the crowd so as not to be seen, but it was too late. Sylvia had spotted her. Wearing a splendid white St. Laurent suit, the older woman approached her boldly.

"Why, we meet again Miss Andres." Eden could hear the veiled venom in her voice.

"Miss Reardon," Eden got out, with Dutch courage.

"Malcolm, darling," Sylvia called out to the man a few feet away, "I want you to meet one of Ben Alexander's friends. Miss Andres, this is my fiancé, Malcolm Eldridge III."

The man in a navy blazer lifted his hooded eyelids revealing pale blue eyes. Eden couldn't believe his frank appraisal of her and felt terribly uncomfortable. He was too many things at once, too polished, too practiced, and too sure of himself. He was just too good looking, almost effeminate with those long lashes and slight build. Eden shuddered – she didn't care for his type.

"Enchanté, Miss Andres," he crooned as he extended a smooth hand to her. Eden didn't like his touch either. It was too cold and told her that he'd never done a day's worth of work in his whole pampered life. She didn't want to sound severe, but in her estimation, the couple in front of her deserved each other. Not to miss a trick, Sylvia took advantage of Eden's discomposure.

"I hear that Ben is in Thailand. You know, my dear, my advice is to forget the louse. It's too unfortunate that you had to find out the hard way. Second best can be so deflating." Eden cringed. The woman had no manners whatsoever.

"Eden! There you are!" Abby's advent saved the day. Eden was so glad to see a familiar and loving face.

Mrs. Malcolm Eldridge III to-be had not been prepared for Abigail. She materialized out of nowhere, still decked out in her modeling makeup and the latest in Leimoni's Fashions, a purple and white sheathed mu'umu'u that hugged her curvaceous figure. Malcolm, instantly bowled over with her theatrical beauty, had to be led away by the haughty heiress like an unwilling dog on a leash. Having witnessed the scene between Sylvia and her vulnerable sister, it was too much for Abby. "Cat," she hissed at Sylvia's undignified exit, hips swaying like mad.

Eden tried to brush off the encounter, but Sylvia's wicked words had already hit their intended mark. Abby placed a protective arm around her sister and led her to the waiting taxi. After a bowl of saimin, she got Eden to take a nap. They had the whole night to catch up on news and to share the secrets of their hearts.

They weren't the only ones sharing secrets. Later that day, O-ma Alexander opened the email from Ben. Her heart skipped a beat. He was leaving Thailand and coming home. No explanations except that he had accomplished his task. Not daring to hope, she prayed somehow that he had come to his senses. There had been too many unnecessary hurts and misunderstandings lately, and she wanted the chance to make things right between her grandson and Eden. She could only wait.

Out on the patio of her home on Maui, she called for Ipolani, her housekeeper and cook, to bring her a glass of iced tea. With the April issue of Tropics magazine in hand, she leaned back into her Adirondack chair. She flipped through its pages, enjoying the coolness of her drink. An ad for Hawaiian Perfumes caught her eye. There, in the gazebo in the garden of the Alexander estate, stood Eden and Ben in a lover's embrace. She adjusted her reading glasses upon her nose and stared. The tiny note printed on the bottom on the page contained three words: Anthony Robertson, photographer. "Why, I'll be, that young rascal!"

She had heard that Tony had won some big prize but had paid no attention to the news. Her dear friends, the Robertsons, had informed her of it. Tony was due home soon, and they had canceled their planned visit to Hawai'i. When she had learned that he had been the inadvertent cause of the breakup between Ben and Eden, she had washed her hands of him. Not being successful in obtaining information from either Ben or Eden, she had learned through Amo'o and the plantation grapevine about the prize money and Eden's new job. Looking at the picture in the magazine, so many unanswered questions were answered. She turned the succeeding pages. Eden looked out at her, each page from a different setting. Delight spread over the old woman's face. "Good for you, my girl!" she said out loud. She was secretly pleased that Eden had done well for herself. If only she hadn't interfered or had persuaded Ben to stay, maybe things would have worked out for her grandson and this darling girl. She sighed deeply as she hadn't heard from Eden in a long while, and she thought it was best to let things be. Ben couldn't get back home soon enough, as far as she was concerned.

"O-ma," Ipolani called from the living room, "there's a phone call for you!" Marguerite Alexander hurried into the house, allowing the ocean breeze to turn the pages of the magazine lying there on the stool.

~

CHAPTER 21
God of the Second Chance

The H-1 Freeway was not too crowded because it was still early in the afternoon. As the baby blue Mini Cooper purred along, Eden slipped a CD of slack key music by Barry Flanagan into the player. The exquisite guitar fingering of 'Sleep Walk," filled the tiny car and soothed her. Her mind was preoccupied with thoughts of her next assignment for "Paradise." She needed a well-deserved rest, having just finished a grinding but successful schedule for the major presentation of Island Fashions at Monte Carlo's, Honolulu's newest and trendiest boutique. A few days break at the plantation would do wonders for her.

Her long hair had been cropped at the shoulders and showed off her fabulous neck and shoulders that photographers were constantly raving about. She wore a white cotton sundress, lavishly silkscreened with Hawaiian quilt patterns in bold colors. It suited her new look. In fact, she did present the very image of the beautiful young sophisticate, the look the exclusive boutique had wanted to project. Yet, deep inside was a restlessness and perhaps a longing for the good old days, simpler days of college life on Maui pursuing her culinary training.

Eden turned onto H-2, which led to Mililani and on to Wahiawā, and dismissed her thoughts. After all, today was a happy day for her family, and she wanted to arrive home in a lighthearted mood. As much as she enjoyed her new occupation, it was always a relief to leave the hectic pace of Honolulu behind and head for pineapple country. What was even better than the amenities that her job provided her was the fact that she could help her parents financially. The back seat of the car was stacked with gifts for the family. Her brother Robert had proposed to his high school sweetheart, Natalie, and the whole family was invited to an engagement luncheon. Abby, however, was still in the throes of another modeling gig, and would join them later in the weekend, so Eden found herself going home alone.

As she neared Mililani there was an immediate change in temperature. The Wai'anae Range was free of clouds and, glorying in the sight of the towering trees surrounding Wahiawā, Eden hummed as she neared her old home. A light mist was falling as she pulled into her parents' driveway. The old house looked the same, gently aging and still dear to her heart.

"Momsy," she called out, "I'm home!"

Mrs. Andres looked up from the sofa. It was Eden's voice alright, but all she could see was a pair of knees and a bundle of packages. Eden deposited the packages onto the coffee table.

"Eden, your hair! Oh, it looks great!" Eden gave her an affectionate hug. The last few months had drawn them close.

"Like it? It's the newest style. My agent, Mark Benton, suggested it for my shoot on **The Big Island**. I leave at the end of this week."

"Well, it will take some getting used to, but I must say that it's very becoming. I remember how I used to badger you to do this. That's a charming dress, dear."

Eden modeled it for her mother and at Janie's delighted laughter, handed her mother a stack of packages. She protested as she always did when Eden brought her gifts, but she loved being pampered.

"Go on, open them up. I found yours at Laura Ashley's. I can't wait for you to see what I got for Natalie." Janie loved her new linens and tut-tutted when she pulled out Natalie's nightie. It was peach, Natalie's favorite color, and was nothing more than a wisp of satin.

"The dear girl will freeze in this Wahiawā weather. I'm a flannel pajama person, myself." Mother and daughter enjoyed a throaty laugh together. "Oh, by the way Eden, you're not going to believe this, but the most amazing thing has happened." Janie appeared to be tickled with her news, and Eden decided to humor her mother.

"You've found the perfect someone for … Abigail!" she teased with mock seriousness.

"Too bad, dear," Mrs. Andres pursed her lips together, "but I've retired from that matchmaking business. It was too stressful."

"Thank you, Lord," Eden looked heavenward and sighed. "I'm glad that you've finally given up on that. You had us all worried for a while. I mean, we all wanted to win the bet."

"Bet? What bet?"

"Oh, never mind. Let's just say that I'm glad you've given up that idea of finding the perfect match for each of us. Look at Robert and Natalie!"

"Yes, they turned out rather well, didn't they?"

"They did it all by themselves, too. Don't you worry, you'll be busy babysitting grandchildren soon enough." Janie felt content. She was expecting this to be her year.

"Anyway," her mother continued, "I have better news than that!"

"This must be good. Well, out with it. What's the news?"

"Lefty Shimizu got religion!" There, she said it! Janie couldn't help the pleasure she felt when she saw that she had totally captured her daughter's attention.

"What? What did you just say?"

"I told you it was good news," Mrs. Andres chuckled. "When he saw your father after the surgery, he was overcome with guilt. Seems he confessed to both Mike and Phil Castro that he had started that talk about you and . . . Well, to make a long story short, he's repented and is living a changed life! He even apologized to your father."

Speechless, Eden sat still in her father's old recliner and took the news well. Her mother's words sank in. For the omission of Ben's name, she was grateful, but it pained, nonetheless.

"Why," her mother continued incredulously, "he gave up gambling and quit drinking cold turkey, although he still puffs on his cigars occasionally. You should see the way he dresses these days, suit and all. A bit old fashioned, if you ask me, but he attends church every Sunday and sometimes on Wednesday and attends Bible study regularly. Everyone's amazed at the change in him."

"Wow, that's very good news, Mom. I'm glad for the guy. You know me, I have no ill feelings towards him, but why would he start such a rumor in the first place?"

Seeing her daughter's wrinkled brow, Janie sought to explain further. "Well, according to Mike Castro, he blamed your engagement as the source of Dad's stress, and somehow didn't realize until the surgery that he had contributed to it himself! Also, he's been dating Gracie Sato. I think there will be wedding bells soon."

"Gracie Sato, do wonders never cease? They were always at each other's throats." Eden shook her lovely head, and on further reflection added, "Perhaps they acted like that because they were attracted to each other all this time!" Janie looked a bit flustered as she handed an envelope to Eden.

"Here sweetheart, this is from Lefty. He didn't know how to tell you in person, and he wasn't sure when he'd see you again, so he gave your dad this letter for you."

Eden was slightly taken aback. Lefty writing letters? She opened it up slowly and read the contents. It was handwritten in pencil, with a few misspelled and crossed out words, but it was what he said that brought tears to her eyes.

"It's an apology for spreading rumors about Ben and me," she shared with her mother. "He wants me to talk with Ben too, and he is truly sorry about our ended engagement."

Mother and daughter hugged, then sat there on the old couch for a long while, both teary eyed, not saying another word to each other for a long time.

Later in the evening, Eden rang Phil. She couldn't wait to talk to her old friend. They did talk, long into the night in fact, and she listened patiently as Phil told her that the Lord works in mysterious ways. He expounded on the importance of Lefty's born-again experience and conversion. She was gently surprised and secretly thrilled when she learned that Michiko was going to have a baby. Wishing Phil and his wife a happy birth, she hung up feeling in need of a visit to her beloved tree. She needed to think.

After the festive luncheon with Natalie's family, Eden took a walk around the plantation and ended up at her favorite place. It seemed to her that everything in life came in stages. Just a little while ago, she and all her friends were kids playing in the mud. Then, before they knew it, everyone had gone off to college or trade school. Now, one by one, they were getting married and having children. It was going to take some getting used to, seeing her good friend Phil or her brother Robert as doting fathers, not to mention as loving husbands, remembering their madcap adventures as kids! Yet, she had to admit, they all had matured in the last year.

She sat herself down at the base of the great tree, her mind still awhirl with so many thoughts. So, Lefty's life had been changed for the better. Phil had come to love Michiko. Now, what about herself? Hadn't she loved Ben, and hadn't he loved her? Yes, she loved him with all her heart, and she knew that a part of her would always love him. She could feel his absence more keenly as she leaned back against the great tree. Ben was gone, and the place felt so empty without his endearing spirit.

She closed her eyes tight to shut out the memories. The thought of him possibly married to someone else was hard to bear. Dear Lord, would she be able to trust in love again? Tony's cheerful face came to mind. Yes, she was fond of Tony, but he deserved more than fondness from a wife. She looked up at the hanging branches of her dear friend and nodded. She had to face the truth and would have to tell him she couldn't marry him. Why had she waited? Was it because of indebtedness or procrastination? Perhaps, it was a reluctance to hurt his feelings? Sighing, she was determined to tell him while they worked at the shoot on the Big Island. She watched the swordtails swim peacefully in the stream for several minutes, patted her tree, and walked home full of resolve.

That very week, a travel-weary Ben Alexander arrived on Maui one night earlier than planned. It had been a long time since he had visited his grandmother at her beach home on Maui, and he was glad for the break before returning to the plantation. The blond hair was long and untidy, and he had grown a beard which made him look like the adventurer he had been the last few months. Passing the car rental booths, he decided to save O-ma the trouble of coming to get him and rented a car. Waiting for the vehicle, his eyes fastened onto a poster tacked on the wall behind the clerk at the Avis counter, and he did a double take. The girl in the blue monokini looked remarkably like Eden Andres. On closer inspection, he saw that the girl's hair was cut bluntly, barely touching her shoulders. This model was posed in the break of a small wave. It couldn't be Eden, he reasoned, the model had a different look and appeared too comfortable in the ocean. After examining it for a few minutes, he remained unconvinced and asked the clerk where he could get one like it. The homely salesgirl looked him over. The fantastic looking man with the gorgeous hair and scraggly beard looked like any maiden's answer to prayer. She took the poster down and handed it to him. Surprised at her gesture, Ben rewarded her with a playful wink. The girl positively swooned.

Before driving out to O-ma's home in Spreckelsville, he rushed into Kahului and stopped at the grocery to purchase some flowers for her. At the check-out counter, he spotted the **macadamia chocolates** and Kona coffee. His mouth started to water as he inspected the picture on the box of chocolates. He grabbed one of each. Dumping his purchases onto the passenger seat, he headed for the beach home on the North Shore. The house was still lit up. His grandmother was quite the night owl. He slipped quietly into the carport and knocked at the back door.

"O-ma!" he called out, "where are you?"

Alika, Ipolani's husband and Marguerite's major domo, appeared at the door. He smiled when he saw who it was. A cautious O-ma in her housecoat standing behind him, clapped her eyes onto her beloved grandson.

"Benjamin!" she cried out, "you're not supposed to be here until tomorrow!"

Ben handed her the bouquet and followed her inside, as Alika took his bags to the guest room. His grandmother immediately placed the flowers in a lovely Dresden crystal vase. His long arms wove around her.

"Oh, how good to have you here, darling. Let me look at you." He smiled down benevolently at his grandmother. "That beard makes you look like your grandfather. Oh, what am I doing? You must be tired."

"You're a sight for sore eyes, my adorable O-ma. Yes, I'm tired maybe, but I'm mostly starving. What do you have to eat around this joint?"

His grandmother immediately brewed a pot of the Kona coffee and served him a cup along with a bowl of her **Portuguese bean soup** and a plate of cornbread sticks that Ipolani had made earlier in the day. Ben tucked in like a starving man, and after seeing him to his room with the promise that they would talk more on the morrow, O-ma retired for the night.

After a couple of minutes, she knocked on his door and called out to him. She could hear the shower running and popped her head in the door. "Benjamin, this package has mail that was sent to you in the Philippines but missed connection. It was forwarded back to you, care of Aloha Nui Loa. Since you were in Thailand, Amo'o passed it on to me for safekeeping. I think you should see who it's from."

"Just leave it on the dresser there, will you," he called out. "I'll have a look at it later!" His grandmother sighed deeply. She was so relieved to have him back.

The shower took all the kinks out of him. He felt refreshed. The lights of Kahakuloa caught his attention and he slipped out onto the patio and sank into one of the Adirondack chairs. It felt great to be on Maui. That magical tropical touch on a clear night was like balm to him. He sat there enjoying his chocolates, relishing in the sea air.

Feeling the impact of his long trip at last, Ben decided to call it a day. He spotted the Tropics magazine on the stool, and picking it up, returned with it to his room. Yawning, he opened the mosquito netting and threw the magazine onto his bed and flicked on the TV. After the cool night air, the room was too warm. He took off his terry towel robe and threw it onto the chintz covered chaise lounge. The pajama top soon landed on top of the robe. A glance at his watch told him that the ten o'clock news would be on soon.

Presently, he sat on the bed and opened his briefcase. Out fell the poster. He unrolled it and studied it once again. Not convinced that it was Eden, he wondered how it would be to see her again. He had buried the memory of her while he had worked like the dickens during his time in the Philippines. When he had sorted out his feelings and gotten a proper perspective on their relationship, he had the courage to continue with his plan to return to Thailand.

Looking hard at the figure in the poster, he couldn't believe the pang he felt in his heart. Lord, he had made one whopping mistake, he didn't need to make another. The great longing for her was temporarily pushed down, and he rubbed his tired eyes.

What a crazy wild goose chase this trip to Thailand had been. He had gotten into Bangkok with the intention of carrying out his promise to George O'Shaunessy. For a few minutes, his memories took him back into time.

It was three years ago that his good friend George had fallen in love with the Laotian orphan Tai. Ben himself had imagined himself in love with her. In fact, the whole male engineering staff did. She had chosen George, the jolly brash Irishman, and Ben had been the best man at their wedding.

Their marriage had been short lived when tragedy struck. Without much warning a sudden storm had destroyed the village where George and Tai were visiting, and, in rescuing a young child from a fallen tree, George had been seriously injured. He passed away a few days later in a makeshift hospital, after extracting a promise from Ben to take care of Tai even if it meant marrying her. Honorable Ben could not make himself deny George his last request. Tai, carrying George's child and all alone, had been inconsolable. Ben had contracted malaria and when he was too ill to fulfill his promise, Tai had slipped away to friends somewhere in Bangkok, not to a refugee camp as he had previously thought. It took some time to locate her with the help of an agency while he was in the Philippines.

Ben came back to the present. How foolish he had been in making that wild promise to marry George's wife on his friend's dying bed, or to believe that she would wait for his return. He must not have been in his right mind. In fact, he was now convinced that he had been unhinged by grief, and by his loyalty to his dear friend. George was gone. Ben had contracted that strange illness. Where had honor fled in a time like that?

What a shock it was to discover that the exotic beauty had transformed so quickly into a plump housewife. He once thought Eden reminded him of her, but he was mistaken. Has he himself changed that much in the last three years? Maybe. Perhaps the traumatic events they had encountered still affected them both. She had made George incredibly happy, but now lacked spark and seemed nervous about meeting Ben again, or at the prospect of meeting George's family in Ireland. George's parents were overjoyed to learn from Ben that he had found Tai and their grandson in Thailand. Yet, Tai was happily married with two toddlers in tow and another on the way. The oldest, George's son Michael, was the spitting image of him. The mop of curly hair was black, but the face was George's. If only he had lived to see his handsome son. Perhaps, Ben thought, George's parents would have more success in winning her over, once George's estate was settled.

Ben felt like he had awakened from a nightmare and had blamed everything on his memory loss. Funny thing about it all was that he had liked Tai's husband Keo, a thin, serious young man. The Alexander ego had taken a severe beating. "Imagine!" he chuckled at the thought of being thrown over for a young lad with not much to recommend him except a fierce loyalty to Tai and a willingness to work hard. They were crazy about each other. He envied them their happiness and had congratulated them sincerely on their marriage, after presenting them with a belated wedding present and a generous monetary gift for the children. Hugging George's son was something else again. Tears filled his green eyes, and he left immediately after extracting a promise from Tai to keep him abreast of things in the future. The closure of the most stressful part of his engineering career left him feeling spent emotionally. He decided then and there to fly straight to Maui from Honolulu. He needed O-ma. He needed to sort things out in his mind, and she was always so patient, so willingly approving of him. It seems he was doing a lot of sorting lately.

During the long plane ride to Hawai'i, he was able to gain some equilibrium to his inner turmoil. He looked up to heaven and said in a prayerful voice, "He's an angel, your son, George. I found her, I found Tai. I am so sorry I was late, but you will be glad to know that she is happy with her new family." His eyes teared and the thanked the Lord for closing that painful chapter of his life. The burden of Tai was gone, and he felt so liberated, he decided to quit smoking cold turkey!

He came back to the present when the whiff from the perfume ad of the magazine caught his attention, and he picked it up. Flipping the pages idly, he came to the same shot as the swimsuit poster. Lines formed on his forehead as he inspected the page and blinked wildly. The picture had been shot at Makapu'u Beach, on O'ahu. The poster model's name printed in the credits was "Sabina." It felt like a blow to his solar plexus. It had to be Eden!

He turned the pages, allowing the scent from the perfume to lead him on. The magazine automatically separated at the ad for Hawaiian Perfumes. Ben found himself staring in disbelief at a photograph of the gazebo on his family's estate on Aloha Nui Loa. He wasn't too sure if he could handle any more shocks tonight, but there before his incredulous eyes stood a young couple --it was Eden and himself dressed for the Summer Fête.

"Paradise," it read in bold letters across the bottom of the page. The photographer's name, Anthony Robertson, was printed below it. At the sight of his cousin's name, anger –or maybe it was resentment– stirred up from deep within him, but his face instantly turned tender when he looked at Eden's lovely image. In an instant he realized how much he had really lost. "It's all my fault," he admitted begrudgingly, he hadn't given her the chance to show him the winning photograph.

His attention was held as he turned the succeeding pages, and Eden's face stared back at him. The debutante standing in front of the Sydney Opera House, dressed in an off shoulder, lime green, sequined evening gown bedazzled him. The college kid clad in a jaunty khaki safari outfit in the hot Australian sun with Ayers Rock in the background caught at his heart. How beautiful she looked with that wonderful tan, with just a hint of sadness around the eyes. The next shot showed her posing with a shepherd and his dogs at a sheep station in New Zealand. She was wearing jeans, a checkered shirt tied at the waist and rubber Wellingtons. The photo brought a tender look to his face. Turning the page, he about fell over when he took in the princess in a fuchsia and gold sari, standing in the foyer of a hotel in Nandi, Fiji. The black framed glasses were slipped on as he hungrily studied the photographs. She was even thinner than he remembered. The last picture hit him hard. Dressed in a red and white **pareo** with flower leis adorning her perfect form, she resembled the tremulous young bride on her Tahitian honeymoon. "The many faces of Woman," he groaned out loud.

Seeking relief from the shock he was feeling, he put the magazine down and turned his attention to the TV. The last night's competition of the annual **Merrie Monarch Festival** on the Big Island was coming to an end. It was a live broadcast, and the announcers were showing off their colorful apparel.

"**Mahalo** again especially to Island Fashions for providing the whole television crew with our gorgeous aloha wear! Don't forget folks, catch their Spring Collection fashion show Wednesday night at the Keauhou Beach Hotel in Kona." A short clip of a fashion show held in Hilo that day was shown, and Eden's comely form flashed by. Astonished, Ben's eyes were glued to the TV as she strutted down the catwalk, her body draped in a red and gold **sarong**, with her hair pulled severely away from her face and intricately wrapped with several strands of **crown flower** leis.

"My God," was all he could utter. He felt shell-shocked.

"This is Kinau Amano wishing you **ā hui hou mālama pono** and a pleasant goodnight."

The news came on immediately, finding Ben standing, eyes blinking furiously. He flicked off the TV and sank into the wicker chair. Drawn once again to the magazine, he flipped through it until he came to the photo he wanted, the one of Eden at Ayers Rock. He always knew that she would look fabulous in fashionable clothing, but this was too much. She looked chic and alluring all at once. Where was the young innocent he had fallen in love with? Where was she? Was she happy? What had he done to her? "Oh God," he exclaimed out loud, "what have I done?" He looked back at the photo and studied her face with memories of the previous summer flooding his soul.

Suddenly, he felt hot and confused. Indecision was written all over his handsome face. What should he do now? How can I make everything right, he asked himself? He had forced himself to believe that the love he had for Eden was only fleeting and was somewhat shocked at the pain he felt in admitting he still loved her. He didn't believe it was coincidence that had led him to all these reminders of her. Was it divine providence? He couldn't be sure.

He emptied his briefcase until the battered Bible fell onto the bed. Quickly turning the pages, he found what he wanted. It was one of his mother's favorite quotes. "By the mouth of two or three witnesses every word may be established."

A piece of paper fell onto the carpet. Ben stared at the faded photo of George, Tai and himself. Carefully holding up the old print, he remembered what Eden had said so long ago. He had wondered how she had discovered another girl was involved. Now, he knew. Lighting a match, he watched as the flames engulfed the old photo, letting the ashes drop into the fireplace.

He looked up and saw the package on his dresser, and quickly tore off the wrapping paper. With the prescription fitted diving mask in his hands, he brightened up. It had to be from Eden. He searched the box and found two letters that were postmarked the year before. He opened the thicker of the two letters which began, "Ben darling . . ."

CHAPTER 22
Faith Is the Substance of Things Hoped For

Hawai'i, the largest of the eight major islands in the Hawaiian chain, more than intrigued Eden. Also called "The Big Island," it was remote, even wilder than Maui and appealed to her sense of adventure. Reading Armine von Tempski's novels about the Big Island only perpetuated this attraction. Seeing it through the author's eyes, she had promptly fallen in love with **paniolo** country, especially **Waimea** with its rolling hills, tall grasses and eucalyptus groves. Earlier in the week, a savored lunch with her co-workers at the popular Merriman's proved delightful. Yet, as much as she loved **Kamuela**, as the Hawaiians call Waimea, there was something about **Kailua-Kona**, urban developed as it was, that still retained its old Hawai'i flavor and caught at her heart. Having spent her growing up years at Aloha Nui Loa, near the mountains, it was a delicious treat to be close to the ocean, and the weather on this western coast of the Big Island was heaven itself. Eden felt that the soft sea breeze that blew through Kailua-Kona, or Kona town, as the locals call it, could cure almost any ills. She'd read that Robert Louis Stevenson had come here to convalesce, stating that the air was like fine wine. Surely, her heart didn't ache so painfully over Ben Alexander when she was in this lovely seaside town.

Today, she had gotten back to Kona town much later than she had expected because she and Chrissie, one of the models in her show, had decided to check out the **Kīlauea Volcano** output at Kalapana. It might be their only opportunity to do so, and they didn't want to miss seeing it. They weren't disappointed.

The sight of all that steam rising hundreds of feet into the air where the lava flow met the sea kept Eden's attention far too long. Chrissie had pleaded with her to quit that historic site if they were going to make it back in time for their show. They were forced to backtrack because of closed roads, and Eden had driven back to the Keauhou Beach Hotel from Kalapana like a madwoman. Chrissie had affectionately nicknamed her the "Marathon Woman." The Island of Hawai'i, twice as large as her beloved Maui, made driving around it in a hurry close to impossible.

Joining the photographers Niall McKay and Tony after their show, the two women raised a number of eyebrows. By now, Eden was constantly recognized around the islands as the poster girl for "Paradise," and Chrissie's silvery hair and alabaster skin made many a folk gasp at the sheer delicacy of the British beauty. The girls had thoroughly enjoyed being tourists, but after working for several hours, they were bone-weary. Now seated at the lounge of the refurbished hotel, Eden finally felt she could let her hair down. She could relax in the old hotel that was built over the water. After a pleasant dinner and the companionship of Chrissie and their escorts, she excused herself to repair her make-up.

She happened to glance across the dining room as she headed for the lady's room. Partially hidden by a small **fish tail palm**, a familiar looking figure sat drinking coffee. Eden stopped in her tracks, heart pounding, hands clenching. The Indy Jones look-alike gent with the reddish-brown beard sitting alone resembled Ben Alexander! It couldn't be Ben, she mentally rebuked herself.

Suddenly, she felt unsure of herself and stopped to lean on the back of a dining chair. Regaining her composure, she made a dash to the lady's room, and once there had to pinch herself.

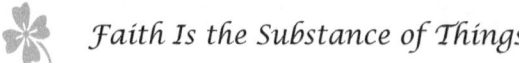

What was the matter with her? She couldn't believe she was reacting like this, after a mere glimpse of a man who just happened to look like Ben Alexander. In the past few months, she felt she had succeeded in purging herself of the memories of her ex-fiancé. She splashed her hot face with cold water and dabbed the moisture off with a tissue. After applying blush and lip-gloss, she tidied up her hair, and dabbed behind her ears and wrists with "Paradise." Looking herself over, she adjusted her black knit dress, which left her shoulders bare and was a bit too short for comfort. A glance at her frivolous strappy shoes brought comic relief. She had to wear so many different kinds of shoes these days, the thought of which boggled her mind. These were flimsy and cramped her feet a little, but she couldn't resist them because they were so pretty.

Warily making her way back to the table, a great weight of anxiousness fell off her shoulders as she noted that the bearded stranger had gone. Upon reaching her table, Tony placed a possessive arm around her, but she stiffened and pulled away. He was surprised at her withdrawal.

"Niall and Chrissie have gone on to meet the others for a walk along Ali'i Drive," Tony cooed persuasively. "Do you want to join them, or would you rather do something else?" Eden shook her head.

"I'm not up to it, Tony. I think I'll have an early night. Plus," she pointed to her shoes, "I need a break from these things."

"Are you sure, doll?" Tony asked, frankly admiring her loveliness. "You get your beauty rest then. I think I'll join them, and perhaps stop by for a night cap later."

Once out of the elevator, Eden removed her shoes and rushed to her room. The door was opened in a hurry, and in her haste was left slightly ajar. She dumped her shoes onto the floor, and catching sight of the moon over the water, she sailed to the balcony. The sea breeze, carrying the scent of tropical flowers, caressed her. All the weariness of the day left her, and lost in thought, she sat for a long while and barely heard the light knocking at her door.

"Come on in, Tony," she sighed, "I'm on the balcony."

"You shouldn't leave your door open, Eden," a deep male voice spoke from the depths of the dimly lit room. Eden stood and turned around suddenly, startled. The bearded man of the dining room paused on the threshold, a bouquet of flowers under one arm. That voice, so familiar, yet so strange, where had she heard it before? When the stranger came into the light in the sitting area, Eden gasped as Ben Alexander stood before her. Her mind had not been playing tricks on her. It had been him in the dining room. As if hypnotized, she was frozen to the spot.

If it weren't for the blinking eyes, Ben could have sworn she was a mannequin. He watched as her expertly made-up eyes fell onto the roses. They were her favorites. He'd remembered.

Her gaze travelled from his stone washed jeans, up to his white knit shirt and then to his brown distressed leather bomber jacket. Finally, she looked up at his beard, so surprisingly auburn. His golden hair was longer than she had ever seen it, and it struck her how unfair it was that he, the brute, should look as handsome as ever. Her errant heart started to pound with longing for him, and it took all her strength to keep from throwing herself into his arms and running her hands through the silky strands of his golden hair. After a long moment of silence, she steeled her resolve and turned back to face the sea. The sight of him filled her with mixed emotions, and her lovely eyes brimmed with hot tears.

Ben gently placed the flowers on the coffee table. Eden looked quite ethereal in the moonlight and more lovely than ever. He couldn't get enough of looking at her. The long hair was gone, and that blunt cut accentuated her fine cheekbones. He had expected hurt and anger perhaps, but this? What was this anyway? It was something he had never encountered in Eden before. On that china face was cool remoteness, a stiff indifference, and she seemed eternally unapproachable. He could feel his confidence slip. He waited for her to speak, but she remained as silent as the stars. Slowly, he approached her and joined her on the balcony, and for lack of something to do, rummaged his long fingers through his hair.

"Nice view," he offered lamely. "Have you been here long?"

Eden turned slightly to look up at him and frowned. She knew he was nervous, but did he have to sound like a dreamboat? She looked up at the sky. The moon rose higher. Life is a dream, she thought. This scene is a dream. No, it couldn't be a dream. He was here, standing just a few feet from her. Isn't this what she wanted, longed for all these lonely months? Yes, yes, she wanted him close to her. No, no, a thousand times no, this is not what she wanted. No, not like this at any event, when she felt caught off guard and feeling exposed and vulnerable. How could she be such a spineless idiot? Well, what did she want anyway? Hadn't she rehearsed the scene many times over in her dreams? Could life be this cruel? She hadn't figured on how upset she would be once she saw Ben Alexander again. This time it was her turn to host the battle between her heart and her mind.

"No!" she cried and leaned against the rail, as his arms came around her. She stepped away.

"Eden, please . . . listen to me," he begged in earnest. Ben grabbed her arms and turned her to face him. This time she didn't resist.

"How did you know I was here?" she asked in a strangled voice.

"Would you believe, the TV told me? Also, I attended tonight's show." He smiled, but she wasn't impressed and pulled away from him to face the sea once more.

"Would it help, sweetheart, if I told you I made a terrible mistake?"

"Don't call me sweetheart!" Eden refused to be swayed and found courage to speak her mind boldly. "Also, how dare you come waltzing in here and expect everything to be the same as it was. It isn't. I haven't heard from you in eight months. Not a phone call, nor a letter, not even one lousy postcard. Ben, don't you see, it's finished between us. I'm not the same green girl I was last summer. Go away! I don't need you."

Her spate of words hit hard. His handsome face fell. He realized the truth of her words and for a moment his courage failed him. She had changed, the little minx. He saw a steely strength he never knew she possessed, and at once, he felt more admiration for her. His mind raced for a solution out of this predicament. He wasn't getting through to her as he had hoped, and for a moment he felt a measure of fear of losing her forever. With the solo trump card left, he decided to throw caution to the wind, and give up his Alexander pride.

"Eden, you're not the only one who's changed," he pleaded wearily. "I've been through a lot of changes myself, and I've never before admitted this kind of thing to anyone. Look, I've been a complete jerk, a blind fool. Call me what you want. There is one thing I know. I've hurt you and I've felt enough remorse to last me a lifetime. I'm truly sorry for the pain I caused. Can you find it in your heart to forgive me? I don't think I can live with myself if you don't."

His voice caressed like the breeze. Ben turned her around slowly and Eden tried to turn her head away, but his hands held her chin firmly. She closed her eyes tight. She knew that if she looked into his eyes, it would be her undoing, and she would lose her resolve.

"Eden, look at me!" he commanded, and then added placatingly, "Please. If you can look at me and tell me to my face that you don't love me, then I'll believe you. I'm not going to go until you forgive me. I don't want to make another mistake." He dropped his hands down to his side, feeling quite helpless. The sudden movement caught Eden by surprise, and she stumbled against his hard solid chest.

Ben groaned and pulled her to him. Her tears fell onto his soft shirt. He walked her into the room to look for some tissue. Not seeing any, he sat her down on the chaise lounge, and went in search of a washcloth in the bath. He saw the white handkerchief on the counter, grabbed it, and helped to dry her eyes. Clutching the hanky, Eden composed herself, but she still wouldn't look up. Ben waited for her to speak. When she did, the tears threatened again.

"Why don't you just go away," she pleaded softly.

"Eden, please, don't turn me away. Give me a chance. I've not just come to ask for your forgiveness. Ray was right. I made this misguided promise to a dying friend. I've never loved Tai. It's you I love and need. It was only yesterday that I received the letters you sent to me when I was in the Philippines." Eden wouldn't look up, and when she spoke again, her voice was shaky.

"I forgave you a long time ago, Ben, but as you can see, things can't be the same between us." Her eyes teared up again. Ben pulled the hanky from her and dried her eyes. Something was very familiar. His eye caught the initials B. A. A. embroidered on the hanky, and he couldn't help but smile his little smile. Hope rose in his heart.

"I wondered what happened to this. Where did you find it?"

Eden looked up finally and tried to grab it away from him. Instead, her arm was held imprisoned by his hand. He looked at her eyes. She looked at his. She had never seen him look so hopeful yet so desperately afraid before. There was that vulnerability that always caught at her heart. Who was she fooling? She couldn't stay angry at him, and she had never stopped loving him. She had prayed with all her heart that he would come back to her. The look of hope told him all he needed to know. He felt his confidence return, and on the chance, opened his arms wide.

"It's been hell and I've missed you, kid." The nickname was her undoing. Her eyes softened, and she went to him fully and placed her arms around his neck.

"Oh Ben, what took you so long? I've been miserable without you."

Ben's face lit up exultantly. This was the same Eden he knew and fell in love with. He crushed her to him and kissed her deeply. They sat there, arms wrapped around each other, whispering reassurances into one another's ears, laughing and hugging as the mood took them. The world felt right again. Eden heard his brief account of his stint in the Philippines. She saw his eyes tear up as he told her the story of Tai, and heard the sob in his voice as he described how he felt about seeing George's son.

"I was so wrought up, I decided to go visit O-ma on Maui. She sends her love." Eden sighed.

"How is our dear O-ma? I have really missed her, you know."

"Oh, O-ma is doing very well, she's in fine health. When I got to Maui, we had a long talk that really comforted me. What about you and the family, and your dad?"

"Dad has recovered well although it was pretty scary when he was going through the surgery. He is back to work part time. Robert and Natalie are planning their wedding and Albert and the twins should be back in the summer. By the way, I have something to show you." She pulled out Lefty's letter from her carryon and handed it to Ben. "I've been reading it over and over since I got it a few days ago." Her eyes shimmered with tears as she watched Ben's reaction to Lefty's apology. He was surprised, but very touched and pleased.

"I guess," he sighed deeply, "we've all made changes these last few months. I don't have any hard feelings, and I'm glad the issue is settled. We'll have to touch bases with him when we get back to the plantation. What do you say, sweetheart?" Eden smiled in answer. More than anything, Ben was grateful to have her back in his arms.

"Working with Hawaiian Perfumes can be demanding at times especially when I have to make appearances, but it is very rewarding work. I get to meet so many good people. I do miss cooking, and maybe I can take up my culinary studies in the future. I haven't made you your pineapple upside down cake, you know."

Ben chuckled and then looked repentful. It was then that he tried to sincerely apologize for his previous nasty comments about her new job, because after all, if he hadn't seen that poster, they wouldn't be here together again. As far as he was concerned, she could go on with her new career.

"I wasn't thinking clearly then," he emphasized, "and I truly want to support you in your work."

"You're not the only one who wasn't thinking clearly, I was too upset myself." Eden hushed him with more kisses. She had better ideas about her future.

"Got some glasses handy, Eden? We have some celebrating to do!" Ben got up to open her tiny fridge. He found a bottle of sparkling French grape juice. It would do. They toasted, drank, and laughed some more. That happy calm was there again, and Eden rejoiced at how simple it was to slip back into their groove of familiarity. She would always feel safe and protected with Ben.

"Were you that sure of me, Benjamin Alan Alexander?"

"Well, a man has to hope you know. It wasn't until I read your letters that I realized how wrong I had been." He brushed her hair away from her face and looked into her happy eyes. Solemnly he vowed, "I promise never to intentionally hurt you, Eden. We both tried to please our fathers and look at what happened. I guess we should have listened to our hearts as well." Eden gave a silent prayer of thanks to Phil and his maker, then demurred and snuggled into his beard. He smelled of musk and wonderfully sweet and earthy. This was where she belonged. How easily the pain of the last few months eased away. Ben held her happiness in the palms of his hands.

"Is that 'Paradise' you're wearing, my beauty?" he asked after a while.

"Yes," she whispered, "I'm wearing 'Paradise,' but why do I detect the scent of chocolates?"

"Uh," Ben chuckled, "I quit smoking! Chocolate is the one thing that really helps." Eden's eyes crinkled with laughter. This was the Ben she loved and missed.

Eventually, they heard voices outside the door, and Chrissie, followed closely by Tony, chose that inopportune moment to make a grand entrance. On his way up, the Kiwi had met up with the flower girl. With a spring bouquet under his arm, he burst in confidently. His jaw dropped as he took in the celebrating couple. Shock, then disappointment showed on Tony's transparent face.

"Ta ta, I'll be back in a little while," Chrissie called out, breaking into a big smile as she made a beeline for the door. Ben was first to recover and stood up, Eden's hand still in his. "Hello cousin," he said measuredly.

"Ben, ah . . . didn't know you were back from Thailand. When did you get back, old boy?"

"As a matter of fact, I just arrived in Honolulu Saturday."

"Tony, I'm …," Eden attempted to explain.

"No, don't say anything, doll." Tony admitted ruefully, "I've always known how it's been between you two. Am I to offer congratulations?"

Eden looked up glowingly into Ben's loving eyes, and he answered for them.

"Yes."

"Well," Tony said with false cheer as he put the flowers under his arm and stuck his hands into his jacket pockets, "I wish you both the best. I guess it's back to Hillary for me, isn't it?"

Eden tried to stand up, but Ben held her firmly.

"Listen, don't get up," Tony insisted, feeling quite de trop. "Um, I'll, uh . . . talk to you both, later." He turned on his heels and rushed out of the room. Once out in the hall, he handed the bouquet to a passing tourist from Atlanta who was in the hallway getting ice from the ice machine. Taken aback, the old woman opened her mouth to speak, but the young gentleman quickly disappeared down the stairway. Feeling like a young 'un all over again, she took a sniff of the flowers and continued on her merry way.

"Oh Ben," Eden lamented, "I feel dreadful. He asked me to marry him, and I never had the chance to give him my refusal. I was planning to tell him this weekend. I never meant to hurt him."

"Leave him be, Eden, he'll be alright." Ben wouldn't relinquish his hold on her. He had come too close to losing her. He vowed, "Now that I've got you again, I'm never letting you out of my sight! Get it into your pretty head, sweetheart, you're getting married, but not to him. Understand?"

"Yes, dear."

It had taken quite some time before Ben could say goodnight, but as he wanted to fly back to Honolulu the next morning, he kissed Eden one last time and retired to his room. Whistling down the hallway, he passed a smiling Chrissie and gave her the okay sign. He couldn't wait until morning to give O-ma a call.

Back in Waikīkī the following day, Ben insisted on replacing Eden's ring. They decided to surprise her folks that night and were in for a pleasant surprise themselves.

Janie Andres was in a state of excitement. With one son engaged and this, too, it was more than she could take in. She held the letter in her hand and hurriedly read it a second time. Upon hearing her loud shriek, Gil came swiftly in from the backyard. His wife stood in the middle of the parlor with her spectacles low on her nose. She was in a state of shock, he could see.

"Janie, my dear, are you alright?"

As she nodded dumbly, he pried the letter from her hands and slowly read its contents. For once, the garrulous spokesman for Local 133 could not think of a single word to say. He sat down and scratched his head while his wife knelt at his feet and looked up devotedly at him. Gil patted her arm as she placed her head in his lap.

"It's a dream come true, Gil," she said softly.

It was quite late by the time Ben and Eden arrived at the old house. The porch light was still on. They held hands and walked across the lawn, avoiding all the toads. It was that time of year when toads seemed to come out of the woodwork. Eden held back her desire to squeal. She hated toads. Ever since she had to dissect one in biology class, she panicked whenever she encountered one. Ben laughed at her silliness, gallantly picked up his beloved, and carried her to the front step. He let her down gently and reminded himself to remove his shoes. They joined hands once more and slipped into the old house quietly. Janie Andres, looking rosy from her shower and wrapped in her old robe, looked up from her favorite chair. Spread out on the coffee table in front of her were her *House Beautiful* magazines.

"Eden! What a surprise! We didn't expect you back from the Big Island until tomorrow evening." She turned up the lamp and saw that Eden was not alone. "Ben! I mean, Mr. Alexander!" She peered at Eden and then back at Ben. She saw the glow in their eyes and Eden's ring. She stood up cautiously. "Does this mean what I think it does?" she asked expectantly.

Ben placed a possessive arm around Eden. "We wanted to surprise you. Sorry we got back so late. Is Gil around?"

"Well, ah, yes, but he's already asleep. Maybe I should wake him."

"No, Mom, don't do that. Let him sleep. Our news can wait until tomorrow."

"Oh my ... my, I don't think I can take any more excitement. Come into the kitchen and I'll make a pot of tea. This has been the day for glad tidings!"

As they sat around the table, an excited Janie Andres disclosed her news. The expression on Eden's face went from anxiousness to delight.

"Oh! Now, I've really heard everything! Will you have enough to buy the lot and build the house, too? Or will you need a down payment?"

"Listen Janie," Ben interrupted, "we can help you there, you know. Money is not a problem, I assure you."

"Now stop it, you two. Let me finish. I do appreciate your offer, Ben. You are a generous soul and when the time comes, you may buy us all the furnishings you desire, but first, let me explain." She opened the envelope from the law firm in Canada and adjusted her glasses. Eden and Ben exchanged looks.

"This is a letter from my Uncle Ah Gi's lawyer. It says here that he left a generous portion of his estate to Annie Chen Wang's eldest child. That's me. The legacy must be used to purchase a home and there is enough here to pay for a house and lot in that new subdivision close to here. Don't you see? The Lord has provided for us."

The pair read the letter together. "Well, I'll be . . . this is remarkable," Ben chuckled.

"Hmmm, Mom, we hardly knew him," Eden added, "and he really wasn't a blood relation, but a friend of your mother's family. Why would he do such a thing as this?"

"I'm not exactly sure, my dear," Janie shook her head. "I've been thinking about it all evening. I knew he made a fortune with his import-export business in Vancouver, but why he would stipulate me in his will, I haven't a clue. He had no issue himself. He never married." Her eyes twinkled. "Oh my, could it possibly be that the old rumors were true after all. If I remember correctly, he left Hawai'i when my mother married your grandfather Wang. Yes, he must have had unrequited love for my mother, your popo, Grandmother Ah Lin!"

This was all too much for Ben and Eden. They huddled closer together and felt relieved to have each other, and Janie, seeing their happiness, laughed. Yes, indeed, what a day for glad tidings it had been. Their merriment woke up Gil, and he appeared in the kitchen looking much like a disgruntled Rip Van Winkle.

"What's all the racket?" a sleepy-eyed Gil demanded.

The laughing ended abruptly. Ben stood up. "Mr. Andres . . .

Gil rubbed his eyes in disbelief. "Ben, is that you? Where did you come from?"

Once more laughter filled the tiny kitchen. It was happy, joyous laughter, straight from the heart. The disgruntlement was short lived, because Eden's dad went to bed that night the second time around, an even happier man.

CHAPTER 23
The Wedding

With the advent of Eden's twenty-first birthday and her parents' blessing, she and Ben eagerly set their wedding date for late August. They were to be wed in the gazebo where they had pledged their love the summer before. Announcing their engagement at the year's Summer Fête had brought applause from the ball goers. Reverend Steve Jamison, an old friend of the Alexanders, was called upon to officiate at the ceremony. The whole plantation was invited to the wedding, including friends who had moved away. Once more there was great rejoicing on Aloha Nui Loa, especially by the father of the bride, who rightly insisted that they serve local style food at the reception catered by Kemoʻo Farms.

The excited women in both families busied themselves with preparations. At her brother's request, Brigitte had come home, and, as Ben had predicted, Eden loved her new sister. She had seen pictures of Brigitte, but she had not been prepared for the leggy, raven haired, violet eyed beauty. Being reconciled with his daughter at long last, Barnes Alexander was brought to reason, and had given the couple his consent with gruff affection. He had pulled Eden aside at the engagement banquet that was held in lieu of the fête's traditional midnight feast.

Contrite, he opened with, "My daughter has totally chastised me, and I've seen the error of my ways. Benjamin is my only natural child, you understand. I've wanted what I thought was the best for him, but I have to admit, I haven't thought about his interests, only of my own." Eden tried to excuse him. "Oh yes, don't deny it, my girl. I've seen the look in your eyes.

Yes, I've interfered. I have not been kind to you, and I'm quite ashamed of myself. How could an Alexander presume to be so sanctimonious, I wonder? Can you find it in your heart to forgive a doddering old fool?"

"Father," Eden called him. These Alexanders, she learned, were great at apologizing.

Overcome with emotion because of his future daughter-in-law's generosity, Barnes Alexander had taken the happy couple into the library, and there behind the portrait of his grandfather, he revealed the small safe. Out came a koa jewelry box. He opened it and pulled out several pieces of jewelry and laid them on the teak table. They looked vaguely familiar to Ben and a muscle in his jaw twitched. His father looked up with moist eyes. In his hands he held a strand of Mikimoto pearls with matching earrings. On the table were several pieces of exquisite jewelry: **Hetian** and Burmese jade, a diamond tiara with matching bracelet, rings and earrings of various gems, several antique brooches, and a gold and silver locket with the Alexander family crest strung on a fine gold chain.

"These were your mother's, Benjamin. I want you and your bride-to-be to have them. This is a wedding gift to you."

It was the first time since her passing that Barnes Alexander had ever talked openly to his son about his mother, his beloved Amelia. Eden looked from father to son, and then thanked her father-in-law to-be ever so kindly. Her lovely eyes shimmered with happiness as Ben and his father embraced, eyes misty. For a moment, she was excluded from their intimacy, but it was joy she felt, not hurt. She left the room quietly to give them privacy to make their peace and joined the guests in the great ballroom.

Eden was extremely popular, and everyone wanted a hand in her wedding. Island Fashions presented her with the entire trousseau and a wedding dress by Tallie, her favorite muʻumuʻu designer. Eden's attendants, Franny, Abby and the twins, Gwen and Vera, were fitted for their dresses. Thank goodness, to Ben's relief, the two teenagers turned out to be still on the chubby side, sporting braids and braces! They, of course, idolized the handsome Ben and hung on to his every word. Tony offered to do all the photographs. Not to be outdone, Marguerite Alexander happily presented the couple with the deed of her family's Tudor home, in Wahiawā. Eden was flabbergasted. It was the wonderful estate that Phil and Eden had discovered the year before. Wise Ray Mulroney had consulted privately with Gil and had insisted on contributing to the wedding expenses. It was more than Eden could take in. Everyone wanted this union as much as she and Ben did!

What a day it was, too. It rained overnight and Janie fretted about the garden reception. Miss Emily, flying home from her annual trip to Michigan, was delayed in Los Angeles and had to take a later connecting flight home. Robert volunteered to pick her up, and got a flat tire and a speeding ticket for his efforts. With the humidity up high, Gramps felt like a stuffed bird, and refused to wear his wedding finery, causing the mother of the bride to burst into tears. Nerves were fraught until Abby came to the rescue and finally, after tall glasses of iced tea, everyone calmed down.

Amid the commotion, Eden slipped away to talk to her tree. The grass was still damp, but she made her way to her favorite spot. Standing so magnificently, Eden looked up at the great height of the Mindanao Gum. The guardian of her girlhood secrets and dreams passed the mantle to the young master. Saying goodbye to the old house would be another matter.

The gazebo was covered with roses of every color. Hushed excitement filled the air as the guests, seated on white wooden chairs, waited in the garden. To the one side there was O-ma, queenly in a pale blue Dior, next to Barnes Alexander and his petite adoring wife Ethel. Brigitte, between Julia De Ponte and Mark Benton, nodded her gorgeous head. There was Amoʻo crying buckets of tears with Kimo patting her back. Of course, there was Tony, camera in hand, smiling wistfully and giving Eden a mock salute, with his parents Reginald and Bunty Robertson, seated near him.

Across the aisle sat Janie Andres, preening with motherly pride in a lovely Tori Richard muʻumuʻu, flanked by Robert and Natalie, and Albert looking spiffy in his Air Force uniform with his date, the adorable Gigi. There was loyal Phil with a pregnant Michiko, the Castros, Lefty, decked out in his newly affected suit, with Gracie, their elderly parents and lovely Charlotte MacDougal escorted by a very proud Ray Mulroney. In back of them sat Miss Emily, looking grayer and dearer, and the Chang ʻOhana with her former boss who looked satisfied that Eden had made up her mind. Aunty Michelle, looking youthful as ever, and her family were thrilled as they sat with Gramps, who himself was looking mighty pleased as he gazed upon his granddaughter with unshed tears. How her life had been enriched by all of them!

Her shining eyes fell on Ben clad in his white coat, the emerald green cummerbund and **maile lei** to match his glorious eyes. With his golden hair combed back, chin clean shaven once more, and wide smile, she knew he was feeling on top of the world, if somewhat nervous.

"This is it, Eden girl," Gil spoke reassuringly and pressed his daughter's arm, as Alika and Ipolani and their musicians started up the old Hawaiian wedding song, 'Lei Makamae,' and hushed all the buzzing. Eden and her dad were preceded by Franny and Abby in pale gold taffeta dresses and the twins in satiny pink. The guests were all smiles as each one walked down the path and stood opposite best man Ray and Ben's groomsmen, his engineering buddies from college. The bride had chosen to wear a haku lei poʻo of **pīkake** flowers instead of the traditional veil. The fitted silk **holokū** shimmered in the sunlight. In her hands she carried a bouquet of white orchids and deep red roses.

Ben watched his bride on her father's arm, as she walked daintily over the koi bridge and up the steps of the gazebo. How serene and radiant she looked in the afternoon light that sparked the locket with the Alexander family crest hanging over her tiny bosom. To him she would always be the most beautiful girl in the world, and he would remember how she looked on this day as long as he lived. Their eyes met and held. When Ben repeated his vows, Eden felt him tremble with emotion. He meant every word with all his heart. Her vows were spoken so softly, almost a whisper that Ben had to incline his head. He knew she also was feeling the emotions of the moment.

Ray, standing by his side, couldn't help but feel smug. He could see all the future little Alexander keiki running around the old mansion. He hoped they named the first boy after him. After all, he patted himself on the back, this whole thing was his idea in the first place, and the best engineered plan of his career.

At the edge of the koi pond, Phil's young brother Ken, who had slipped out of his seat, reached in and pulled out the shiny object. It was Eden's first engagement ring. Pleased with his find, he wiped it clean on his shirt, and tucked it in his pocket. At that very moment, Ben placed the new ring on Eden's finger and Reverend Jamison pronounced them man and wife.

"You may kiss the bride, Benjamin," the reverend urged the groom. The crowd cheered when Ben didn't hesitate. "Ladies and gentlemen," he continued, "may I present to you, Mr. and Mrs. Benjamin Alexander!"

Ben pulled the SL up to the front door of the ranch house. The porch lights were the only exterior lights on. He carefully removed the cans that had been tied to the back bumper, opened the passenger door for Eden and led her up the steps. Once the front door was opened, he picked up his bride and carried her over the threshold.

"Welcome home, Mrs. Alexander." He kissed her thoroughly and put her down gently. For a moment they just looked into each other's shimmering eyes. "I'll bring the suitcases in. Go on ahead if you want to freshen up. Emma, our housekeeper, has everything ready for us. I gave the rest of the staff the night off."

Eden gently picked up her train and walked towards the lighted and winding stairway. This house of dreams was her home now, and she felt a bit awed at the prospect of being its mistress. Something caught her eye. In the open kitchen sat a bright red two oven AGA, wrapped in white ribbon and a huge bow, a gift from the Robertsons. Delight spread over her face. They remembered how much she admired the one in their kitchen in New Zealand. Touched, she couldn't get over how generous everyone had been on her wedding day.

She entered the master suite which was softly lit from two antique Tiffany lamps on either side of the beautiful koa four poster bed with carved pineapple spindles. The room had been redone white on white and a tropical fragrance caught at her breath. White flowers in white vases and white candles were everywhere. Eden eyed it all with widened eyes. Ethel, it seemed, had surprised everyone with her decorating expertise. She lit the candles which gave the room a soft glow.

A fire was blazing in the fireplace. On the nightstand sat a bowl of freshly picked mountain apples with a note from Francesca. "Well, what's his comment?" it read. Eden laughed. Her best friend thought of everything.

She surveyed the room and saw the mosquito net and brass ceiling fan over the bed. She ran her fingers over the Battenburg lace duvet. It was exquisite and so soft. She was feeling a bit nervous and wasn't quite sure what to do next. The lamplight revealed the tall trees in the ravine. Drawn by the view, the new bride walked to the balcony and pulled back the glass sliding door. The night air was damp and smelled of eucalyptus. It immediately cooled off the heated room. A dog barked in the distance. Ben came in and smiled to himself when he saw his wife dithering on the balcony.

"Careful Eden, the mosquitoes can be bad after all the rain we've had." Eden came in quickly, secured the screen, and looked uncertainly at her husband. Ben had brought up their suitcases and had also managed to bring up a bottle of Ariel's king of bubbly and two glasses. They laughed together when the bottle was opened with a large pop and the cork hit the ceiling. He poured, toasted "To us, my sweet." and downed the contents of his glass in one long gulp. Eden stared at him, her glass still held up in the air. Getting married was a thirsty business.

"Eden, uh, you're supposed to drink it," Ben smiled indulgently.

"Huh, oh ... oh yes." She took a sip and shuddered because it was so unexpectedly sour. Heat spread over her rosy cheeks. Ben threw back his head and roared. Gently, he removed the glass from her hand and downed its contents too. They sat on the love seat in front of the fireplace in silence. Eden's wedding dress glimmered in the flickering light. She could see all the planes in Ben's face. This beautiful man was now her husband. Feeling warmed by the fire, Ben got up and removed his coat.

"Sweetheart, what's that in the bowl over there?"

Eden's eyes followed his finger. "Um," she replied, "they're mountain apples. Franny brought them over from Maui." Eden stood up and handed her hubby the best of the bunch. He bit into the succulent flesh.

"Yum! It's excellent! So juicy and refreshing. I wonder why I've never had one before."

Eden beamed and wondered why, too. Someday she would tell him, but for the moment, she threw her arms around her husband. "Benjamin Alan Alexander, I love you!"

"And I love you, Eden Sabina Alexander!"

Ben glanced at his watch. "Hmmm, it's almost midnight, Mrs. Alexander. We'd better get some sleep. We have an early flight tomorrow. Leave the sliding glass doors open tonight. This fire is too much for this time of year." Ben bent to stir the embers.

"Oh, please leave it," his wife pleaded. "I love a fire in a fireplace." Ben looked into Eden's anxious eyes. She looked mighty worried about something.

"Eden, darling, I know it's been a long day, but are you feeling alright? You look a bit . . .."

"Ben," she interrupted.

"Yes, my beauty," he answered obligingly.

"Am I supposed to feel different?"

"Different? What do you mean by that?"

"Well, you know, am I supposed to feel married?"

The bushy brows went up and he couldn't help but chuckle. Eden could make him laugh faster than anyone he knew. She had taught him how to love again and that the Lord is the God of the second chance. What could he teach her? The warm glow of love shone in his eyes.

"This way, my beloved." He took his nervous bride by the hand and led her to the four-poster bed. He untied the mosquito net, and they were immediately shrouded with the feeling of intimacy. The rain chose that moment to come down hard. That night, in the soft firelight with the rain beating upon the roof, Ben taught his wife the meaning of those wonderful words from the Bible: "For this reason a man shall leave his father and mother and be joined to his wife, and the two shall become one flesh." The end, but really, the beginning.

Epilog

Barnes Alexander sat out on the patio with his grandson Harry Raymond bouncing on his lap. The boy was not quite three years old, but he already had his grandfather eating out of his chubby little hand. They made quite a pair, the gallant silver haired gentleman and the exotic Eurasian child.

"Master Barnes, Master Barnes! Yoo-hoo. Master Barnes, it's a girl. It's a girl!" Amo'o came running out of the house, huffing and puffing, sweat beading on her brow. Grandfather Alexander stood up.

"Good gracious!" he exclaimed. "The doctor said this one was a kicker, but it wasn't due to arrive for two more weeks!"

Harry Raymond Alexander, pleased with the appearance of his favorite Amo'o, screamed with delight. "Mo-o! Mo-o, coogies and muk, Mo-o."

Amo'o laughed and took Harry from his grandfather. "I swear this kid love me for my cookies."

Barnes Alexander patted his grandson's reddish-brown hair. He was fast learning to enjoy his role as grandfather, or Pop-pop, as Harry called him.

"A girl did you say? My, my, won't O-ma be pleased. How is my daughter-in-law doing? And Ben?"

"Master Ben say she mighty tired, and they both very pleased it's a girl. They naming her Amelia Jane. She tiny, just 6 pounds!"

Pleased at the compliment, Barnes chuckled. "Have the Andreses been informed? What a time for Ethyl and O-ma to be out shopping! Perhaps I ought to go to the hospital now!"

"Master Ben say the Andreses are already on their way there! I tell Mrs. Ethel and O-ma the good news and tell them to join you there. You go, I watch the boy. Say bye-bye to Pop-pop." Harry, happy in the arms of his favorite Amoʻo, capitulated.

Mr. Alexander arrived at the hospital just in time to see baby Amelia, wrapped snugly in a pink blanket, placed in Eden's arms. Flowers in vases and baskets were stacked all around the room. Gil, Janie and Abby were already there, hovering around mother and child. As Ben was passing out pink banded cigars, his cell phone rang. It was O-ma.

"We're on our way, darling. So thrilled it's a girl," she gushed and rang off.

"That was O-ma, sweetheart. I'm relieved and happy she will be here to welcome Amelia." He looked at his wife, proud she did so well in the delivery room. She was worn out after being up all night going through labor, but she looked so beautiful to him.

Yes, she is feeling tired, thought Barnes, observing her, the mother of his grandson, and now his granddaughter. In fact, she looked angelic and serene. "She's a perfect wife for Ben," he thought, "a loving mother and an excellent hostess."

He patted Ben on the shoulder. "Congratulations my boy, Eden." Eden looked at her father-in-law tenderly. The birth of

Harry had changed their relationship, and Eden had quickly become the favorite in the family. She felt incredibly blessed, and now the good Lord had given her a baby girl.

Ben was jubilant. "Dad, you're not going to believe this, but the baby looks just like Mother!"

Barnes Alexander bent to take a closer look at his little granddaughter and trembled. The tiny babe with ivory skin and almond shaped, dark blue eyes looked indeed like his beloved Amelia. His eyes misted. For a few moments, he was all choked up. Becoming a grandparent had brought a new dimension to his life, but to be given back his dear Amelia was more than he deserved. Eden handed her daughter to her paternal grandfather. He took the pink bundle from her gingerly and gazed upon the baby's sweet face.

Gil patted his back. "She's a beaut, Barnes!"

"Yes, yes," was all he could say.

Meanwhile, Janie and Abby were in the background, looking very pleased. Janie smiled because she now had two mo'opuna, and, thanks to Robert and Natalie, another one on the way. She couldn't wait to swap pictures of this little princess.

Everyone in the room wore exceptionally happy and satisfied faces, but Abby took the cake. She could have just won the state lottery, judging by the smile on her lips. In her mind, she had crossed Eden, Robert, and Albert, who was engaged to local girl Gigi, off her list. All she had to do was wait for the twins and, knowing them, she figured it wouldn't be too long before they found spouses. She resembled the Cheshire cat who had gotten the cream because she knew most definitely that she would win the bet! She didn't see Ray Mulroney hurrying down the corridor with flowers in his hand. Plan B was definitely in effect! Praise the Lord!

Glossary

Adobo: Filipino, marinade or to braise with vinegar, soy sauce, garlic, bay leaves, and is the unofficial national dish of the Philippines

AGA: Acronym for renowned enameled cast iron cooker oven designed by Gustaf Dalén, originally manufactured in Sweden

Ā hui hou, mālama pono: Hawaiian for until next time, take care

Aliʻi: Hawaiian, royalty in old Hawaiʻi, Hawaiian ruling class

Almond cookie: Chinese, cookie made with blanched almond pressed into center, or marked with red food coloring, symbolizing good fortune

Almond Float: Chinese, gelatin dessert made with milk and almond essence, sweetened very lightly with sugar and eaten with fruits

Aloha: Hawaiian for unconditional love, used as greeting, farewell; to respect and love one another, and live in harmony with everything around you

Aloha Nui Loa: very big aloha, also "all my love"

Aloha shirt: a loose-fitting, short-sleeved, collared, brightly colored or patterned shirt, designed by and coined the "Aloha Shirt," by Musa-Shiya Shoten in Honolulu in 1935

Aloha spirit: the coordination of mind and heart within each person, mutual regard and affection and extends warmth in caring with no obligation in return

And then: Hawaiian slang pronounced "An den," means "What next" or "Go on"

Anthurium: a low plant with heart shaped flowers and a spadix that is like a spike, very prized among gardeners in Hawai'i. Native to the Americas

Anuenue: Hawaiian for rainbow

Après la Fête: French, "After the Party," title of a painting

Au poivre: French, a steak, usually filet mignon, coated with loosely cracked black peppercorns, seared to form a crust and usually served rare with a wine cream sauce

Baba au Rhum: a small moist yeast cake saturated in syrup, usually made with rum, invented in Paris

Banyo: Filipino, (Visayan) toilet or bath, like a mud room, small outdoor room attached to house

Bark cloth: a soft, thick, slightly textured fabric of cotton, especially made in tropical and mid-century modern prints, used for upholstery, drapery and slipcovers

Bete Mu'u: brand of Hawaiian mu'u mu'u designed by Betty Manchester

Bibingka: Filipino, rice cake made with sweet rice flour, coconut milk, eggs and sugar, baked or cooked over a fire

Bitter melon: tropical and subtropical squash resembling a cucumber, very bitter in taste, highly nutritious, very popular in Hawai'i, called in Filipino, Ampalaya (Tagalog) Paria (Visayan) and Goya (Okinawan)

Black beans: small black fermented soybeans preserved in salt, used for flavoring. Chinese in origin

Black Forbidden rice: Chinese, highly nutritious black rice, once only served to the emperors for health and longevity. Now grown in Japan and California.

Black pineapple bugs: tiny black flying beetles that multiply in profusion around pineapple fields, especially at harvest time

Blini: (blin or blintz) small Russian style pancake eaten with caviar

Bonsai: Japanese, art form of growing miniature trees or plants in containers

Bouillabaisse: a traditional fish stew from the Provence, France, originating in Marseille, consisting of the red rascasse, sea robin, the European conger and served with a saffron mayonnaise called a rouille

Breadfruit: 'Ulu in Hawaiian, a flowering tree found in Southeast Asia, India and the South Pacific. The name is derived from the texture of cooked moderately ripe fruit which has a potato-like flavor and is similar to freshly baked bread. To the Hawaiians, traditionally, the breadfruit pattern is the first quilt to have in a home

Buang: Filipino, idiotic (Visayan)

California Avenue: the main street of Wahiawā, O'ahu. Named by founders, from California

California grass: perennial grass that can reach heights of over six feet.

Camp: housing community in pineapple or sugar plantation in 1900s Hawai'i

Cassava: tapioca plant, woody shrub native to South America

Cheongsam: Chinese, (Cantonese) body-hugging sheath dress usually made with brocade fabric, popular in Shanghai in the 1920's

Chow Mein: Chinese, stir-fried dish of noodles, meat and vegetables, usually flavored with soy and oyster sauces

Crown flower: a small waxy flower, from India, with a lavender cast consisting of 5 pointed petals and a crown that holds the stamen. Lei Pua Kalaunu in Hawaiian, a favorite of the last reigning queen, Lili'uokalani and symbolic of royalty

Cup of Gold: tropical ornamental vine from Mexico, bearing huge flowers, in deep yellow with thick leathery petals. Exudes a coconut scent

Cutting suckers or pulling slips: cutting shoots or pulling slips from the base of pineapple plant stem. Dried, these can be planted to start new fields

Diamond Head: a volcanic tuff cone on the island of O'ahu known to Hawaiians as Le'ahi, (brow of the Tuna). Named by 19th century British sailors who thought they discovered diamonds (calcite crystals) on the crater's slopes

Dinuguan: Filipino (Ilocano) for flavorful stew made from pig's blood, meat and entrails

Duke Kahanamoku: Five-time Olympic medalist in swimming, popularized surfing to the world, "Ambassador of Aloha"

Eh: Hawaiian slang for the word hey

Falsetto: singing in Hawaiian in a high voice, ki'eke'e

Fête: French, a gala, garden party, a ball

Fishtail Palm: Caryota, a genus of palm tree with fronds that resemble fish tails, native to Asia, N. Australia and the S. Pacific

Friesian: a horse breed originating in Friesland, in the Netherlands. Large but graceful, and nimble for their size, and usually black in color.

Gin Dui: (Jian Dui, Gin Doi) fried (usually round) Chinese pastry of glutinous rice flour, with various fillings, coated with sesame seeds, from Tang Dynasty

Guava: plant of the Myrtle family, "Apple Guava" variety grows wild and is very common, native to Mexico, Central and South America and the Caribbean

Hakka: ethnic Chinese group who originated in the North, but migrated South during the fall of the Song Dynasty. Considered a branch of the Han

Haku, haku lei po'o: a style of wreath weaving with flowers and leaves, especially for a lei worn on the head (po'o in Hawaiian)

Hala: Hawaiian, Pandanus, native to Malaysia, eastern Australia and the Pacific Islands. Dried fronds used to make mats, rugs, bowls, jewelry and ornaments in Hawai'i

Hala kahiki: Hawaiian for pineapple, from hala, pandanus, the fruit of which resembles a pineapple, and kahiki, foreign

Haleʻiwa: small town located on Oʻahu's North shore, widely known for its surfing competitions. In the Hawaiian, hale for house and ʻiwa for the frigatebird

Haleʻiwa Rainbow Bridge: the concrete bridge over Anahulu Stream, known as Rainbow Bridge for its distinctive double arches. One of the most recognized symbols of Haleʻiwa

Hāna: Hawaiian, a small, isolated seaside town on the eastern end of Maui

Hānai: Hawaiian, adopted, taken in as one's own. Very traditional common practice in Hawaiʻi

Hang loose: Hawaiian slang means chill, relax. Used as adjective or verb

Hangi: Maori oven, or the social gathering with food prepared on the open-air cooking pit

Hapa haole: mixed breed, from Hawaiian hapa, half, and haole, foreigner or Caucasian

Happi Coat: a loose informal Japanese short robe, made with light fabrics, usually worn at festivals. In Hawaiʻi it is made with colorful fabrics.

Hauʻoli: Hawaiian for happy, awesome, amazing

Haupia: Hawaiian for coconut pudding

Hawaiiana: objects relating characteristically to Hawaiʻi or of Hawaiian origin

Hele: Hawaiian for go, come, walk

Heliconia: tropical plant with brilliantly colored long panicles as flowers, from the Greek, Heliconiaceae, native to tropical Americas, certain islands of the western Pacific and Maluku, Indonesia

Hetian: White jade, (Nephrite) highly prized, very rare, from Kunlun Mountain, China. A seal made of hetian jade was used to document papers for the 2008 Beijing Olympics

High maka maka: Hawaiian slang, to be stuck up or pretentious

Higot: Filipino, (Visayan) for a braided string cord to tether fighting cocks

Hoe-hana: from hoe, English for gardening tool, and hana, Hawaiian for work, weeding

Holokū: Edwardian style, long sleeved, long fitted gown with train, worn on formal occasions since 1820's

Honolulu: Hawaiian for sheltered harbor or calm port. The capital of Hawai'i located on the island of O'ahu

Ho'omalimali: Hawaiian, to flatter, to soothe with soft words

Huli-Huli: Hawaiian, to turn repeatedly; hence, to cook on a rotisserie over a fire

Ikebana: a style of Japanese floral arrangement

Ironwood: common tree planted for windbreaks, especially in sandy areas requiring a salt-tolerant tree, related species called she-oak or beefwood, native to Australia

Jook: Chinese, rice congee soup, or gruel, normally served for breakfast or when one is ailing

Ka'ena Point: A state park and bird sanctuary with a hiking trail at the western tip of O'ahu. Said to be the place where souls of ancient Hawaiians would jump off into the spirit world and meet the souls of their ancestors

Kailua-Kona: town on the west coast of Hawai'i island. Locals call it Kona town.

Kala: Hawaiian for unicorn tang, a fish. Not to be confused with kala: dollar, money

Kalamungay: Filipino (Visayan) for Moringa oleifera, a fast-growing deciduous tree with edible leaves and pods, healthful and nutritious

Kamuela: Waimea on the Big Island of Hawai'i. The name was chosen in honor of Samuel Parker, the son of the area's most famous historical resident, when the postal service asked for a new designation of the town. Hawaiian for Samuel

Kanikapila: Hawaiian, kani for sound and pila for any string musical instrument, or to play music, impromptu

Ka'u orange: Washington navel orange grown primarily in Ka'u, Big Island of Hawai'i. Used mostly for juice

Kau-kau tin: from kaukau (Hawaiian pidgin slang of Chinese origin) for food or to eat, also a tiered metal container with handle, used for meals, especially by field workers

Keiki: Hawaiian for child or children

Kīlauea Volcano: youngest and southeastern most volcano on the Big Island of Hawai'i, still active

Kiwi: In this instance, a New Zealander. Also, a fruit called Chinese gooseberry, native to mainland China and Taiwan

Koa: tree endemic to the Hawaiian Islands; the wood is prized for great beauty, strength and stability

Kolekole Pass: pass in the Wai'anae Range above Schofield Barracks

Kona: sunny district that stretches almost ⅔ of the entire West side of the Big Island of Hawai'i

Kona coffee: coffee from the Kona district of the Big Island of Hawai'i, originally Coffea arabica from Brazil, now grafted with Coffea liberica

Kona storm: a storm coming from leeward, South or West, opposite the typical NE trade winds

Ko'olau Range: windward, also the mountain range that stands behind Honolulu. Highest peak is about 3,100 ft.

Kūkaniloko Birthstones State Monument: Birthstones where Hawaiian ali'i gave birth, on National Register of Historical Places, located outside of Wahiawā, O'ahu

Kukui nut: Hawaiian for the fruit of the candlenut tree, sometimes polished and made into leis. The Kukui is the State tree of Hawai'i

Kūmū: Hawaiian for the white saddle goatfish, a prized reef fish. Also, teacher, as in Kumu Hula (no kahako)

Labor truck: truck with a crate fitted with wooden benches for transporting field workers

La Mer: French for the sea, in this instance, the name of a restaurant in Waikīkī

Lana'i: Name of a Hawaiian island. Lanai (no okina) is patio or veranda

Leilehua Plateau: central Oʻahu plateau, 942 ft. elevation, between Waiʻanae and Koʻolau Mountain Ranges

Lilikoʻi: Hawaiian for passion fruit, originally from South America, purple or yellow skinned

Liquid sunshine: Hawaiian slang for sunshine during a rain shower. Common in Hawaiʻi

Luna: Hawaiian for supervisor or foreman

Macadamia Nut Chocolates: macadamia nuts covered with chocolate, a popular candy from the Big Island of Hawaiʻi

Mabuhay: Filipino (Tagalog) greeting, used by all Filipinos to welcome, greet, cheer or toast

Mahalo: Hawaiian for thank you

Maidenhair fern: common in wet areas, fern with tiny leaves, the name comes from the thin, shiny, dark stems that resemble human hair, native to Australia and South America

Maile lei: Hawaiian, lei made from an indigenous vine or shrub found in wet forests found throughout the Hawaiian Islands, the leaves are fashioned in a long lei not tied together and worn especially for festive occasions; used to communicate respect, blessing, enduring devotion, reverence, friendship and a desire for peace

Mānini: Hawaiian name for the convict tang, a small reef fish; also, an expression for something small or of little consequence

Manju: Japanese, baked confection made with flour and usually filled with sweet bean paste

Matsumoto Store: small store in Haleʻiwa, on Oʻahu's North Shore, famous for its shave ice

Mejiro: Japanese, a tiny green bird commonly called Warbling White Eye for the white ring around the eye

Menehune: crafty, mythical dwarf-sized people of Hawaiian legend

Merrie Monarch Festival: prestigious annual hula festival and competition held in Hilo on the Big Island of Hawai'i. Honors King David Kalākaua, nicknamed the "Merrie Monarch" for his patronage of the arts and is credited with restoring cultural traditions, including the hula, the Hawaiian dance

Mindanao Gum: a tall eucalyptus, with smooth, multi-hued bark, native to the Philippines, Indonesia and Papua, New Guinea, commonly known as "The Rainbow Eucalyptus"

Mochi: Japanese, a confection made with glutinous rice and filled with sweet bean paste

Moi: the threadfin, a prized reef fish, reserved in old Hawai'i for the ali'i

Monoi Tiki Tahiti oil: in this case, perfumed oil from Tahiti in the Tiare (gardenia) scent

Mondo grass: evergreen, sod-forming perennial, native to east Asia, used as a ground cover

Moon cake: Chinese, a pastry made with wheat flour and a rich red bean or lotus seed filling. Formed in a wood mold and originally eaten during the Mid-Autumn Festival

Mo'opuna: Hawaiian for grandchild or grandchildren

Mo bettah: (More better) Hawaiian slang for "it's better"

Mountain apple: fruit or tree, common in wet areas, native to Malaysia. Fruit is succulent, delicate

Mu'umu'u: Hawaiian, a traditional loose-fitting dress, usually made with floral or Polynesian prints

Myna bird: related to starlings, native to SE Asia, especially India, they are gregarious, sassy, loud

Niele: Hawaiian for inquisitive, curious, nosey

Night Blooming Cereus: a cactus from the southwestern US and Mexico, with large fragrant white flowers that bloom only once a year, for a single night

'Ohana: Hawaiian for family, extended family

'Ohi'a-lehua: evergreen shrub or tree, endemic to Hawai'i, with fluffy red or white blossoms, likes higher altitudes, wood prized for floors and wainscots

Okinawan Sweet Potato: vibrant purple sweet potato native to the Americas, brought to Hawai'i via Okinawa, Japan. Flavorful, creamy, high in fiber and antioxidants

'Ono: Hawaiian for delicious. ('ono-licious, slang, a combination of 'ono and delicious) Also, Hawaiian name for a pelagic fish, ono (no okina), the wahoo

Ōpakapaka: Hawaiian for a prized deep water bottom fish, the pink snapper

Ōpihi: Hawaiian for an endemic edible limpet

Osetra: prized, costly caviar from Osetra Sturgeon. Golden osetra is rare and very rich in flavor

Other side: slang for the other side of the island from Hāna, isolated on the east end of Maui

Oyster sauce: cooking sauce used in Asian cuisine, made from oysters, brine, and soy sauce,

Paiute: (Payut) card game originating in Hawai'i that is akin to Poker

Palaka: Hawaiian for a thick cotton plaid, originally navy and white, used to make shirts for plantation field workers

Paniolo: Hawaiian for cowboy

Papered (field): black plastic, about three feet wide, its edges held down by dirt, confines the soil fumigant, helps hold in moisture, controls weeds and pests, and heats the soil to stimulate root growth. It is marked for placement of young pineapple plants, two rows of plants for each strip of plastic

Pareo: French Polynesia for sarong, body wrapping fabric

Pau hana: Hawaiian slang, for the end of work, end of the workday, from pau, finish, end, done, and hana, work

Pīkake: a species of jasmine, originally from India and the Himalayas near Bhutan, derived from the Hawaiian word for peacock, because Princess Ka'iulani was fond of the flower and the bird

Piña Cloth: Filipino, a fiber from the leaves of the pineapple plant used in the Philippines to make cloth for clothing, especially for the Barong Tagalog, the formal shirt for men, now made for women also

Pinakbet: Filipino (Ilocano) vegetable stew of eggplant, yard long beans, bitter melon and bagoong, fermented fish sauce

Plum Pudding: steamed pudding made with dried fruits, eggs, flour, sugar and spices, original to Great Britain, eaten at Christmas. Usually served with Hard Sauce

Plumeria: Frangipani (common name), lovely flowering tree of many varieties and colors, native to Mexico, the Caribbean, Central and South America, used for flower leis in Hawai'i

Powder Puff tree: low branching small tree, with evergreen binnate, oblong leaves and auxiliary with showy pink flowers, native to Bolivia, named after Suriname (Calliandra surinamensis)

Poi: Hawaiian, the famous dish made from the corm (the root) of the kalo (plant) cooked, pounded, and mixed to a pudding-like consistency. A must at a luau (feast)

Poi dog: local slang for dog of mixed breed, from the word, poi, a primary staple of Hawaiians, made of the corm of the kalo (taro) plant, which is mixed before eating

Poke: Hawaiian, diced raw fish with seasonings, usually served as a pupu (appetizer)

Portuguese bean soup: a hearty soup of red beans, vegetables, hambone or hocks, Portuguese sausage

Portuguese sausage: linguica, a smoke-cured pork sausage seasoned with garlic, chile powder and paprika

Pouchong tea: Chinese, a light oolong tea from Fujian, China

Prayer of Hannah: 1st Samuel chapter 1, a barren Hannah prayed for a son, and God heard

Protea: a genus of flowering plants of S. Africa and Australia. Over 14,000 species

Puhi: Hawaiian for moray eel

Puka: Hawaiian for hole. Puka-puka, many holes, or tattered

Rainbow Warriors: in this case, The Hawai'i Rainbow Warriors football team representing the University of Hawai'i at Manoa, O'ahu

Red soil (red dirt): deep red color of the soil where most of the pineapple fields are located on O'ahu island

Reyn Spooner aloha shirt: exclusive brand of aloha shirts (Hawaiian shirts, with short sleeves and a collar, brilliantly colored with floral patterns or other Polynesian motifs, can be worn casually or formally)

Royal palm: a large single stemmed palm with pinnate leaves. Native to Caribbean

Sabitan ng pera: Filipino, (Tagalog) a wedding money dance

Saimin: a noodle soup developed in Hawai'i, inspired by Japanese Ramen

Salade Niçoise: a salad from Nice, France composed of lettuce, tomatoes, tiny black olives from Nice, with cooked green beans, potatoes and eggs, topped with tuna fish (usually canned) and anchovies

Sarong: of Malay in origin, a body wrapping fabric, used most often as a cover up. In Hawai'i, most are very colorful with beautiful prints

Schofield Barracks: Home of the 25th Infantry division since 1941, as well as the Command Headquarters for the United States Army Hawai'i. Located in the Wahiawā District, City and County of Honolulu

Sea Grape: a flowering plant of the buckwheat family, native to Florida, Mexico, Central America, western South America and the Caribbean, can grow at the high tide line

Shaka: Hawaiian salute, consists of extending thumb and little finger while holding the three middle fingers curled, presenting front or back of hand. Can wag hand for emphasis

Shave ice: Hawaiian ice-based dessert of fine ice chips topped with fruit syrup

Shoji: Japanese, a door, window, or room divider of rice paper, over a wood frame

Shower tree: Cassia javanica which is the pink blossomed variety, (also comes in white, yellow and orange) native to southern Asia,

Slack Key: Kī hō'alu, Hawaiian for 'to loosen'; to slacken the strings of a guitar so they form a single chord, frequently G Major, style of music originated in Hawai'i

Sotto voce: Italian, lowering of the volume of one's voice for emphasis

Star anise: a star-shaped spice that resembles anise in flavor, native to NE Vietnam and SW China

Stollen: German, a bread-like cake with raisins and almonds, rolled to represent the Christ child in swaddling clothes

Swordtails: species of small, brightly colored freshwater fish with an extended lower lobe of male's tail fin, native to Mexico and North and Central America

Talking story: Hawaiian slang for chatting with friends, shooting the breeze

Tapa: Tahitian (kapa in Hawaiian) for bark cloth made with the bark of the Mulberry tree, with designs from natural dyes, especially of earthy colors

Taro: kalo in Hawaiian, a tropical plant grown primarily for its edible corms and leaves, a staple to Hawaiians

Tatami: Japanese, a rice straw mat

The Big Island: the largest of the eight major Hawaiian Islands, also called Hawai'i, or Moku 'o Keawe

Tinikling: Filipino (Visayan) bamboo pole dance, means tikling like, after the tikling bird because the dance steps mimic the bird's movements in eluding bamboo traps

Tinola: Filipino, (Tagalog or Visayan) chicken soup, made with ginger, onions, green papaya and kalamungay leaves

Tradewinds: Winds that reliably blow east to west just north and south of the equator. The winds help ships travel west, and they can also steer storms such as hurricanes

Tūtū: the most used word in Hawai'i for grandmother, it is an Anglicized version of the Hawaiian grandmother, kūkū

Uhu: Hawaiian for parrotfish. Among the most beautifully colored of all reef fish. To about 15 lbs.

U.H.: University of Hawai'i

Umami: Japanese, umai for delicious and mi for taste. One of the 5 basic tastes which include sweet, sour, bitter and salty. First coined by Professor Kikunae Ikeda

Uni: New Zealand, short for university

Up Country: area on the island of Maui, located on the upper slopes of Haleakala, famous for its flower, vegetable and fruit farms

Ute: New Zealand (Aotearoa, Maori), short for utility vehicle

Velouté sauce: a white cream sauce in French cuisine, from French word for smooth

Wahiawā: Hawaiian for "Place of loud noises," because the surf from the North shore could be heard, a city located in central Oʻahu, 22 miles NW of Honolulu, on the Leilehua Plateau, 942 feet above sea level. Founded in 1898

Waiʻanae Range: Hawaiian for "water of the mullet," the mountain range on the western side of Oʻahu, includes Mt. Kaʻala, highest point on Oʻahu at 4,025 ft.

Waikīkī: Hawaiian for "Spouting fresh water," a vibrant neighborhood in Honolulu County known for its popular surf beach

Weke: Hawaiian for any of several white, yellow, or orange goatfishes

Wun tun: Chinese, also won ton, a type of dumpling made with a flour wrap, boiled and served in soup, or crispy fried

Zabuton: Japanese, a cushion for sitting, normally 20 to 30 inches square in size

Zori: Japanese, flat sandals, thongs, can be of straw, cloth, leather or rubber; flip flops

More from our readers...

"*Aloha Nui Loa* is a wonderful story, written from the perspective of a girl who grew up on a thriving pineapple plantation in Hawai'i. The characters are so realistic, and the settings are described in such a way that they come to life in your imagination. The author, ever the romantic, tells a sweet tale of love in this beautiful setting." Bonnie McMurtray Evans, Florence, MS. Quilter, Designer, Seamstress, Crafter

"I often visited my Obachan who lived in a plantation house in Paia, Maui. The place was filled with chickens, mountain apple trees, and other country smells. So, I thank you, Yvonne McIntire, for sharing yourself in your novel. It is full of big joy, lots of love, food and family. Your story of old plantation Hawai'i brought back precious memories. I thank God for a person like you!" Ann Okamoto, Kahului, Maui, HI. Teacher, Vegan chef

"I am usually not one to read romance novels; however, *Aloha Nui Loa* was centered on a pineapple plantation which brought back good memories of being a part of a plantation community. Life was so much simpler then, no worries, be happy." James H. Abear, Lake Elsinore, CA. Consultant, Right of Way & Governmental Affairs,

"Heartwarming story, I could not put the book down. I loved hearing about life on a pineapple plantation." Virginia Van Pelt, Ha'iku, Maui, HI. Vacation Rentals, Manager

"*Aloha Nui Loa* recreates life on a pineapple plantation in Hawai'i where two 'opposites' fall in love. It is an array of delightful, but determined characters inspired by real people whose lives changed for the better. The author's knowledge of diverse Island culture is amazing. If you want to learn Hawaiian vocabulary, reading this book would be a good starting point." Elizabeth Ladao, Henderson, NV. Teacher

"The best of this book is simply that a 'local girl makes good.' The author combines her ethnic background and vivid imagination to create an awesome love story. Yvonne Lee McIntire has done what I wish I could have done. As a small-town girl, we dream and fantasize about writing a hot romance. *Aloha Nui Loa* is a wonderful mixture of actual places and is flavored with ono small-town umami that satisfies our soul. The story is typical but unique in its inspirational Christian values. Thoroughly enjoyed this book and I hope you will too as it shared the values that still exist in small town Hawai'i. A-l-o-ha!" Gerrie Nakamura, Wahiawā, HI. Teacher

"This book captured the true feelings of the love and life of living on a Hawaiian island. It leaves a lingering taste for more!!!!" Nida Bautista Abear, Las Vegas, NV. English tutor, Japan

"No Ka Oi!" (Is the best) The smell of pineapple and the fresh ocean breeze is where this story takes you. You will fall in love with hope again as you follow the main characters, Eden and Ben, through courtship. It took me back to the islands. Take the journey yourself, as you read *Aloha Nui Loa*." Terri Krupp, Rockwall, TX. (By way of da Islands) Business entrepreneur

"Memories of Love, 'Ohana, Pineapple and Red Dirt. Mahalo 'sistah' for writing *Aloha Nui Loa*." Linda Ringor

Turqueza, Henderson, NV. RN, Hula dancer, choreographer, Hula 'O Mahina,

"*Aloha Nui Loa* refreshed my memories of Wahiawā town and of life living next to the pineapple fields. A romance story that filled my mind with all the food, flowers and cultural differences that I remember. I love how the author described the appearances of the characters and the happy ending!" Jennifer Kaitoku, Wahiawā, HI. Teacher, Ed. Asst.

"I made a journey on the U.S.S. Leilani to the beautiful island of O'ahu, where I grew up on a military base called Schofield Barracks. Who knew I would be living in Hawai'i when it became our 50th state, on August 21, 1959. I was known as a malihini (newcomer) while attending a wonderful school in Wahiawa known as Leilehua High School, where I became an awesome 'mule,' class of 1966. With love and friendship from all my Hawaiian friends and classmates I became a kama'āina (native). *Aloha Nui Loa* not only brought back memories but reminded me of this love Hawaiians show to everyone, newcomer and native alike." Bennie Sue Mayfield Houck, Marietta, GA. University System of Georgia

"So enjoyed the book. I reread it and loved it even more. You will feel like you are on the plantation road with the hot Hawaiian sun shining on you and trade winds blowing your hair. As you get to know the characters and see their relationships unfold you will not want to put this book down. An excellent and joyful read!" Shauna Gibney-Fawcett, Rotterdam, NY. Mom of 3, lifelong friend, Elementary School Educator

"At age 12, I was given the name of a Hawaiian girl, Yvonne McIntire, who would become a penpal and life-long friend. In penning this book, Yvonne shows skill and compassion. The story is filled with the experiences of a girl's love of her plantation life on a tropical island. A must read." Mary Bird Drahos, Lufkin, TX. Writer, Vidor Vidorian and Mauriceville Country Chronicle, Poet, life-long pen pal of author

"I have visited Hawai'i many times. But it took Yvonne McIntire's *Aloha Nui Loa* to give me a full awareness of what it was like to be one of the plantation workers during the heyday of pineapple cultivation. Through her winsome heroine, Eden, we meet a spectrum of the men who operated the plantations and the women who created welcoming homes for them in the standardized estate housing. Her tale brings to vivid life this era in Hawaii. And buy a pineapple to relish while you're reading!" Gwen Allmon, Wailea, Maui, HI. (By way of Barbados)

"I really enjoyed reading this book because it reminded me of the happy times growing up on a pineapple plantation on O'ahu. It helps me remember everything about the island I left 33 years ago. The story tells you how our parents took care of our family." Allan Michael Abear, Los Angeles, CA. Albert in *Aloha Nui Loa*, Vietnam Vet

"*Aloha Nui Loa* brought me back to my childhood days, too. All about plantation life – it was the greatest experience growing up. It was simple living, fun, and filled with lots of love from not only family but from neighbors and friends as well. Your story was like mine living on a sugar plantation. This story tells it like it was, all so true ---the good old days. It was a joyful time when we got together at fiestas, cooking the best yummy ethnic dishes. Looking back, we took things for granted and the years passed by. We miss it, HAWAI'I!" Georgia Wabinga Abear, Los Angeles, CA. Tūtū, Waialua Girl

"An enchanting story packed with local flavor that reminded me of my island home, every time!" Q. Gabumpa, Seattle, WA. Library Associate, Suffolk U. Boston, Psychology/Drama

"Reading *Aloha Nui Loa* brings back fond memories of growing up in the pineapple community featured in the book. I wouldn't exchange the experiences for the world!" Edith Barcina, Sunset Beach, HI. Hula dancer, Collector of Pineapple memorabilia

"A wonderful story that brought back so many fond memories of my childhood growing up on the island of Oʻahu." Jeannie Tubania Dinwoodie Atwater, CA. Nānākuli Girl Forever

"Who doesn't love a love story? Especially when it takes place in beautiful Oʻahu. Written by a lovely Hawaiian lady who had the good fortune to grow up on a pineapple plantation with so much adventure! A great read." Renee Supola, Grants Pass, OR. Retired Secretary

"I loved reading a story written by someone who lived in the time." Cheryl Johnson Mahin, Minnetonka, MN. Piano Teacher

"If you love the feel of the Hawaiian Islands, you will enjoy this book. It brings you back to what island living was like in earlier days, especially for a family on a pineapple plantation. Yvonne has peppered this book with many fun and interesting island phrases and words. The aloha spirit is everywhere in *Aloha Nui Loa*." Patrick Lee Mahin, Minnetonka, MN. Retired Naval Officer and Missions Pastor

"A good read through the relationships of those who lived in the close community culture of the old Hawaiian (pineapple) plantation. Worth the read from many aspects. I Applaud!" Susan Kokus, Haʻiku, Maui, HI. RN, Prayer Warrior